Depth Psychology and the Digital Age

Edited by
Bonnie Bright

Depth Insights™

Cover Image:
Sergey Nivens/Shutterstock

Book Layout and Design by
Stephanie Kunzler, GreatGraphicLayouts.com

Cover Design by Bonnie Bright

Printed and bound in the United States of America.

Library of Congress Cataloging-in-Publication Data

Depth psychology and the digital age / edited by Bonnie Bright

p. cm.

Includes bibliographical references

ISBN: 0997955007
ISBN-13: 978-0997955002

1. technology and culture   2. Jungian psychology   3. Popular culture—Psychological aspects

1. Bright, Bonnie

Table of Contents

Acknowledgments

The editor would like to acknowledge the following individuals for their contribution, assistance, encouragement, and support:

Jordan Shapiro, Ph.D., who first visioned and launched this project, as well as Drew Foley, Jason Butler, Diane P. Coffey, Priscilla Hobbs, John Woodcock, Dorene Mahoney, Jennifer Selig, Robert Romanyshyn, Glen Slater, and Christophe Morin among many others for editing, support, inspiration, and/or encouragement to finish the project, especially after it faltered midstream. Special thanks to the authors for their passion on the topic, and for sharing their gifts through writing.

Acknowledgement is also extended to the following for permission to reprint previously published material:

An early draft of Glen Slater's essay was first presented in an online discussion forum of the International Association of Jungian Studies, May 2014.

A version of Aaron Balick's essay entitled "The Real Motivation Behind Social Networking" first appeared in *TILT Magazine: Therapeutic Innovations in Light of Technology*, Winter 2013: Volume 3, Issue 2

A version of Sharon Heath's essay originally appeared in *Jung Journal: Culture & Psyche*, 2012, Volume 6, Number 2.

About the Authors

Aaron Balick, Ph.D., is a UKCP registered psychotherapist, supervisor, and social networking and media consultant working in London. Dr. Balick holds the post of honorary senior lecturer at the Centre for Psychoanalytic Studies at the University of Essex. He has a special interest in relational psychoanalysis and psychotherapy and is a founding member and chair of The Relational School, UK. In addition to his academic and clinical work, Aaron is a media spokesperson for the UKCP, a media consultant and a blogger and mental health writer for a variety of print and online publications. Aaron is the author of two books, *The Psychodynamics of Social Networking: Connected-Up Instantaneous Culture and the Self* (2014, Karnac) and the children's book, *Keep your Cool: How to Deal with Life's Worries and Stress* (2013, Hachette).

Bonnie Bright, Ph.D., spent fifteen years in the corporate world working in media and technology before earning Master's degrees in Psychology from Sonoma State University and in Depth Psychology from Pacifica Graduate Institute, where she also earned her Ph.D. She is the founder of Depth Psychology Alliance, an online community for everyone interested in Jungian and depth psychologies, and of DepthList.com, free-to-search database of Jungian and depth psychology-oriented practitioners. She is the creator and executive editor of Depth Insights Journal, and she regularly produces audio and video interviews on depth psychological topics. She has completed 2-year certifications in Archetypal Pattern Analysis via the Assisi Institute and in Technologies of the Sacred with West African elder Malidoma Somé, and has trained extensively in Holotropic Breathwork™ and the Enneagram.

Jason Butler, Ph.D., is a licensed clinical psychologist and core faculty in the Holistic Counseling department at John F. Kennedy University. He has a psychotherapy practice in Oakland, California where he sees adults and couples. He received his doctorate in Clinical Psychology from Pacifica Graduate Institute and his master's degree in Transpersonal Psychology from Saybrook University. His writing and research interests include archetypal psychotherapy, dreams, depth psychological research methods, technology and the body, and aesthetic modes of relating to psychopathology. He recently published a book entitled *Archetypal Psychotherapy: The Clinical Legacy of James Hillman,* in the Routledge series on Research in Analytical Psychology and Jungian Studies. His most significant passion, however, resides in the pursuit of the perfect blend of tomato, cilantro, onion, and pepper in the dish we all know and love as salsa.

Craig Chalquist, Ph.D., is department chair of East-West Psychology at the California Institute of Integral Studies in San Francisco and adjunct faculty at Pacifica Graduate Institute, where he teaches ecopsychology. He is Executive

Editor of the Journal of Holistic Psychology and the author of several books, including those of the *Animate California Trilogy* and *Terrapsychology: Reengaging the Soul of Place*, editor of *Rebearths: Conversations with a World Ensouled*, and co-editor of *Ecotherapy: Healing with Nature in Mind*. His website is www. Chalquist.com.

Diane P. Coffey, Ph.D., has a long history convening and collaborating with nonprofit organizations serving the imperfections of being human. Her international humanitarian work has traversed rural areas of China and crisscrossed through Central and South American countries. She holds a certificate in Chinese Art and Culture from the International Living Tao Institute in Fujian Province, China and a Ph.D. in Mythological Studies and Depth Psychology from Pacifica Graduate Institute. She is also a certified canine behavioral therapist. Current art and writing projects include a book reflecting the art of forgiveness, and an illustrated series of picture books about healing abuse. Her 2010 essay "Abu Ghraib Enhanced Interrogation: The Iconography of Evil" appears in the anthology *Challenging Evil: Time, Society and Changing Concepts of the Meaning of Evil*. She writes on archetypal patterns and the dynamics of canine companion relationships at www.dianepcoffey.com. She resides in Philadelphia, PA, with her loving husband and routinely returns to her multigenerational family homestead in Santa Barbara, CA.

Drew Thomas Foley is an educator, researcher and entrepreneur. His interest in depth psychology and the digital age traces back to his undergraduate studies in Psychology at Willamette University in Salem, Oregon. For the last 25 years, he has lived and worked in Southern California where he earned a Masters of Business Administration from Pepperdine University and a Masters of Arts in Human Development from Fielding Graduate University. In 2012, Drew earned his PhD in Human and Organizational Systems from Fielding Graduate University. His dissertation, *Navigating Mythic Space in the Digital Age*, focuses on the how digital technology shapes the ways that we live, work and learn. He continues his research as a Fellow for the Institute of Social Innovation and teaches course in organizational development and technology management.

Sharon Heath, M.A., M.F.T,. is a certified Jungian analyst in private practice and a member of the faculty of the C. G. Jung Institute of Los Angeles. A previous Associate and Manuscript Editor of Psychological Perspectives, she guest edited the special issue The Child Within/The Child Without. She has written articles for *The Journal of Jungian Theory and Practice, Psychological Perspectives,* and *Jung Journal: Culture & Psyche*. She has blogged for The Huffington Post and TerraSpheres, and she maintains her own blog at www.sharonheath.com. She contributed a chapter, "The Church of Her Body" to the anthology *Marked by Fire: Stories of the Jungian Way*. Her novel, *The History of My Body*, was published by Fisher King/Genoa House in October 2011. Its sequel, *Tizita*, is forthcoming.

Priscilla Hobbs, Ph.D., earned her doctorate in Mythological Studies from Pacifica Graduate Institute and is the author of *Walt's Utopia: Disneyland and American Mythmaking*. Articles she has published or presented at conferences concentrate popular culture as a modern, living mythological system, including: "The Tri-Wizard Cup: Alchemy and Transformation in Harry Potter," "The Wizarding World of Harry Potter: From Book to Embodied Myth," "Rewriting Fairy Tales: Disney's Silly Symphonies and the Great Depression," and "Every Pony Has a Story: Revisions of Greco-Roman Mythology in My Little Pony: Friendship is Magic." Dr. Hobbs is constantly looking critically at the relationship between popular culture and cultural identity, with current research focusing on theme parks, Disney studies, and American studies.

John B. Loghry, M.A., M.A., Ph.D., is a social worker, writer, and artist in Oklahoma.

Donna May, M.A., L.M.F.T. is a therapist, consultant, educator and author of the upcoming book *Psyche's Call: Putting the Soul Back into Psychology*. She is an adjunct faculty member at College of the Siskiyous, where she has taught courses in dreams, life story writing and human services. Donna graduated from Pacifica Graduate Institute, where she studied counseling psychology with a specialization in depth psychology. She has conducted classes, groups and workshops on writing and story for over twenty years. She also has extensive training in dreams, and dreams, writing, art, and active imagination are key elements in the work that she does with others. Donna lives is beautiful Etna, CA with her husband Bruce and their three dogs and three cats, where she loves to read, write, walk and explore the wild nature all around. Donna can be reached via her website: www.psychescall.com.

In elementary school, **Lola McCrary** read myth and folklore. In high school she read science fiction and fantasy. In college she read theology, philosophy, and history. In graduate school she read C. G. Jung and Joseph Campbell, and began to understand why she read (and reads) all those other things. Her master's degree senior project at JFK University in Concord, CA was on how theorist Ken Wilber didn't understand C. G. Jung. Presently she is looking at genealogy from a depth psychology perspective. She also works at as a first reader, proofreader, and fact checker for both fiction and non-fiction writing. She is on the editorial board of *Immanence: The Journal of Applied Mythology, Legend, and Folklore*. She can be reached at lolamccrary@yahoo.com.

Andrés Ocazionez, Ph.D., (AGAP) is a psychotherapist and Jungian analyst with a private practice in Berlin. Andrés is a graduate from the C. G. Jung Institute Zürich and has received a cum laude recognition for his thesis, The Psychology of Analytical Training, presented in the Faculty of Philosophy of Universidad Complutense de Madrid. His main concerns orbit around psychological creativity, psychological becoming, depth-psychological epistemology, and the possibilities and challenges of technological tools in the practice of psychotherapy. Andrés also works with sculpture, poetry and digital illustration. Andrés dances like a lobotomized person but continues trying to catch up with rhythm… a mysterious phenomenon for him (this has been endearing and even inspirational to some).

Robert D. Romanyshyn is an Emeritus Professor at Pacifica Graduate Institute. Author of seven books including his most recent *Leaning toward the Poet: Eavesdropping on the Poetry of Everyday Life*, Robert has published numerous book chapters along with more than forty articles in psychology, philosophy, and education journals. Robert has done numerous radio, television, and online interviews, and has given keynote addresses at conferences around the world.

Elizabeth Shepherd is a writer, therapist, and all-around creative. She received her M.A. in Counseling Psychology from Pacifica Graduate Institute. This past summer, she completed her coursework for Pacifica Graduate Institute's Ph.D. in Depth Psychotherapy program, and is currently working on her dissertation. In her ongoing research, she is passionate about exploring storytelling and collective phenomena. When Elizabeth is not writing, engaging in projects, or seeing clients, she can often be found relaxing with a glass of wine, adventuring in the nearby Pacific Northwest's mountains, shooting her longbow, or chasing after the occasional unicorn.

Glen Slater, Ph.D., has studied and trained in religious studies and clinical psychology. For the past 18 years he has taught Jungian and archetypal psychology at Pacifica Graduate Institute, where he is a professor in the depth psychology programs. He edited and introduced the third volume of James Hillman's Uniform Edition, *Senex and Puer,* as well as a volume of essays by Pacifica faculty, *Varieties of Mythic Experience* and has contributed a number of essays to Jungian journals and collections. He is currently writing a book on the psychology of the posthuman movement and related implications for living in the digital age.

Jason Sugg, MA, LPC is an Austin-area counselor and a Ph.D. candidate in Pacifica Graduate Institute's Depth Psychotherapy program. He has a strong interest in the cultural and political applications of depth psychological theory. He also holds B.S. and M.Eng. degrees in Computer Science from the Massachusetts Institute of Technology. He lives in south Austin, TX, with his wife and two children.

Steven P. Wood, Ph.D., is a psychological philosopher who lives and works in Venice, California.

Editor's Introduction

Google "the digital age" and you'll discover it is rather broadly defined as "the present time"—when most information is available in digital form, as compared to the era before the rise of computers in the 1970s. Now, I know what you're thinking—and I don't need an FMRi machine, Google Glass, or even a web browser to predict it: If you're familiar with depth psychology, you may well be of the mind that depth psychology and the digital age go together about as well as oil and water.

Depth psychology is the study of the soul, first and foremost associated with uncovering and exploring the unconscious. The Greek word *psyche* means "butterfly," as one of the key founders of depth psychology, C. G. Jung, pointed out in *Modern Man in Search of Soul*.[1] The word is also linked to the Greek *aiolos*, meaning "mobile, colored, or iridescent," and to the Greek *anemos*, meaning "wind" or "breath," as well as "soul" and "spirit"—all concepts that appear distinctly unrelated to technology.

Your Google search for "the digital age" will return a multitude of opinions on the pros and cons, with some contending the digital age is "good" because browsing the Internet stimulates our minds, and video games are teaching us new skills. However, if you entertain the notion that there are a multitude of detrimental side effects and disorders initiated by the digital age—illustrated by creative new terms such as "cyberchondriacs" (those who self-diagnose medical symptoms online), and "Facebook Addiction Disorder,"[2]—and if you experience moderate concern, as many of us do, that as a digital culture we are becoming hooked on the web; that we are ruder, less empathetic and we procrastinate more; that our memory is deteriorating; and that we are developing increased anxiety about "missing out" because of the rash of information on social media—you might quickly see the benefit of looking at the digital age from a depth psychological perspective to begin to understand the archetypal aspects at work in our individual and collective lives.

In his seminal work, *The Discovery of the Unconscious*, Swiss medical historian, Henri Ellenberger (1905-1993), suggested that an exploration of the unconscious might offer a "renewed knowledge of the conscious mind, with a wider application to the understanding of literature, art, religion and culture."[3] Ellenberger didn't make mention of the study of the unconscious to better understand technology specifically, but it is clear from his writings that even C. G. Jung himself believed depth psychology might shed light on a multitude of topics, including modernity and all its challenges.

When Sigmund Freud, Jung, Eugene Bleuler, and other pioneers of the depth psychology movement first contributed their unique perspectives to the fledgling field of psychology in the late 1800s and early 1900s, the so-called digital age was simply not conceivable. In truth, however, Jung was deeply desirous of making depth psychology an aggregate of many of the sciences of the time—philosophy, medicine, physics, biology, and so many disciplines that were growing in both application and credibility in the early twentieth century. "Psyche is the mother of all our attempts to understand Nature," Jung wrote, noting its connection in particular to the natural sciences. He even went as far to wonder whether "the sciences themselves ultimately rested on psychology."[4]

Fast-forward to modern day. The debate about the digital age is every bit as alive in depth psychological discussions as it is in the collective forum. Technology is the magic of the modern world and plays a key role in our relationship to earth, writes depth psychologist Robert Romanyshyn in his timeless book, *Technology as Symptom and Dream*.[5] He refers to technology in conjunction with the *imagination* of earth. In a still, quiet place like an African Sahara, he asserts, one "can still imagine technology as a vocation as the earth's call to become its agent and instrument of awakening."[6] But technology can be both a danger and an opportunity, becoming a threat when it is too literal—when imagination falters.[7]

Jungian Dolores E. Brien, who has written about technology from a depth psychological perspective for over two decades, sees the digital age as a rich new resource for understanding ourselves. "The Internet is an extraordinary locus for fathoming the depths of the collective unconscious of our time," she writes, suggesting:

> It can be as fertile a psychological field as fairy tales, folk lore, and ancient myths have been. On the Internet new myths are being formed, hitherto ignored archetypes are coming into their own, and new adventures for the psyche await us.[8]

For Jung, who was born in 1875 and died in 1961, the "digital age" remained *in potentia*, but even more than half a century ago, he had significant concerns about the challenges of a growing mind/matter split and the excessive focus of western cultures, at least, on science, technology, and rational thinking. Jung believed this trend toward "modernity" emerged at the expense of more soulful, reflective, poetic ways of being and he even issued a strong caution against our increasing reliance on machines and technology:

Our intellect has created a new world that dominates nature, and has populated it with monstrous machines. The latter are so indubitably useful that we cannot see even a possibility of getting rid of them or our subservience to them. Man is bound to follow the adventurous promptings of his scientific and inventive mind and to admire himself for his splendid achievements. At the same time, his genius shows the uncanny tendency to invent things that become more and more dangerous, because they represent better and better means for wholesale suicide.[9]

A Seismic Shift

Besides the rise of agriculture millennia ago when hunter-gatherers began to embrace new technologies in the form of the harvest and the plow, the 16th and 17th centuries CE were the most critical in human history. It was then that the dominant worldview shifted from one of an organic living universe to a mechanistic view of nature, a view which held the material universe as a machine governed by precise mathematical laws.[10] The scientific work of prominent men such as Copernicus, Galileo, Isaac Newton, Francis Bacon, and especially of French scientist and mathematician Rene Descartes (1596-1650), initiated a scientific revolution that produced sweeping changes. These men focused on generating understanding via empirical methods, insisting on quantifiable criteria and measurable physical properties in lieu of what was deemed more subjective input coming from sensory feedback, aesthetic sensibilities, beauty, nature, and spirit. Descartes, often credited as the founder of modern philosophy, believed understanding required assessing any complex system by reducing it to its smallest parts.[11] Descartes is perhaps best known for his dictum, "Cogito, ergo sum," translated as "I think, therefore, I exist," which sums up what has been referred to as the *Cartesian split*, the contention that mind is the primary element of consciousness and is what separates humans from nature.[12] Nature, including animals, therefore becomes the equivalent of a machine, lacking emotion or spirit.

Even from his vantage point of the mid-twentieth century, Jung issued further warning against what he foresaw as severe consequences that might ultimately propel our civilization toward collapse, unless they were adequately acknowledged and dealt with from a psychological view. He wrote, "Coming generations will have to take account of this momentous transformation if humanity is not to destroy itself through the might of its own technology and science."[13]

The rapid growth of technology in recent decades, combined with what is arguably a decided lack of psychological context around it, has contributed intensively to concerns for some regarding the speed and quantity of information we encounter on a minute-by-minute basis and whether we have lost (or ever really had) the capacity to navigate such a tsunami of data. Technology has profoundly amplified the speed and efficiency at which we accomplish certain tasks, but at the same time has served to expedite the very pace of our lives, leaving us with little time for reflection and reconnection with things of the soul.

According to best-selling author of *Care of the Soul*, Thomas Moore, "soul" is not a thing but rather a dimension of experience. It is related to depth, to substance, and to relationship to the world.[14] James Hillman, contemporary Jungian and pioneer of Archetypal Psychology, outlines various functions of soul, including that it makes all meaning possible, turns events into experiences, and is communicated in love, among others.[15] This depth of essential experience is so vital for our existence, Jung believed, that he referred to the "daily need of the soul"[16]

We must question, then, whether this has pushed us in great part toward an increasing loss of soul and a dearth of meaning, a disconnect that may be illustrated by the sheer amount of screen time logged by both adults and children today as they interact with gadgets and machines at the expense of quality time spent connecting with our fellow human beings and with nature. Long before the mass technological advances of the last several decades, Jung observed the price we pay for adopting "gadgets" that seem beneficial on the surface, but which may not live up to their promise from a more soulful standpoint, noting that in the long run they are "dubious" and that they only accelerate the pace at which we live our lives while leaving us with "less time than ever before."[17]

The Technology Debate

One individual who is rightfully concerned about the level of abstraction presented by the Internet and the extent to which it tears us away from the tangible world, is Sven Birkerts, a modern-day literary analyst and author. Since the mid-1990s, Birkerts has voiced strong concerns about the speed with which we have adopted the Internet and corresponding technology, all the while not knowing where we are going, and lacking both depth and the desire for depth. To what extent is technology responsible for people's alienation from nature and geography, Birkerts wonders, insisting that "for the average urban or suburban dweller today…a communications net…has fallen over everything" to the point where even trees and rocks have receded.[18]

Birkerts goes further to articulate concerns about loss of individualism in the face of interconnectedness. As far back as 20 years ago, he foresaw "private, subjective space dwindling until 'one day we will conduct our public and private lives within networks so dense, among so many channels of instantaneous information,' " and that even a *reference* to subjective individualism would be ridiculous.[19] Clearly he was intuitively tuning in—nearly two decades ago—to the emergence of social media, particularly Facebook and Twitter, which didn't arrive on the scene until almost ten years later. In his most recent book, *Changing the Subject: Art and Attention in the Internet Age*, Birkerts continues to observe the negative effects of technology, particularly in terms of how it affects our relationship with art and literature.[20]

In 2010, Nicholas Carr, who has written for *The New York Times*, *The Wall Street Journal*, and *Wired*, put forth a similar cautionary to Birkerts' perspective with the publication of *The Shallows: What the Internet is Doing to our Brains*, in which he correlates human brain plasticity with our changing habits based on use of the Internet.[21] Carr reveals that the capacity of the brain to essentially rewire itself to work in short shallow bursts rather than deep sustained reflective thinking is becoming the new norm and suggests we are, collectively, experiencing less and less capacity for focus, for depth of engagement with content, or for contemplative thought. In a similar vein, Jaron Lanier, inventor of virtual reality and author of *You Are Not a Gadget*, argues that the Internet has the potential to create "mass-mindedness,"[22] coalescing people's thoughts and feelings into a soundbyte culture where large numbers of individuals endlessly proliferate the same unexplored and unverified details that emanate from a limited number of sources. This, Lanier believes, leads to collectivization and blatant *groupthink*.

Meanwhile, from a depth psychological perspective, Joseph Henderson, one of Jung's early students and supporters, wrote about the metaphor of a "plural psyche" in which the "Net" is a projection or externalization of the psyche, a concrete way in which we can actually visualize how all the separate parts interact—in conflicts, complexes, subjects, objects, subparts, internal objects, and relationships.[23] Not only do the individual parts relate to one another, sets also relate to other sets, creating a complex interweaving of relationships, images, and entities.

Henderson's contemporary counterpart, Andrew Samuels, describes our psyche as an "imaginal network" made up of various parts, characters, and subpersonalities that all have roles that relate to one another and which interact. He doesn't acknowledge one central organizing archetype, but rather clusters of archetypes, a shifting state of relationships between the many archetypes that exist.[24] Sometimes, Samuels remarks, the web represents one archetype or is influenced by another, but primarily it is what happens *between* themes and archetypes that is important.

I would also add that it is what happens *between* the user and the technology—and not wholly one entity or the other—that is in control of the outcome of the interaction, so it is critical to note that technology itself must not be demonized. From a depth psychological viewpoint, everything has its unconscious and its shadow. As Jung's colleague Erich Neumann noted, the effect of conscious attitude on the unconscious demands that responsibility be carried by the totality of the personality and not just the ego—that is, we must own the shadow and not simply assign everything to opposites of good and evil.[25]

If we look at technology in general—and the Internet and social media specifically—in a more archetypal way, identifying and owning the shadow and looking with symbolic eyes as both Neumann and Henderson[26] suggest, we can actually begin to see there is a greater intelligence at work. With social, psychological, aesthetic, and philosophical lenses, a more whole truth emerges. While technology may present specific challenges to a soulful way of being in the world, it can also contribute to it. The rapid growth of online video conferencing platforms and increased speed and availability of high speed Internet access increasingly bring people from diverse reaches of the globe in new and more deeply interconnected ways. Game designer and author Jane McGonigal writes about how, in spite of what we know to be record amounts of screen time that goes to playing video games these days, gaming is positively changing the world for the better on the social front, actively offering opportunities for combating everything from depression to chronic pain to obesity to climate change. There's no going back, she insists, as from here on out, "every generation will be a gamer generation."[27]

As long as we are vastly intertwined with our cultural ideals of advancement, our thirst for new technologies that will make us more efficient and that will offer more opportunities for success will not be assuaged. All the touted tools and processes in the world, however, will still not be enough to usher us back into the profound interconnection with each other and with other elements of the "real world" which we require to thrive, both individually and as a collective.

"All time-saving devices, amongst which we must count easier means of communication and other conveniences, do not, paradoxically enough, save us time but merely cram our time so full that we have no time for anything," Jung wrote in 1941, suggesting that this is the cause for the "breathless haste, superficiality, and nervous exhaustion with all the concomitant symptoms—craving for stimulation, impatience, irritability, vacillation, etc." that we observe so commonly in ourselves and in those around us.[28] "Such a state may lead to all sorts of other things," Jung went on, "but never to any increased culture of the mind and heart."

Beyond Technology: Self, Soul, and Shamanism

Yes, technology can connect us, distract us, lend us a sense of quick fulfillment, but it will never complete us without the inclusion of mind and heart that lends itself to that wholeness, that inherent sense of connectedness to something more ancient and deep than all the gigabytes of data that have ever existed. Technology alone will never be that thing that enlivens us, enforces our sense of soul in a fast-moving world, and roots us in something which is inherently already there. Technology is neither good nor evil, neither wholly to blame nor wholly independent; technology is a thing that is whole. What is asked for is that we each meet it in a place from which we are also whole and conscious in the ongoing engagement, thus rendering each transaction not psychologically infectious, but healthy, productive, and whole as well. We must plug into the part of our selves that is indigenous to earth, reconnect with what is real, and re-boot our understanding of the psychological and soulful aspects of technology in order to adopt a new way of being in a digital world.

Jungian analyst and author, Fred Gustafson, believes it would behoove us to discover our indigenous self, the self that is grounded in the depths of nature, the patterns of the seasons, and the meaning of the moon and the natural elements: in short, in the soul of the world.[29] Others such as philosopher Edward Casey emphasize the importance of connection and communication with land and place as a way to root ourselves into the greater Self.[30] Yet others specifically honor the role of the shaman who serves as a critical connector between the people, nature, and the great mystery, and the *axis mundi*, the world tree, as the link between heaven and earth, the world of matter and the world of spirit.[31]

With the proliferation of digital advances in an increasingly globalized culture, we tend to take "technologies" lightly, without giving them their proper ritual due. In earth-based cultures, "technologies of the sacred" have always encompassed ceremonies, invocations, and rites that created containers in which something very special could occur.[32] Shamanism was only practiced within the proper context by individuals who were designated and prepared to enter sacred space. Over time as the ritual has been lost, the container has also crumbled, and technology is no longer wielded in sacred space but rather is used haphazardly by virtually all members of our society. Now we check email or Facebook on the bus or at the dinner table, even walking down the sidewalk as people attempt to rush past. Each random, haphazard instance only blurs the boundaries between what is appropriate for the moment and what serves to distract us, eating away at meaningful moments; disregarding the inherent magic in technology in short, uncontained bursts that are indistinguishable from other mundane activities of the profane.

While on some level, aggregating a collection of essays on the digital age seems like its own form of madness due to the rapidity with which technology is subject to change, this book contains themes that will resonate with readers for decades to come as technology continues to evolve, and as our relationship as both individuals and a culture responds in kind. At this time, even as the era of wearable computers, nanotechnology, self-driving cars, and virtual reality is already upon us, this collection of essays is an effort to re-engage the imagination when it comes to the topic of technology, particularly in regard to the advancing digital age and its affiliated trends. Each of our contributors expounds (and *expands*, using a depth psychological lens) on many of the different facets that comprise what we know as the digital age today. Social media, video gaming, virtual reality, digital media, screen time, mobile devices, electronic music, "smart" technology, and electronic waste are all imperatives in our current culture, and will continue to be future realities for decades, if not centuries. Some of us have been engaged in the digital world for years; others of us are resistant—for good and obvious reasons.

James Hillman asserted that a world without soul offers no intimacy.[33] Depth psychology has a mission, then. "Technology is not necessarily the enemy of the heart; technology is not inherently soulless," insisted Hillman. "Technology becomes psychopathological when, like any other phenomenon, it is deprived of soul."[34] I honor each of the authors who have contributed to this work in the face of the intensity of a fast-changing world, who continue the good work of authentically seeking soul in the face of the many facets the digital age delivers.

In "Going Somewhere: Implications of Electronically Inflated Psychological Acceleration," **Steve Wood** addresses the factor of "speed" in our current cultures, and points to the ways in which the integration of computational devices with our body—smartphones and screens among them—have accelerated our reality at the cost of the loss of reflection and contemplation. He wonders how memory has been sacrificed in the face of the "empty self" that is constantly seeking meaning.

In "Jung and the Posthumans," **Glen Slater** delves into the image of "posthumans," wondering how Jung's concern with the "loss of instinct" results in increasing fragmentation correlates with the impending "human-machine hybridization" becoming ever more real due to advances in artificial intelligence, robotics and nanotechnology. When such pervasive challenges as dissociation and denial are pervasive in contemporary culture, we are encouraged to remember the "age-old forgotten wisdom" that resides in each of us.

Craig Chalquist does not fail to deliver a creative approach to the theme in "Allegory of the E-Cave," a metaphoric commentary on our cultural milieu which utilizes *Plato's Republic* as an engaging vehicle. In an exploration of the confinements and distractions characteristic of the digital age, Craig captures how key archetypal mythemes—basic plot elements that reappear in every time and place—correspond and interact with our own cultural perspectives in much the same way that prisoners chained in a cave might experience them. This essay reconnects modern, contemporary situations to which we can all relate back to the metaphor of the e-cave.

Robert Romanyshyn penned "Terminal Talk: Reflections on Thinking and Saying in the Digital World" in response to his own first experience leading an online webinar. Here, he initiates a call to consider transitions, and articulates the uncanniness of teaching in a sort of vacuum when one can't see or hear the audience at hand. He goes further to expound on the shortcomings that are still inherent in our modern technology. "Where is the sky in the digital world? Where is the earth, the flesh of nature? Where is the depth of this space?" Romanyshyn wonders, while delving into the image of the individual as "spectator" and the body as "specimen" in a world where reflection no longer plays a role in our experience as it once did.

The role of the virtual world and the way in which video and online games have manifested in recent years is a critical topic explored by several of our contributors: **Priscilla Hobbs** illuminates how "virtual hyperrealities" reflect our collective "hungry imagination" in "Virtual Hyperrealities: Redefining the Real World for the Hungry Imagination Through Digital Media." **Lola McCrary** delves into how the power of mythology, especially according to the legendary Joseph Campbell, translates into the experience of computers, social media, and technology in general in "Be the Story, Change the Story: Engaging Gender-based Archetypes in Online Science Fiction and Fantasy Fandom." Her exploration of gender-based stories shines a light on cultural attitudes. In "Interplay: Bridging Dynamic Systems through Video Game Narrative," **Elizabeth Shepherd** highlights how storylines in gaming are inherently linked to individual players and points to how collective material is often unconscious and universally inherited, while **John Loghry** looks at how reincarnative gaming correlates with mindfulness found in yoga and Hindu traditions in his insightful "Reincarnative Gaming: The Hard Death and The Intransient Self."

The role of social media takes a front row seat in the explorations of **Aaron Balick**, **Sharon Heath**, **Donna May**, and **Eva Rider**, who each recount profound experiences of their own forays into social media from the perspective of both therapists and individuals in contemporary society. Sharon, Eva, (and also Drew Foley) all synchronistically—but not surprisingly—found meaning in the metaphor of Alice in Wonderland with their respective essays. Sharon's "A Jungian Alice in Social Media Land: Some Reflections on Solastalgia, Kinship Libido, and Tribes Formed on Facebook" and Eva's "Through the Looking Glass: Musings and Adventures in Social Media," each focus on a soulful exploration through archetypal images, while Donna and Aaron each express the implications of such global interconnectedness when it comes to both individual identity and client relations, Aaron via "Online Social Networking: The Digital Face of Relational Psychodynamics," and Donna in "Finding the Connection: Depth Psychology and Social Media."

Drew Foley contends that the Internet serves as a map of the world's information, drawing parallels between the term *map*, which implies a product of reason—and which represents a gain in organization, but a loss of meaning—and the term *myth*, which suggests an act of the imagination, and which aids us in navigating an increasingly electronic world.

Jason Butler explores the role of electronic dance music and its inevitable invitation to both expansion and pulling back in a technologically fluid world where boundaries are blurred through "Electronic Dance Music and the Indomitable Imagination." **Andrés Ocazionez** details and shares insights based on the surprising visitations by digital entities that manifest themselves as instances of objective reality in his playful and informative "Paintbrush Ramblings." In "Mythic Ringtones: Hello Hermes! We've Come to Talk with You Again,"

Diane P. Coffey dives into the implications of smartphones and the influence of mercurial god, Hermes, who plays a critical role in our individual and collective psychological capacity to establish relationships. **Jason Sugg** outlines how the very act of engagement with the online world entangles one in metaphor, noting that to "surf" the "Web," to "chat," or to "game" are all activities that are only possible via analogy, via seeing the physical world through a particular metaphorical lens that channels one into a different mode of thinking. This is a mode that analytical psychologist Carl Gustav Jung referred to as "dreaming or fantasy-thinking."

Finally, I, **Bonnie Bright**, round out the collection of essays with an inquiry into the "selfie" phenomenon and a reminder of the consequences of the digital age to the culture and planet with "Century of the Selfie: Culture and Context in the Era of Electronic Waste." This essay links our growing issue of electronic waste and the perils of attempting to fulfill the Empty Self through consumerism and technology, while speculating on how the trend toward "selfies" is an unconscious urge to help us find context and meaning. Poets Brian Michael Tracy and Dennis Patrick Slattery deliver an antidote to the Empty Self with soulful poetry—"The Universe is Only This Big," and "Elevator Football"—respectively.

While it's easy to predict that the digital age will always produce consternation, scintillation, and debate—no matter the pace of growth or decline, the essays and themes that appear in this collection are timeless; that is, they tap into underlying ideas that can offer context and meaning for generations to come. The authors in this anthology proffer a chance to redeem ourselves, to re-invent our relationship to the digital age and re-infuse these sacred tools with meaning and soul. The details of our technologies may morph, but the contents of this volume are profoundly archetypal, offering patterns upon which we may predicate our own relationship to the depths and breadths of the digital age. May each of these essays serve to help bring us back into balance, then, to create the sacred place where meaning arises, where depth psychology and the digital age converge.

Notes

1 C. G. Jung, *Modern Man in Search of Soul*, 1933/2001.
2 Paul Kendall, "Is the Digital Age Rewiring Us?", from *The Telegraph* online, http://www.telegraph.co.uk/technology/9913452/Is-the-digital-age-rewiring-us.html
3 Henri Ellenberger, *The Discovery of the Unconscious*, 1970, 490.
4 In Sonu Shamdasani, *Jung and the Making of Modern Psychology: The Dream of a Science*, 99.
5 Robert Romanyshyn, *Technology as Symptom and Dream*, 1989.
6 Ibid.
7 Ibid, 3.
8 Dolores E. Brien, "Archetypes of the Internet," The Jung Page, 1997. http://www.cgjungpage.org/learn/articles/technology-and-environment/680-archetypes-of-the-internet, para. 2
9 Jung, The Spiritual Problem of Modern Man, 1964, 90-91.
10 Capra & Luisi, *The Systems View of Life: A Unifying Vision*, 2014.
11 Ibid.
12 Ibid, 23.
13 Jung, "The Undiscovered Self," *Collected Works Volume 10*, 1957, para. 585.
14 Thomas Moore, *Care of the Soul*, 1992.
15 James Hillman, Re-Visioning Psychology, 1975.
16 Jung, "The Symbolic Life," *Collected Works Volume 18*, 1939, para. 627.
17 Jung, *Memories, Dreams, Reflections*, 1961/1989, 237.
18 Sven Birkerts, *The Gutenberg Elegies: The Fate of Reading in the Electronic Age*, 1994.
19 Sven Birkerts, Dolores E. Brien's essay, "A Psychology for the Age of the Internet," in *The Soul of Popular Culture*, 1998, 286-7.
20 Sven Birkerts, *Changing the Subject: Art and Attention in the Internet Age*, 2015.

21   Nicholas Carr, *The Shallows: What the Internet is Doing to our Brains,* 2010.

22   Jaron Lanier, *You are Not a Gadget: A Manifesto,* 2010.

23   Joseph Henderson, *Cultural Attitudes in Psychological Perspective, 1984.*

24   Andrew Samuels, *The Plural Psyche: Personality, Morality and the Father, 1989.*

25   Erich Neumann, *Depth Psychology and a New Ethic, 1990.*

26   Henderson, *Cultural Attitudes,* 1984.

27   Jane McGonigal, *Reality is Broken: Why Games Make Us Better and How They Can Change the World,* 2011.

28   Jung, "Return to the Simple Life," CW 18, 1941/1989, para. 1343

29   Fred Gustafson, *Dancing between Two Worlds: Jung and the Native American Soul,* 1997.

30   Edward S. Casey, *Getting Back into Place: Toward a Renewed Understanding of the Place-World,* 2009.

31   Mircea Eliade, *Shamanism: Archaic Techniques of Ecstasy,* 1974.

32   Stanislav Grof, *Psychology of the Future: Lessons from Modern Consciousness Research,* 2000.

33   James Hillman, *The Thought of the Heart and the Soul of the World,* 2007, 120.

34   Ibid, 123.

Bibliography

Birkerts, Sven. *Changing the Subject: Art and Attention in the Internet Age.* Minneapolis, MN: Graywolf Press, 2015.

Birkerts, Sven. "Into the Electronic Millennium." *Boston Review,* October 1991. http://new.bostonreview.net/BR16.5/birkerts.html

Birkerts, Sven. *The Gutenberg Elegies: The Fate of Reading in the Electronic Age.* Boston, MA: Faber & Faber, 1994.

Brien, Dolores E. "A Psychology for the Internet." In *The Soul of Popular Culture: Looking at Contemporary Heroes, Myths, and Monsters,* edited by Mary Lynn Kittelson. Chicago, IL: Open Court, 1998.

Brien, Dolores E. "Archetypes of the Internet," The Jung Page, 1997. http://www.cgjungpage.org/learn/articles/technology-and-environment/680-archetypes-of-the-internet, para. 2

Capra, Fritjof, and Luisi, Pier Luigi. *The Systems View of Life: A Unifying Vision [Kindle Version].* Cambridge, U.K.: Cambridge University Press, 2014.

Carr, Nicholas. *The Shallows: What the Internet is Doing to our Brains.* New York: W. W. Norton & Company, 2010.

Casey, Edward S. *Getting Back into Place: Toward a Renewed Understanding of the Place-World.* Studies in Continental Thought. 2nd ed. Bloomington, IN: Indiana University Press, 2009.

Eliade, Mircea. *Shamanism: Archaic Techniques of Ecstasy.* Princeton, NJ: Princeton University Press, 1974.

Ellenberger, Henri F. *The Discovery of the Unconscious: The History and Evolution of Dynamic Psychiatry.* New York: Basic Books, 1970.

Grof, Stanislav. *Psychology of the Future: Lessons from Modern Consciousness Research.* Suny Series in Transpersonal and Humanistic Psychology. Albany, N.Y.: State University of New York Press, 2000.

Gustafson, Fred. *Dancing between Two Worlds: Jung and the Native American Soul.* Jung and Spirituality Series. New York: Paulist Press, 1997.

Henderson, Joseph L. *Cultural Attitudes in Psychological Perspective*. Toronto: Inner City Books, 1984.

Hillman, James. *Re-Visioning Psychology*. New York: Harper & Row, 1975.

Hillman, James. *The Thought of the Heart and the Soul of the World*. Dallas, TX: Spring Publications, 2007.

Jung, Carl Gustav. *Memories, Dreams, Reflections*, edited by Aniela Jaffé and translated by R. Winston & C. Winston. New York, NY: Random House, 1989.

Jung, Carl Gustav. *Modern Man in Search of Soul*, translated by W. S. Dell and C. F. Baynes. New York, NY: Routledge. (Original work published in 1933), 2001.

Jung, Carl Gustav. "Return to the Simple Life," translated by R.F.C. Hall. In *The Collected Works of C. G. Jung, Volume 18*. Princeton, NJ: Princeton University Press. (Original work published in 1941), 1989.

Jung, Carl Gustav. "The Spiritual Problem of Modern Man." In *The Collected Works of C. G. Jung*, edited by R.F.C. Hull, 226-54. Princeton, NJ: Princeton University Press. (Original work published 1928), 1964.

Jung, Carl Gustav. "The Symbolic Life." Translated by R.F.C. Hull. In *The Collected Works of C. G. Jung, Volume 18*, edited by Herbert Read, Michael Fordham, Gerhard Adler and William McGuire. Princeton, NJ: Princeton University Press. (Original work published 1939), 1989.

Jung, Carl Gustav. "The Undiscovered Self." In *The Collected Works of C. G. Jung, Volume 10*, edited by R. F. C. Hull, Michael Fordham and Gerhard Adler. Princeton, NJ: Princeton University Press, 1957

Lanier, Jaron. (2010). *You are Not a Gadget: A Manifesto*. Waterville, ME: Thorndike Press.

McGonigal, Jane. *Reality is Broken: Why Games Make Us Better and How They Can Change the World*. New York, NY: Penguin Books [Kindle edition], 2011.

Moore, Thomas. *Care of the Soul: A Guide for Cultivating Depth and Sacredness in Everyday Life*. New York: Harper Collins, 1992.

Neumann, Erich. *Depth Psychology and a New Ethic* (1st Shambhala ed.). Boston: Shambhala, 1990.

Romanyshyn, Robert D. *Technology as Symptom and Dream*. New York: Routledge, 1989.

Samuels, Andrew. *The Plural Psyche: Personality, Morality and the Father*. New York: Routledge, 1989.

Shamdasani, Sonu. *Jung and the Making of Modern Psychology: The Dream of a Science*. New York, NY: Cambridge University Press, 2003.

Going Somewhere

Implications of Electronically Inflated Psychological Acceleration

By
Steven P. Wood

We live in a time of exponentially increasing speed, occurring at the intersection of electronics, miniaturization, and mind that is perhaps so rapid that its tempo can only be approximated through a kind of psychological Doppler effect. This is to say that these various means of connectivity as mediated via computational devices (cell phones, computers, iPads etc.) have created an explosive velocity that is vaguely sensed, hardly understood and whose effects are felt everywhere. This speeding up has been afoot for some time as cultural theorist Paul Virilio, writing in 1977, apparently understood. From his vantage point he could see that the shrinking and miniaturization of space were compressing events, shortening distance and enhancing speed, and not for the better. In fact he said plainly:

> In this precarious fiction speed would suddenly become destiny, a form of progress, in other words a "civilization" in which each speed would be something of a "region" of time.[1]

Virilio is a member of a long lineage of writers and thinkers who have remarked on the rapidity and dramatic up-tick in speed visited on our societies at various times of technological jumps. Jung fretted that we needed to control our machines lest they control us, and worried, "the whole of reality will be replaced by words."[2] Heidegger, while writing a considerable number of words, evinced some serious issues with the technology of the typewriter and in the nineteenth century, even Nathaniel Hawthorne bemoaned at length his difficulties dealing with the noisy locomotives that were disturbing his reverie and thought. These earlier worries seem quaint compared to our present technological concerns as we sense consciously and unconsciously this element of speed intersecting with an accelerating environmental degradation. Although the phenomenon of technological transformation and its after-effects is not totally novel, the scale is much grander and the pace much, much more accelerated. It is worth reflecting on Bill Joy's (co-founder of Sun Micro Systems) words of caution:

> The experiences of atomic scientists clearly show the need to take personal responsibility, the danger that things will move too fast, and in a way in which a process can take on a life of its own. We can as they did, create insurmountable problems in almost no time flat. We must do more thinking up front if we are not to be similarly surprised and shocked by the consequences of our inventions.[3]

Indeed, we are moving with such a technological rapidity that we can scarcely comprehend the pace. Ten years ago hardly anyone had wireless Internet or an electronic smartphone and now a huge percentage of the world's population carries a computational device of some sort as an extension of their body. Constant checking. Texting. Multi-thinking and tasking are altering biological pathways of neurons to accommodate these new machines and their cultural fetishism. Now we are all holding and stroking the little machines, which are accepted by common narrative as pathways into future progress and interconnection. Parents pushing children in strollers and diners at meals are visually riveted to these devices and apparently strangely dissociated from their immediate surroundings. As an interested observer, I wondered what they were doing. Exactly what had come over them and psychically where were they? What were the emerging psychological implications of these handheld devices? These are not easy questions to answer.

I can imagine that, culturally, the computational devices are possibly our most recent ancestral legacy, an extrapolation from past generations desirous for control of nature. A portable improvement to effect change and control reality operated with one finger, actively turning on, off, and changing locations, connecting and terminating at will; nicely backlit for nighttime viewing. They look a lot like remote controls, too.

Considered on a deeper personal level, through the use of our computational devices we may be gaining an accelerated access to knowledge and an exaggerated extension through space-time, but the exchange entails a loss of our interior solitude, reflection, and privacy. This is a troubling trade-off that is being addressed by a number of researchers, inventors, and early adopters of the electronic era such as Sherry Turkle, Andy Clark, and Jaron Lanier, to name a few. Among them is Stuart Brand, a founder of the Whole Earth Catalogue, who is now also active in the *Long Now Foundation.** This foundation is imagining and designing a clock to measure longer spans of time in the order of tens of thousands of years. The foundation's intention is that by measuring these very long periods of time, human beings might regain a healthy planetary perspective and create a compensatory structure to counter-balance the fast-moving computer technology whose tempo, they sense, is a growing problem.

This sensation of time compression is being exacerbated by changes in our thinking and the speedy replication of technology itself. This is a contentious point argued fiercely from a cognitive perspective by scientists like Andy Clark, who suggests in his recent research regarding thought, language and cognitive extension that:

> We self-engineer ourselves to think and perform better in the worlds we find ourselves in. We self-engineer worlds in which to build better worlds to think in. We build better tools to think with. We tune the way we use these tools.[4]

From Clark's vantage point, both language and thought are technologies that we as "engineers" refine and transmute in order to extend our human-ness across space-time. He concludes his argument regarding this transformative effort with a degree of finality when he suggests that:

> Work on embodiment, action, and cognitive extension likewise invites us to view mind and cognition in a new and, I believe, illuminating manner. Such work invites us to cease to unreflectively privilege the inner, the biological and the neural.[5]

Certainly now, and in the near future, the memory contained in and transmitted over generations within the artifact of computational devices *could*

---

* See: http://longnow.org

allow us to recall bits of history after the fashion of remembered photographs and this very persistence of memories, and our ability to contact them *could* allow us to imagine a collective memory and provide a primitive metaphor of a collectively viewed life vastly extended through these electronic capacities.

However, in spite of Clark's arguments, there are still numerous compelling reasons to *reflectively* privilege our ancient biologic and psychic roots. Chief among them is that together they provide a home* for us, anchoring our cognitive extension and consciousness, which Jung has referred to as "the avant-garde of our psychological existence."[6] Biologically, our genetic roots are transmitted through our DNA and our psychic memories are derived from our interactions with our living surround, and it is doubtful that machines of any sort could supplant our bio-system.

Additionally, as Stuart Brand points out, "By constantly accelerating its own capabilities (making faster, cheaper, sharper tools) the technology is just as constantly self-obsolescing. The great creator is the great eraser."[7] Basically his thesis is that the newer and newer iterations of computational devices cannot access the older versions.** Many people, myself included, have begun to encounter this dilemma as computer hardware and software rapidly "improves." In my case, I have poems and stories written in old formats that my computer cannot read and, for all intents and purposes, they are lost. Brand is also worried about our loss of memory due to the very speed of this technology:

> Just when you think at last, thanks to digitization, everything we want to keep can be preserved perfectly forever, the reality is precisely the opposite. Never has there been a time of such drastic and irretrievable information loss. If this seems extravagant, consider the number of literate people in today's world, the bulk of whose work is knowledge-based, which means increasingly relying on computers. The world economy itself has become digital.[8]

Although, it is possible that we risk a type of amnesia as we increasingly embrace computer mediation, our present circumstances have been underway for a considerable period of time and indeed, these fast-moving technological

---

* Most literally, our lived surround that provides the air that we breathe, the food and water necessary to sustain our lives.

** Jaron Lanier, the inventor of immersion technologies called *Virtual Reality* tells this story: I was asked last year by a museum to display an art video game ("Moondust") that I had written in 1982. It ran on a Commodore 64, a computer that had already sold in the millions by the time of the game's release. It turns out that after my game cartridge was introduced, there was a slight hardware change to the computer (in 1983), which caused the sound not to work. So I had to find a 1982 Commodore 64. But then it turned out that all the joysticks I could find only worked on the later version. Once I finally had a matching trio of computer, joystick, and cartridge, it turned out that I didn't have a working video interface box. All this trouble with a machine whose operating system was fixed in ROM and had been available at the time in the millions! (After months of effort, Lanier gave up.) (1999, Brand as quoted: p. 83)

changes that we are sensing have not happened in a vacuum. They have paralleled, if not out-stripped, the way we imagine, think about, and even experience our sense of self. For most of our human history, what was felt and experienced in our lived surround was boundary-less, an instinctual perception via our senses. As external screens developed, our senses began to become inscribed and bounded as they were exposed to a synthetic imagery that was not always derived from the viewer's immediate surroundings.

Screened Acceleration

With the development of art, drama, dance and music, an artificial screen came into being; an objective screen of fixed thought, which was transitionally viewed, each according to the individual viewer's perception: co-creating a fantasy as it were. With the advent of the cinema the concept of a screen congealed and became extant as a surface on which the scene was shown. Initially the movie theater was embraced as a socially-experienced screen. Theaters with a large screen hosted hundreds of viewers at once within the building's confines to share images projected on screen. In a very condensed period of time, the concept and the actual size of the screen began to shrink exponentially. Within a period of fifty years or so, this large screen began to give way, telescoping into the smaller television screen situated within the intimacy of the living room.

Experiencing television, there were fewer viewers together in one building, though a larger audience scattered over a greater demographic was affected. Following television came the introduction of the computer with its smaller screen meant to be viewed by a solitary viewer. More recently, this screen has shrunk further through the proliferation of the portable, small computational devices, and smart phones. Increasingly intimate, these screens are no longer visited and left as with the movie theaters, televisions or computers, rather they are being carried about: "hand-held." Adjuncts to the body, these objects have become intimations of the co-mingling of machine and human.

Consulted and handled, but seldom left alone, these neo-transitional objects are bridging a future into one-to-one virtual reality. This type of virtual reality is entered through wearable devices, the progeny of these shrinking screens. The telescoping screen can now be embedded in your glasses, or in the near future, directly into your body, further hollowing out a rapidly-emptying self that can be entered and re-entered visually with the tap of a key or a directed thought, anytime, anywhere. It provides an increasing tempo of machine-mediated information, thoughts and images augmenting, and in many cases, replacing those derived from our lived surround. A pixelated photo of a rose caught on the wink cam of Google Glass is substantially different from that of the garden grown rose with its distinctive spicy fragrance.

The Empty Self

In his book *Constructing the Self, Constructing America: a Cultural History of Psychotherapy,* Dr. Philip Cushman refers to the empty self as the "predominant psychological configuration" of our era. Cushman traces the origins of this empty self to "the rise of the industrial state, the attendant loss of community and the press of consumerism."[9] He suggests that the empty self's "insatiable, gnawing sense of internal emptiness drives individuals to yearn to be filled up; to feel whole, solid, self-confident, in contact with others."[10]

Cushman contends that it is not just material commodification alone that makes media and its siren, advertising, so compelling to the empty self, but it is through the emptying process itself that previously subtle regions such as thoughts, emotions, and indeed the unconscious are also rendered into commodities. The composite of this amalgamation is presently called *Information Technology.* When considered this way, it is easier to understand the attraction of the sleek little computational devices with their promise of connectivity and access to that commodity called *content.* At the "click" of an electronic button these devices function as the high-speed delivery links for the empty self that enables a passive consuming of screened images delivered directly through the threshold of our pupils.

In addition to this *consuming* aspect of our devices, they also provide an illusion of control in various aspects of our daily lives. Ecologically, as our emerging situation becomes an increasingly troubled one, and as the earth's disposition becomes more atypical (from a human standpoint) as expressed through erratic, extreme weather and temperature fluctuations that become progressively uncontrollable, we look for control. As bio-diversity dwindles, we invent narratives of connective realities in such a manner that we feel we are not left alone and abandoned; we network. Socially we look for control in an increasingly unstable world of friction, discord, and warfare. Seeking respite we imagine that dominance can be found via the click and the tap that opens the familiar screen replete with its familiar tempo; we crawl into our electronic niche imagining our computational acceleration to be a match for that of our rapidly degrading environment.

Electronic Re-situation

In the 17th century, Descartes articulated "a re-situation of the geographical *location* of 'the order of things,' from an external world to the internal, intra-psychic world of the mind."[11] So too, at present, through machine–mediation, we seem again to be "re-situating" parts of the intra-psychic location of our thinking self into our computational devices. A movement in consciousness is taking place that is the broad intellectual change of the Post-modern era. It seems possible, if not probable, that through this activity a tension is being created between instinctual thought and that of a simulated sort.

As Clark takes pains to explain, "Our sense of self, of what we know and of who and what we are, is surprisingly plastic."[12] However, perhaps we are not really as plastic as Clark seems to suggest since the compensation necessary to absorb an increasingly skewed and unstable environmental habitat creates severe psychological and physical "difficulties." These difficulties are the result of our attempts to balance untenable situations, which typically leave us holding our smooth little devices in order to connect.

For a few moments we can be absorbed electronically, forgetting that we may be lost and powerless, imagining instead that we have found shelter from the storm. With a few tapping gestures we are transported thousands of years back to the fringe of the savannah, perhaps perched in an electronic simulacrum of a tree alert to *something*—another tribe, or an animal perhaps, that wishes to take our food or consume us. *It* is stalking us and we need our group, our nest—this is our shelter. Connected electronically, we engage in a rich active metaphor of our lived surround, but the weather outside is threatening and in the end, a metaphor isn't alive like we are. It holds a place for us to think about aspects of conglomerates of water, minerals and air, but the viscera is lacking.

This fact of aliveness is ultimately our true shelter and our place is biologic in spite of being motivated by very ancient instincts whose outlines are discernible through our connections with computers and our stated need for increased connectivity with various electronically -mediated interest groups. As E. O. Wilson suggests:

> Modern groups are psychologically equivalent to the tribes of ancient history and prehistory. As such, these groups are directly descended from the bands of primitive pre-humans. The instinct that binds them together is the biological product of group selection.[13]

Aside from its computational and communicative uses, the computer also multi-tasks as a psychological metaphor and it can be used as a psychic retreat.

Depending upon our needs and utility, this latest technology can function as a thoughtful refuge of remembering or a hiding place of forgetting. When thought of as a metaphor, the computer mirrors various working aspects of the brain, and the computer's web of communicative nodes calls to mind our neurological constructions. Using the entire communication spectrum and the Internet in whole as a metaphor allows us to model various ideas of the unconscious mind and opens up some interesting avenues of thought. However the same computer when used as a psychic retreat is quite something other. Becoming a sort of second self, we inhabit a make-believe shell world composed of telescoping windows and imagine that we are nesting and cocooned inside this electronic construction encased within a fantasy that a bright future awaits:

> [A future that] leads to the creation of extended computational and mental organizations: reasoning and thinking systems distributed across brain, body and world. And it is in the operation of these extended systems that much of our distinctive human intelligence inheres.[14]

A Wonderful Dream

In the end this is all a wonderful dream—until it is rudely interrupted as the wind wails its weathered instinctual call. It is the wind, via nature, that will call us home and remind us of our needs for shelter. What, after all, is this earth if not our shelter, providing the water and breath needed for life, and the source of all of our instincts? What do we retain if, through our flight of fancy, we soil our prime refuge, waste our inheritance, and engage in an inflationary fantasy of control? Ultimately the planet will speak to us in our instinctual language of earthiness whether we like it or not.

Computer models, it's true, can allude to our instinctual base via the composite of an aggregate memory and our facility to access it from anywhere, at any time, coupled with our ability to share parts of this memory through an instantaneous connectivity. It is possible that over time, these capacities may demonstrate and accentuate human similarities and in effect break down long standing borders lessening our tribal differences through *inter-mingling* (both physically and electronically). This new mixing may create within us a larger scope of what it means to be human by shrinking the distances between us electronically as we expand psychologically. That said, at the end of the day, we remain instinctual creatures standing upon a planet that is our home, and with its singular wild voice, our home is calling us to pay attention.

Virtual Inhabitation

Implicit in this concept of virtual inhabitation is to actually live within the simulated environment of fantasy. Where previously we "had" a fantasy or "indulged" in one, living within a fantasy puts considerably more skin in the game than theatrical viewing with its willing suspension of disbelief. This suggestion of inhabiting also infers pretending that our screened fantasy is real, or at least questions the nature of the real. This is a problematic situation at best.

The research of Dr. Sherry Turkle, a psychologist associated with the Artificial Intelligence lab at M.I.T., has shown that when the boundary between simulated reality and our lived surround is blurred, "a split develops . . . [We are] newly free in some ways, newly yoked in others."[15] Indeed within a wholly electronic inhabitation there is no aliveness, no breath. Our respiration diminishes and vanishes through our increasing dependence upon content providers, a growing intimacy through texting, virtual realities, and their reinforcing networks. This burrowing into electronica and blurring of boundaries creates a breathless electronic refuge that is but a splintered reflection of our lived surround.

The computer and its various offspring are interesting enabling devices that, with gestures, keys, and glowing pixels, create and engender a feeling of control. However, this idea of control is ultimately at the very heart of our present ecological predation. There has emerged a wish to rule the wild, the savage, and the unknown, to manage the horizon, and when dropped into its final resting place, to manage the indeterminate origin of these very words. Civilizing, by its very nature, sets up a tension between what once was and an imagined will be. The present is lost.

Perimeters of Inflation

The perimeters of human settlement have now been extended outward from the soiled wildness into an electronic spectrum with its lure of connectivity and so forth. Lost in the gap between virtual and vital is the fact that we are insignificant specks pretending to dominate a very large rock ball, its vital inhabitants, and its atmosphere of surrounding radiation. Consequently we have split off into our unconscious the vast scale of this wild creative matrix, and as a result, we have immeasurably inflated our sense of self.

In previous times, myth functioned as a bridge to our deeper psychic layers, linking them to the mysteries of our vitality. Now, however, this bridging is potentially being constructed by machine coding. As Wertheim points out, "The growing view [is] that man is not defined by atoms of his body, but by an information code. This is the belief that our essence lies not in our matter, but in a *pattern of data.*" Wertheim continues, "Perhaps not since the middle ages has the fantasy of leaving the body behind been so widely dispersed through the population, and never has it been so strongly linked with existing technologies."[16]

Historically, our human view has been from the outside in. Now it has very rapidly shifted to viewing from *within* the inside. As a researcher, I wonder if this obsession with our various devices is a sign of our leaving our bodies behind or something more elusive? Without perfunctory glances up from these devices, there is no acknowledgment of a shared "lived" humanity. As a participatory inhabitant of simulated worlds, the body of the lived surround is exchanged for an electronic avatar body, so in a sense, the body is not really left behind but rather exchanged for another body without breath.

A body animated by fire, carried within the wires, animating silicon-based chips—but unlike the primal fire of our ancestors, there is no breath in this wired body. Claustrophobically encased within the wire, a vibration, a pulse moves through a sheath with bits of a Hermetic message pre-destined by a mathematic protocol—no wandering, no dawdling, no consideration, and no deepened breathing. No air. A message goes from point A to B. The question is asked and an answer received, and a computational problem is processed. I am doubtful that this environment can be successfully inhabited. After all where in this virtual world would there be room for the animation of flesh with its smells, odors, and heaving breath. These are all missing from the shrunken screens—carried in hands or found on desktops and pockets that are easily destroyed by an errant glass of water.

The Entering In

The activities of entering and influencing the realm of our private interior are central aspects of the field of psychology. This has been traditionally accomplished through the use and creation of narrative, either consciously through the medium of art, reading, writing and oral narratives, or most formally engaged as psychoanalytic theory. More frequently, however, we experience this psychological manipulation unconsciously through the aegis of advertising, with its provocative visual imagery and iconography.

Now, with the spread of computational devices and their attendant languages, another pathway of entering into narrative is being provided to us. The computer narrative is presented by the rapid excitement of electrons on a screen creating a visual stimulation that plays directly into our unconscious. This dance of light is attractive as it comes streaming through our various screens bearing countless visual cues, often distended from spoken language. These bits of information, icons encased in pixels, act as symbolic referents, which often slip unconsciously into our psychological terrain and are the bedrock of our accelerated psychological stimulation. This transmutation from a spoken, verbal linguistic base to a visual one has been stirring for a considerable time. Alfred Crosby, in *The Measure of Reality*, makes this point in an interesting way by noting,

> The practice of communicating and preserving information by means of a stylus, quill and ink surged in the thirteenth century. England's Royal Chancery used on average 3.63 pounds of wax per week for sealing documents in the late 1220s and 31.9 pounds in the late 1260s. A society in which the chief conduit of authority was the ear, tilted to the recitation of Scripture and the church fathers, to the somniferous repetition of myths and epics, began to become a society in which the recipient of light ruled: the eye.[17]

Quickly through the passage of a few centuries, the eye has indeed come to dominate our senses, our psychology, and more recently it seems, our instincts. Initially, visual entry was focused through written text and the printed word. Our embrace of silent reading has allowed for *solitary* imaginal fantasy and the development of directed thought, the sum of which is the configuration known as the psychological self: the thinking self, replete with its imaginal screen of mind and a vivid bubbling unconscious.

The Thinking Self Quickens

As the thinking self quickens through the utility of computer mediation, aspects of our memory are being out-sourced to our computers and various content providers. This has happened so rapidly that we are scarcely aware of the changes. The equivalent measure of "modern sealing wax," by which we can begin to understand the magnitude and rapidity of change, is perhaps found within our dinner conversations, where, without the slightest pause at a puzzling question, a guest or two will reach for their "phone." This allows them to quickly Google the answer to a question, and speaks to how easily they assume that what shows up on their screen will in fact blend into the conversation—whether it be about the weight of butterfly wings or Jupiter's diameter. Just as quickly, these facts are forgotten or left re-posited in the memory of Google or some comparable search engine. Psychologically, as we are provided content to assist in "remembering" and increasingly utilize our computers to provide analysis for our thinking, the trade-off seems to be in increased speed and number of computations and a loss of reflection and concentrated thought.

This exchange is a type of electronically-induced domestication. Staring at the little screen in your hand, you are now essentially holding a small electronic computerized version of an unconscious—a very blank slate. Aspects and functions previously thought to belong to our unconscious are now increasingly *product* originating from content providers and aggregation sites connecting through handheld devices. Google again. Perhaps it is good to reflect on Virilio's comments on enclosure* as a creator of inhumanity:

> What else has the proletariat been since antiquity, if not an entirely domesticated category of bodies, a prolific, engine-towing class, the phantom presence in historical narrative of a floating population linked to the satisfaction of logical demands?[18]

Prior to the advent of an *enclosure* of wireless data, solitary individuals could daydream, honoring their unconscious thoughts as they *appeared* in the mind. Fantasies were created willy-nilly while waiting for the bus; worries were indulged and "to do" lists created. This *private* mental wandering was the accepted norm of *wondering*. It is from these meandering thought processes, "the idea of unrelated thought sequences,"[19] that the origins of individual creativity and play in the broadest conceptual consideration can be sensed.

Cyborgization, the melding of machine and biologic body that is implied through the holding of the little electronic devices, has now created a new domestication in the sense that the private wildness of our own unconscious has been set aside, replaced more and more by an increasingly public electronic simulacrum. The electronic version is not entirely dependent on the inner life of the individual per se, rather it is exposed by small taps that open up windows in a computational device that we can think about, obsess into, and fantasize upon. Where once there was a sycamore leaf, a daydream, or sexual fantasy, there is now data and content provided for our psychological consideration by a provider that is not exactly ones' self.

Sherry Turkle concludes her recent book with these thoughts:

> As we try to reclaim our concentration, we are literally at war with ourselves. Yet no matter how difficult, it is time to look again toward the virtues of solitude, deliberateness, and living fully in the moment. We have agreed to experiments: robots for children and the elderly, technologies that denigrate and deny privacy, seductive simulations that propose themselves as places to live.[20]

---

* Enclosure for Virilio is thought of as an aspect of domestication; the pen holding animals limiting their mobility until they are to be "used" for instance or more overtly, domestication of certain human classes in order that they might supply their own type of utility, passively as demanded.

After three decades of research engaged with these ideas, she acknowledges that we are involved in a war to reclaim our concentration, and we need to examine the virtues of solitude, deliberateness, and living fully in the moment. Just as the newer and newer iterations of computational devices *cannot* access the older versions there is a very real possibility that the newer and newer versions of humans may not remember or be able to access their older thoughts and types of thinking either, so dependent are they on their rapidly proliferating electronic minders.

Notes

1. Paul Virilio, *Speed and Politics*, 157.
2. Carl Jung, *The Earth has a Soul*, 138.
3. Phillip Singer, *The Robotics Revolution and Conflict in the 21st Century*, 174.
4. Andy Clark, *Supersizing the Mind*, 59.
5. Ibid, 218.
6. Carl Gustav Jung, *Collected Works 18*, paras.168-169.
7. Stuart Brand, *The Clock of the Long Now*, 83.
8. Ibid, 84.
9. Phillip Cushman, *Constructing the Self, Constructing America*, 245.
10. Ibid, 246.
11. Ibid, 375.
12. Andy Clark, *Natural Born Cyborgs*, 45.
13. Edward O. Wilson, *Social Conquest of Earth*, 57.
14. Andy Clark, *Natural Born Cyborgs*, 32-33.
15. Sherry Turkle, *Alone Together*, 152
16. Margaret Wertheim, *The Pearly Gates of Cyberspace*, 262-263.
17. Alfred Crosby, *The Measure of Reality: Quantification and Western Society 1250-1600*, 133.
18. Paul Virilio, *Speed and Politics*, 98.
19. Donald Winnicott, *Playing and Reality*, 74.
20. Turkle, *Alone Together*, 296.

Bibliography

Brand, Stuart. *The Clock of the Long Now*. New York, NY: Basic Books, 1999.

Clark, Andy. *Natural Born Cyborgs*. New York, NY: Oxford University Press, 2003.

Clark, Alfred. *Supersizing the Mind*. New York, NY: Oxford University Press, 2011.

Crosby, Alfred. *The Measure of Reality: Quantification and Western Society 1250-1600*. New York, NY: Cambridge University Press, 1997. Cushman, Phillip. *Constructing the Self, Constructing America*. New York, NY: Perseus Group, 1995.

Jung, Carl Gustav. *The Earth has a Soul*. Edited by Meredith Sabini. Berkeley, CA: North Atlantic Books, 2002.

Singer, Phillip. *The Robotics Revolution and Conflict in the 21st Century*. New York, NY: Penguin Press, 2009.

Turkle, Sherry. *Alone Together*. New York, NY: Basic Books, 2011.

Virilio, Paul. *Speed and Politics*. Los Angeles, CA: Semiotexte, 1977.

Wertheim, Margaret. *The Pearly gates of Cyberspace*. New York, NY: W. W. Norton, 1999.

Wilson, Edward O. Social Conquest of Earth. New York, NY: W. W. Norton, 2012.

Winnicott, Donald. *Playing and Reality.* New York, NY: Routledge Classics, 1971.

Steven P. Wood, Ph.D. *is a psychological philosopher who lives and works in Venice, California.*

Jung and the Posthumans

By
Glen Slater

The technologist has something of the same problem as the factory
worker. Since he has to do mainly with mechanical factors, there is a
danger of his other mental capacities atrophying. Just as an unbalanced
diet is injurious to the body, any psychic imbalances have injurious
effects in the long run and need compensating.

—C. G. Jung, Letter to *Zurcher Student*, September 1949.[1]

According to C. G. Jung human nature tends towards a holistic state of awareness. Fostering this disposition, he observed, is associated with wellbeing and
purpose; thwarting it leads to neurosis and strife. Most pointedly, to be fully
human stems from the capacity to weave the organic basis of existence together
with the demands and discipline of civilized life. Attempts to deny or dismiss
the instinctive, animal ground of being lead to imbalance and compensatory
expression. Such dynamics, which Jungian psychology holds as intrinsic to the
psyche, seem particularly pertinent when considering the quest to deliberately
merge human and artificial intelligence in order to transcend the organic basis of existence and adapt life for a digitalized reality. Such a quest, which was

once the province of a small circle of futurists, is now, according to one recent reviewer of cultural discourse, quite central to "the worldview that is ascendant" in American culture, typically referred to as *posthumanism*.[2]

Rising high above the instinctual ground of our nature, riding the wave of Enlightenment ratiocination—or reasoned thinking— into the modern era, science and its technological offspring early on created a chasm of human experience that occasioned a depth psychological response. At the dawn of last century, in Europe and America, newly mechanized lives, Victorian strictures, the "death of God" and overconfidence in the rational mind promoted dissociation between the upper and lower portions of the psyche, initiating a trail of neurotic symptoms. Freud addressed sexual repression and Jung described what he termed a "loss of instinct,"[3] commencing a hundred years of soul-searching and existential questioning. Beneath social and political dynamics also lay various states of psychic fragmentation, particularly between humanitarian ideals and the drives for power and greed. Collective neuroses arose in the form of extremist ideologies and religious fundamentalisms, employing totalitarian schemes to compensate for the fragmentation, often leaving a trail of destruction. None of these conditions would yield to conscious will and reason, which could not sway deeper emotions and spiritual longings. In all of these ways the twentieth century punctured post-Enlightenment expectations and showed that directed thinking and egocentric conceptions of self are not enough to contain or regulate the psyche as a whole.

Today a holistic perspective has grown out of a number of critical fields— physics, biology, ecology, neuroscience and some quarters of medicine—at least in part as a response to the mechanistic excesses of science and the exploitative tendencies of industry. The prospect of nuclear destruction and environmental damage has also necessitated a more circumspect approach to technology— at least in terms of the outer world. However, for the most part, our approach to human nature and its *interior* landscape has resisted this perspective, and instead of overcoming the psychic divisions of the last century we're finding more elaborate ways to fabricate around them, doubling down on the idea that computational modes of intelligence might direct human endeavors. We may well refer to this as an *ecological crisis of mind*.

Having the world at our fingertips and automation all around cannot assuage the creeping sense that something about this approach is unsustainable. Unlimited information and worldwide connection evoke images of expansive knowledge and broader understanding, at the same time streams of factoids and sound bites obscure deep or complex comprehension. "The distinction between knowledge and information is a thing of the past, and there is no greater disgrace than to be a thing of the past."[4] Connectivity and social media tease us with a sense of boundless community, yet they are promoting new forms of interpersonal isolation. Virtuality is everywhere eclipsing actuality. Plugged into the endless flow of online media we've become distracted from ourselves; depression and anxiety treated with the latest psychotropic medications has become commonplace. Immersion in technology has produced arrays of momentary satisfactions but left a hunger for more relational, communal and creative accomplishment. Works such as *Artificial Happiness*[5] and *Alone Together*[6] explore the evident shadow of such trends, respectively arguing that over-medicating psychological discomfort short circuits the endurance of unhappiness and renewal involved in human maturation, and that online environments like Facebook and *Second Life* are eroding emotional and relational capacities. The modern mechanized citizen has thus turned into the postmodern digital one, reiterating a now familiar overconfidence in engineering our way through life, this time via the silicon chip. The world has come to our fingertips, but it's also slipping from our grasp. We may have lifted the lid on many of the repressive attitudes of a century ago, but a lingering loss of soul has followed us right into the third millennium. In what may turn out to be a second act of psychological awakening, we're coming to see that neither our emotional ties, nor our sense of place, nor the life of the flesh can be fully lived in a cyber-based existence.

This questionable state of mind is the launchpad for technophiles to redirect the path of human evolution and alter the very basis upon which we perceive and engage the world. The goals and values fueling the push towards human-machine hybridization in particular, present an unprecedented drive to redesign the fabric of being. Artificial intelligence (AI), robotics and nanotechnology are three fields that undergird this movement. These fields are now engaged in potentially irreversible transformations of humanity, with posthumanists envisioning the creation of a new species, known to us through science fiction as the *cyborg*. Part human, part robot this figure has stepped off the page and screen and become a focal point in even the most sober assessments of technological advance. Computer-based intelligence and replacement body parts form the two primary strands of this envisioned human makeover. Both present extremely slippery slopes, involving a submission of psychological function and physical form to the drive for innovation and willful re-engineering of existence. Awareness of how the psyche and its holistic bearing are implicated in redesigning ourselves has hardly entered the picture, and the process of individuation, which Jung situated at the heart of psychological development, appears to be incompatible with these trends. Given posthumanism is essentially a programmed end to our species, these points of collision take on a certain significance.

Constructing the Posthuman

Present day innovations and the psychological attitudes that surround them are laying the foundations for this posthuman future. Gadgets such as Google Glass eyewear, which stream a constant flow of Internet information into the visual field, reflect what has come to be called "ubiquitous computing," a state in which cyberspace constantly enters and alters ordinary everyday experience. Adapting to such a state invites more direct neural-cyber connections. Intel is already at work on a computer chip brain implant that would allow direct operation of computers and other devices.[7] And whereas artificial limbs and organs may restore functionality, *enhancement* as opposed to therapeutic application raises major questions about the psychosocial implications of altered physicality and increased longevity. In the background of these developments stand both the rather unpredictable trajectory of AI and the gradual inversion of actual and virtual reality. One commentator has declared we are already "fyborgs"— functional cyborgs.[8] In effectively allowing technology to define us through its constant presence and expectation for instant access we're creating the conditions for actualizing a hybrid version of ourselves. As Culkin described the worldview of Marshall McLuhan: "We shape our tools. And then our tools shape us."[9] A literal realization of this insight is probably not what McLuhan had in mind.

While posthumanists perceive a utopia built upon what has been called "technological solutionism,"[10] already evident problems and more catastrophic ones on the horizon are either rationalized away or seen as inevitable risks of expanding innovation. The gravity of their interest rests with the pursuit of more computational intelligence, often articulated with an inevitability that rationalizes prospective disasters. For example, many AI specialists foresee the danger of autonomous computer-based "intelligences" exponentially infiltrating worldwide networks and overpowering human control. Think tanks now exist to work on the problem of "unfriendly" AI. And with the US military being a major funder of these new technologies and building more robotic weapons systems—even some that take the decision to kill out of human control—the idea of computers waging war on human civilization has become a matter of serious concern. As many posthumanists and wary commentators predict, AI may well become what one writer recently called *Our Final Invention*.[11] In such writings we find a disconcerting view of human ingenuity beginning to situate itself in subservience to the evolution of artificial intelligence, as if we've already entered a track of research and development that imagines humanity as an "evolutionary precursor" or a "biological way station"[12] for a silicon-based form of sentient life.

The posthuman movement's most prominent proponent, Ray Kurzweil, is an inventor and successful entrepreneur, well placed as Google's chief engineer to exert significance influence. Kurzweil books predict what he conceives as the inevitable moment when artificial intelligence surpasses human intelligence and, expanding exponentially, leaves any unenhanced human in the dust. In the lead-up to this moment, which he and now multitudes of technologists and commentators refer to as the *singularity*, we will seek increasing merger with silicon-based intelligence and remake our physical form via GNR innovations (genetics, nanotechnology and robotics).[13] Although critics have forced Kurzweil to consider what he calls the "promise *and peril*" of such developments, he is taking extreme measures to prolong his life so he may take advantage of this moment.[14] Basing much of his thought on the continual doubling of computation power every two years known as "Moore's Law," as well as Von Neumann's "essential equivalence (of the) computer and the brain,"[15] many of his predications have so far proven accurate. Kurzweil is no cultural outlier; Google also funds Singularity University, a Silicon Valley institute devoted to his ideas. In his latest book, *How to Create a Mind*, Kurzweil begins his first chapter quoting B. F. Skinner, mainstream psychology's favorite son.[16] Whereas his concept of the human mind attempts to embrace the latest findings in neuroscience, it remains mechanistic and behaviorist, with little sense of deeper psychic realities that would maintain a place for character, calling, ancestry or archetypal patterns of thought and perception. Little we would associate with a sense of soul can be found in his view of the mind, nor that of the posthumanists in general. But the neglected soul has a way of returning.

Psychological Ghosts in the Machine

The dovetailed history of psychology and technology was initiated in full by shifts in lifestyle that began with the industrialization of Europe in the 19th century. Neurosis captured the imagination of Freud's immediate predecessors at the same time railways expanded across the continent and factories blew their smoke across cities and towns. Reflections on this era, then and now, suggest that industrialization and the resultant displacement of natural rhythms of everyday life and ties to the land played a greater role in psychological disturbance than did oft-cited Victorian values;[17] the "animal-machine" was already one term being applied to the factory worker of the late nineteenth century.[18] Meanwhile hysteria was exposing the fault-lines of the rationalistic mindset, simultaneously underscoring the fusion of psyche and soma. Jung's "loss of instinct," which he thought was "largely responsible for the pathological condition of our contemporary world,"[19] linked his psychology with the eroding human connection with nature. By the middle of the twentieth century humanistic and existential writers were focused upon the widespread feelings of alienation and anxiety within urban existence and the failed promise of 'time-saving' devices. At that time Rollo May wrote, "the chief problem of people in the middle decade of the twentieth century is emptiness."[20] He then notes, "our relation to nature tends to be destroyed not only by our emptiness, but also by our anxiety."[21]

The technologist's vision of the body as machine and the mind as computer has been a primary vehicle for this state of affairs, leaving little room for any conception of the psyche in the first place. In this hobbling together of a mindless body and a disembodied mind, the witting or unwitting social engineers of our time are blind to the Cartesian and Promethean excess of their vision, pushing to the point of caricature an increasing tendency toward materialism on the one hand and conscious agency and willfulness on the other. In many respects modernity fell into the gap of comprehension left by this division, with postmodernity and its deconstructive, poststructuralism attempting to endure this gap without overcoming it. Depth psychology, particularly that of Jung, directly counters this reductive polarization of being, by recovering the soul as the in-between realm of Platonic *metaxy*, the past as the realm of Augustinian *memoria* and the unconscious as a source of subterranean wisdom. But mainstream psychology, psychiatry and much of neuroscience have largely maintained the reductive position, which enables a comprehension of existence that serves the strident redesigning of bodies and minds. Such fields are supplying posthumanists with their bread and butter; when conceptions of human nature align with this soulless and fragmented mentality, living and working "with the machine without becoming a machine"[22] becomes difficult. If the psyche can be reduced to the brain, and the brain to a computer, wiring our minds with silicon chips seems a shorter step away. In this way the collision of humanism and posthumanism runs parallel with the collision between a depth psychology of the soul and a cognitive-behavioral neuropsychology of the brain.

The implications of these mainstream approaches to psychology are widespread. Today's robotic conceptions of human nature are conveyed to us within the pages of every magazine with the image of the depressed or anxious mind resulting from a "chemical imbalance"—a veritable grooming of the popular mindset for the posthuman ethos. Our emotional lives are being effectively reduced to a mechanism inside a machine in need of reprogramming. Psychological symptoms no longer point to anything meaningful; the soul's pathologizing complexity has disappeared into the synaptic gap. Whereas neuroscience has brought marvelous medical applications and an affirmation of some psychodynamic understandings, it has also instigated a mode of comprehending the human condition that one neuroscientist refers to as "neuromania."[23] The focus on neurology as the basis of thought tends to remove the mind from the phenomenology of being, as if everything that makes us essentially human may be found in the cerebral cortex. The idea that our humanity comes down to a brain-in-a-vat stands behind current endeavors in large-scale computer facilities to "reverse engineer" the brain on the pretext of creating an artificial human mind. But the differences between psyche and mind, mind and brain, and even neurons and transistors, raises the specter that whatever form of intelligence results from these pursuits won't be remotely human.

Other operations of neuropsychological reduction accompany the brain-as-complex-machine trope. Posthuman notions of the mind are based almost exclusively on left-brain modalities and higher cortical functions, pushing aside right-brain function and the more instinctive reptilian brain and limbic system. This literally half-brained notion of the mind, in which neither the body-world-psyche continuum nor the maintenance of psychological patterns generated in the evolutionary process play a significant role, constitutes the mentality reshaping our sense of self. Google founder Sergey Brin is quoted as saying, "we want to make Google the third half of your brain."[24] Removing right brain functions and exchanging virtuality for actuality may just allow this to happen.

Much of posthumanist discourse assumes a basis in science and an objective reading of the course of technology, but posthumanist conceptions of the mind and how to reshape it betray egocentrism and a disregard for emotion, imagination and the phenomenal world Indeed, much of the thought generated by posthumanists reflects a propensity to elevate intellectual endeavors far above other pursuits, and it's tempting to suspect that many hardcore advocates formed an early sense of identity around being a "geek" or a "brain." When life also revolves around gaming, online avatars and status in the world of computation, it isn't difficult to see the appeal of exchanging an organic mind for a computerized one, or swapping flesh for a robotic shell or, eventually, an angelic presence in cyberspace. Most of us may not be there yet, but ominous signs of the slippery slope of the Digital Age are omnipresent: compulsive checking of online communications and social media; preference for texting over interacting; an insatiable need for distraction from the persons and experiences immediately at hand.

I recently stood in front of Van Gogh's "Starry Night" at the MoMA in New York City and watched smart phones readily displace perception and memory. Many people walked away without beholding the painting at all; the experience had been effectively stored in the phone—digitized. This normative embrace of fabrication and facsimile was spotted over thirty years ago by Gaston Baudrillard in his famous treatise *Simulacra and Simulation*, where he argued representations have taken on a "hyperreal" value and originality has become meaningless.[25] Posthumanism is, in essence, an introjection of this hyperreality, a simulation of self that mirrors a simulated world. This would complete the detachment from nature that began with the Industrial Revolution, but it would also fully detach the controlling ego from the instinctual basis of being, as well as anything remotely resembling a phenomenal sense of self in relation to place and world.

From the psychological standpoint, this egocentric embrace of a fabricated self has all signs of a defensive withdrawal from the totality of being—a neurotic response to the unresolved existential crisis of the modern era. The questions of meaning and purpose, which Jung placed at the core of his psychological explorations, are thus still driving the bus of history, with the posthumanist riding in the very backseat. The posthuman fantasy is a reaction formation, an attempt to first perfect what is inherently imperfect and then transcend the conundrums of a fully human life. Promoted as a futurist vision that has been extrapolated from objective scientific understandings, this movement turns out to be deeply haunted, vibrating with the shades of the past—an unconscious backstory in need of analysis.

The Return of the Repressed

Until the posthuman movement succeeds in creating a mode of being that is fully detached from existence as we've come to know it, we are still subject to the compensatory nature of psychological life, wherein that which is avoided or dismissed returns in surreptitious ways. In this vein, notions of redesigning human existence contain unconscious religious and spiritual aims that are rarely acknowledged or comprehended, of which examples have been discussed by David Noble in his book *The Religion of Technology*.[26] Assuming the role of Creator, pursuing immortality, shedding the flesh for a more angelic life in cyberspace, not to mention projecting ultimate meaning and purpose onto technology itself, all indicate a displacement of the religious function, which is an archetypal pattern of the unconscious. Noble cites one software engineer saying that in cyberspace "floats the image of a Heavenly City, the New Jerusalem of the Book of Revelation . . . a place where we might enter God's graces . . . laid out like a beautiful equation."[27] The archetype of wholeness and totality that Jung aligns with this religious function reappears in the images of unlimited access to information, boundless computational intelligence and endless permeations of what remains of our physical form, as if the individual merger with these digital realities would be the fulfillment of existence. Citing his current day reliance on the computing "cloud," Kurzweil says he "feel(s) less than complete if . . . cut off from these brain extenders."[28] The feeling of completion is now already to be found in our access to digitalized information, where the three pseudo-divinities of our time—science, technology and economics—come together, in cyberspace.

This technological religion, promising release from our flawed and limited form and deliverance into a state of perfection, appears to share much in common with what Jung called the rise of "isms"—secular, collective attempts to meaningfully explain and systematize life in the way traditional religion and myth once did. However, there is one distinct difference. Whereas the ideologies and cults of the twentieth century could not eventually escape the mirror of human integrity and the presence of archetypal needs, scientism and technologism, which together background posthumanism, threaten to erode the presence of that very faculty, altering the ground of being to the point most existential questions of consequence will not *make sense*. In other words, we'll no longer be playing with a full deck. As Jung wrote, the individual who has "allegiance to any kind of –ism, loses touch with the dark, maternal, earthy ground of his being."[29] The mutual reinforcement of mechanization and detachment from a deeper integrity thereby becomes the stage upon which we will leave ourselves behind.

The problem with isms is that they leave us with a psychological hangover, a stalking sense that meaning has not been found and a lingering instinctive dissatisfaction. These are the unmet archetypal needs, referred to above. The psychic bridge between the upper and lower realms of experience, between the cultural and the instinctual, occurs via archetypal forms, which maintain a sense of the past at work within us and satisfy what is deep and essential. As "the hidden foundations of the conscious mind," Jung described the archetypes as "the most effective means conceivable of instinctive adaptation . . . the chthonic portion of the psyche . . . that portion through which the psyche is attached to nature."[30] The more absent these mediating archetypal experiences become, the more we find attempts to satisfy primary instinctual needs through secondary technological means—a vicious cycle in which superficial and fabricated ways of life leave lingering dissatisfactions and distracting enticements that are in turn redirected back to technology. Describing this process in terms of a "techno-addiction," ecopsychologist Chellis Glendinning counts nourishing food, strong community, meaningful work and the spiritual connection to the world among the areas now subject to this cycle.[31] With fast eroding means to directly satisfy these primary needs, artificial substitutions are readily accepted, and any lingering dissatisfaction or anxiety is repressed or denied. But anxieties return as compulsions, manias and distractibility, which have become such widespread modes of living as to be normative. This is the collapsing ecology of mind within which the fantasy of a new kind of human takes form.

The 2013 film *Her* portrays a man in the near future searching for love.[32] A computer-based personal companion appears at first to meet all of his needs. However, the disembodied, abstract and—as he comes to discover—highly generic virtual partner eventually conjures a soulless reality. The way this virtual human *almost* satisfies the instinctual need for friendship, love and even sexual gratification strikes the viewer as eerily believable because it's but a short extrapolation from the current day cyber-search for satisfaction. The man, ironically, makes a living writing love letters for those who need to outsource matters of the heart. And in the course of the film, it's as if his eyes are opened to the reality in which he now resides—a world of secondary satisfactions, where actual relationships have difficulty competing with the hyperreal. The film leaves us wondering whether life in that kind of world is sustainable or even worth living.

Anxiety and accompanying forms of dissociation point to neglected dimensions of the psyche, which call our awareness back to the breadth and depth of our humanity. But the return of neglected archetypal patterns can also turn tyrannical and monstrous. The enantiodromic exchange of utopian plans for dystopian outcomes is a recurring motif in science fiction, often in the form of autonomous technology turning on the humans, or rapacious alien life forms appearing alongside the overreach of science and industry.[33] Handing our fate over to computers or robots is another popular plotline, and it usually sets up unforeseen destructive consequences. However, in these stories at least, destruction is followed by insight, often leading to the rediscovery of human values and communal bonds. After the catastrophe comes the reawakening of soul. But can these fictional renderings of new consciousness translate into actual changes in collective awareness?

Posthumanistic Therapy

Standing by Jung's holistic embrace of the human condition and the creation of culture and meaning through dialogue with the archetypal patterns of the psyche exposes the underside of the posthuman vision. The fantasy that human beings are merely complex machines, destined to merge with other machines and then transcend the biological form of existence appears defensive and escapist. It is unconsciously driven by pseudo-spiritual aims, Cartesian flights from body and earth, and unresolved questions of modern life. Posthumanism's aim to adapt our existence to artificial forms of intelligence rather than to evolutionary inheritance is a grandiose redirection of human experience as a whole towards the particular mindset of the technophile, who surfs the wave of simulation that now surrounds us.

Like a patient in therapy, defenses of dissociation and denial must give way to the call for inner integrity before these neurotic patterns can be discerned. Individual conscience must rise above the hive mind. For this to occur, a point of reference is needed outside of science and technology so that the future of *humanity* can first be considered along *humanistic* lines. As one commentator recently noted, "The processing of information is not the highest aim to which the human spirit can aspire, and neither is competitiveness in a global economy. The character of our society cannot be determined by engineers."[34] The bubble of scientism and technologism that surrounds posthumanism must thus be burst by a more circumspect consideration of the actual human condition, one that makes room for "complexly beating hearts" and a "soulful and sensitive existence."[35] For that is the condition that lies within us, irrespective of what trends and futurist aspirations constitute the spirit of times, and its continued denial can only lead to a more haunted and split form of existence.

A century ago, eyeing the American love of technology, Jung said that the country must "make a choice to master its machines or be devoured by them,"[36] and sometime later, addressing the European, "it is sheer poison to suppress his nature, which is warped enough as it is, and to make out of it a willing robot."[37] Psychologically, we're already inside the belly of the techno-beast, long ago swallowed. And we already imagine our selves as robots, with programmable brains and a growing list of spare parts. But the continued embodiment of these states of mind may begin to place in starker relief the soulless and eventually inhuman reality under construction, so that the reawakening of the fully human occurs before we actualize the cyborg stage of existence. Sometimes the patient has to get worse, to cook for a while in the juices of their one-sidedness, waiting for the other shoe to drop. Somewhere along the path of living so detached from the ground of being, with posthumanism pushing us towards a programmed demise, we might just come to see, with Jung, that "Nature is not matter only, she is also spirit,"[38] and that the instincts are "the age-old forgotten wisdom stored up in us."[39] These elemental understandings of the human psyche would reverse the reductive operations of posthumanism and restore awareness of an interior ecosystem. The alternate is a kind of managed madness—a patient that never recovers a sense of self but continues to layer on fabricated reality until any spark of humanity is replaced by a blank, robotic stare, haunted by the absent presence of a former way of life.

Notes

1 In Meredith Sabini (Ed.). (2002). *The Earth has a Soul: The Nature Writings of C. G. Jung.* Berkeley, CA: North Atlantic Press. 153.

2 Leon Wieseltier. "Among the Disrupted." *The New York Times.* January 18, 2015. Book Review. 14. Wieseltier makes a clear distinction between "transhumanism," which would pertain to the goal of moving existence beyond the human form, and "post-humanism," which he maintains is a much broader and more pervasive departure from humanism. In most writings on the topic this distinction is less clear.

3 C. G. Jung (1958). The Undiscovered Self. In *The Collected Works of C. G. Jung.* (Vol. 10). London: Routledge & Kegan Paul. par.562.

4 Wieseltier. "Among the Disrupted," 14.

5 Ronald W. Dworkin (2006). *Artificial Happiness.* New York: Carroll and Graf.

6 Sherry Turkle (2011). *Alone Together.* New York: Basic Books.

7 Sharon Gaudin, "Intel: Chips in brains will control computers by 2020": http://www.computerworld.com/s/article/9141180/Intel_Chips_in_brains_will_control_computers_by_2020

8 Cited in Michael Chorost, *Rebuilt: How Becoming Part Computer Made Me More Human* (New York: Houghton Mifflin, 2005), 42.

9 (1967). "A Schoolman's Guide to Marshall McLuhan." *Saturday Review*, March 18, pp.51-53, 71-72.

10 See Evgeny Morozov (2013). *To Save Everything, Click.* New York: Public Affairs Books.

11 James Barrat (2013). *Our Final Invention: Artificial Intelligence and the End of the Human Era.* New York: St. Martin's Press.

12 Steven Levy. (1992). *Artificial Life.* New York: Vintage. 41.

13 See esp. Kurzweil. *The Age of Spiritual Machines.*

14 Kurzweil. *The Singularity is Near.*

15 Kurzweil. *How to Create a Mind.*

16 Ibid. 13.

17 See George Drinka (1984). *The Birth of Neurosis.* New York: Touchstone.

18 John and Paula Zerzan. "Industrialization and Domestication", 204.

19 Jung. "The Undiscovered Self", para. 1494.

20 Rollo May. *Man's Search for Himself.* (Originally published in 1953). Italics in original.

21 Ibid. 45.

22 May. (1969). *Love and Will*, 32.

23 Raymond Tallis. *Aping Mankind: Neuromania, Darwinitis and the Misrepresentation of Humanity.*

24 Claire Cain Miller, 2010. *Google Unveils Tool to Speed Up Searches:* http://www.nytimes.com/2010/09/09/technology/techspecial/09google.html?dbk&_r=1&

25 Jean Baudrillard, *Simulacra and Simulation.* S. F. Glaser (Trans.). Ann Arbor: University of Michigan Press.

26 David F. Noble (1999). *The Religion of Technology: The Divinity of Man and the Spirit of Invention.* New York: Penguin.

27 Ibid. 160.

28 Kurzweil. *How to Create a Mind*. 279.

29 Jung. *CW* Vol. 10. para. 103.

30 In Sabini, 198-199.

31 Chellis Glendinning. (1995). "Technology, Trauma and the Wild." In T. Roszak (Ed.). *Ecopsychology*. Berkeley, CA: Sierra Club Books.

32 Spike Jonze, (Director/Writer/Producer). (2013). *Her*. Warner Bros. DVD.

33 Glen Slater. (2007). "Aliens and Insects." In Slattery and Slater (Eds.), *Varieties of Mythic Experience: Essays on Religion, Psyche and Culture*. Einsiedeln: Daimon Verlag.

34 Wieseltier. 15.

35 Ibid.

36 In Sabini, 143.

37 Ibid. 124.

38 Ibid. 80.

39 Ibid. 98.

Bibliography

Barrat, James. *Our Final Invention: Artificial Intelligence and the End of the Human Era*. New York: St. Martin's Press, 2013.

Baudrillard, Jean. *Simulcra and Simulation*. Translated by S. F. Glaser. Ann Arbor: University of Michigan Press, 1994.

Chorost, Michael. *Rebuilt: How Becoming Part Computer Made Me More Human*. New York: Houghton Mifflin, 2005.

Drinka, George. *The Birth of Neurosis*. New York: Touchstone, 1984.

Dworkin, Ronald W. *Artificial Happiness*. New York: Basic Books, 2006.

Gaudin, Sharon. 2009. "Intel: Chips in brains will control computers by 2020". Retrieved from http://www.computerworld.com/s/article/9141180/ Intel_Chips_in_brains_will_control_computers_by_2020

Glendinning, Chellis. "Technology, Trauma and the Wild." In *Ecopsychology*, edited by T. Roszak. Berkeley: Sierra Club Books, 1995.

Jung, C. G. *The Collected Works*. Edited by Herbert Read, Michael Fordham, Gerhard Adler and William McGuire. Translated by R. F. C. Hull. Vol. 18. Princeton University Press: Princeton University Press, 1980.

—. *The Collected Works*. Edited by Herbert Read, Michael Fordham, Gerhard Adler and William McGuire. Translated by R. F. C. Hull. Vol. 10. 20 vols. London: Routledge & Kegan Paul, 1958.

Kurzweil, Ray. *How to Create a Mind*. New York: Penguin, 2012.

—. *The Age of Spiritual Machines*. New York: Viking, 1999.

—. *The Singularity is Near*. New York: Viking, 2005.

Levy, Steven. *Artificial Life*. New York: Vintage, 1992.

May, Rollo. *Love and Will*. New York: Norton, 1969.

Morozov, Evegny. *To Save Everything, Click*. New York: Public Affairs Books, 2013.

Noble, David F. *The Religion of Technology: The Divinity of Man and the Spirit of Invention*. New York: Penguin, 1999.

Sabini, Meredith., ed. *The Earth has a Soul: The Nature Writings of C. G. Jung*. Berkeley: North Atlantic Press, 2002.

Slater, Glen. "Aliens and Insects." In *Varieties of Mythic Experience: Essays on Religion, Psyche and Culture*, by D. Slattery and G. Slater. Einsiedeln: Daimon Verlag, 2007.

Tallis, Raymond. *Aping Mankind: Neuromania, Dawinitis and the Misrepresentation of Humanity*. Durham: Acumen, 2011.

Wieseltier, Leon. "Among the Disrupted." The New York
    Times. January 18, 2015. Book Review.
Zerzan, John & Paula. "Industrialization and Domestication." In *Questioning
    Technology*, edited by J. Zerzan and A. Carnes. London, Freedom Press, 1988.

*An early draft of this essay was first presented in an online discussion forum of the
International Association of Jungian Studies, May 2014.*

Glen Slater, Ph.D., *has studied and trained in religious studies and clinical psychology.
For the past 18 years he has taught Jungian and archetypal psychology at Pacifica
Graduate Institute, where he is a professor in the depth psychology programs. He edited
and introduced the third volume of James Hillman's Uniform Edition,* Senex and Puer,
as well as a volume of essays by Pacifica faculty, Varieties of Mythic Experience *and
has contributed a number of essays to Jungian journals and collections. He is currently
writing a book on the psychology of the posthuman movement and related implications
for living in the Digital Age.*

Allegory of the E-Cave

By
Craig Chalquist

In Plato's Republic, Socrates wonders out loud what an ideally just city would be like. He contrasts it with his famous image of the Allegory of the Cave, a dark place in which the confined mistake shadows shifting on the wall for what is true. This essay illustrates how the Allegory has found new life and relevance in the psychological confinements and distractions characteristic of the digital age. Excerpts from Plato's text[1] alternate with current events that parallel them. At the end the concept of an imminent change of "eradigms"—vast, collective worldviews with an archetypal core—introduces the hope that the luminous presence of the living Earth will break through the darkness of the digital cave.

Allegory 2.0

One key archetypal mytheme—a basic plot element that reappears in every time and place—is that of a prisoner lost in the Underworld. For Plato this mytheme took the form of the famous Allegory of the Cave in Book Seven of *The Republic*, where Socrates compares the ignorant to prisoners chained in a dark cave. With even their heads fastened in place, the prisoners mistake the shadows on the wall before them for reality. By contrast, the awakened can see the fire behind the prisoners, the shapes manipulated to cast as shadows, the opening out of the cave, and the sunlit world beyond.

As Joseph Campbell pointed out *The Hero with a Thousand Faces*[2], myths do not stay in mythology books: they come back to life all around us. The same is true for mythemes. When collective consciousness loses its balance, the old plots bubble up in new forms to compensate, to redirect, and to warn.

Has the digital age updated the Allegory of the Cave? Perhaps we can find out by perusing excerpts from Plato's famous allegory interspersed with daily happenings within the all-enclosing world of electronic media.

Inside the E-Cave

Socrates: Compare the effect of education and of the lack of it on our nature to an experience like this: Imagine human beings living in an underground, cave-like dwelling, with an entrance a long way up, which is both open to the light and as wide as the cave itself. They've been there since childhood, fixed in the same place, with their necks and legs fettered, able to see only in front of them, because their bonds prevent them from turning their heads around.

Young children in the U.S. spend an average of 32 hours a week in front of a television set watching live TV or playing electronic games. 71% of children between the ages of 8 and 18 have a TV in their bedroom. In most households, the TVs are on all the time and there are no rules about watching them. 98% of all U.S. computer users are online.

Socrates: Light is provided by a fire burning far above and behind them. Also behind them, but on higher ground, there is a path stretching between them and the fire. Imagine that along this path a low wall has been built, like the screen in front of puppeteers above which they show their puppets...Then also imagine that there are people along the wall, carrying all kinds of artifacts that project above it—statues of people and other animals, made out of stone, wood, and every material. And, as you'd expect, some of the carriers are talking, and some are silent.

Glaucon: It's a strange image you're describing, and strange prisoners.

Socrates: They're like us.

Texas Instruments tablets can wirelessly stream a TV movie and run a game at the same time. OnStar is developing Verizon streaming content such as music and video, games for car passengers. Paro the robot seal built in Japan for "psychological enrichment" now has a homepage on the Internet. The robot responds to greetings and changes of light and knows when it is being held. Adult males retreat into "man caves" of rooms rigged with monitors, flight simulators, and science fiction decor.

Socrates: Do you suppose, first of all, that these prisoners see anything of themselves and one another besides the shadows that the fire casts on the wall in front of them? How could they, if they have to keep their heads motionless throughout life? ...And if they could talk to one another, don't you think they'd suppose that the names they used applied to the things they see passing before them?

Accident rates rise in industrial nations as distracted cellphone users step into busy intersections, walk through plate-glass doors, and even slam into each other. Teens have actually been observed sitting next to each other while texting and phoning each other, an eerie exchange that social scientist Sherry Turkle refers to as "alone together. Students fail exams and essay assignments because they write in abbreviated bursts like they text.[3]

Socrates: And what if their prison also had an echo from the wall facing them? Don't you think they'd believe that the shadows passing in front of them were talking whenever one of the carriers passing along the wall was doing so? Then the prisoners would in every way believe that the truth is nothing other than the shadows of those artifacts.

As record droughts, superfires, and storms ravage the U.S., its politicians, funded by powerful corporate interests, pretend that climate change is either unreal or unimportant, cultivate the image of patriotic Christians, allow exorbitant war spending as half the nation struggles financially, and distract attention from pressing but unspoken issues by waving the flag and talking up "freedom" and "democracy." Reporters and news agencies—whose prime responsibility is to confront this untruth—parade stories about popular baby names, Spandex-wearing celebrities, and how pandas know where to pee.

Socrates: Consider, then, what being released from their bonds and cured of their ignorance would naturally be like... If someone compelled him to look at the light itself, wouldn't his eyes hurt, and wouldn't he turn around and flee towards the things he's able to see, believing that they're really clearer than the ones he's being shown?

Boys in the U.S. spend an average of 13 hours a week playing video games, girls less but gaining. 49% of the games are violent. 2% are educational. As digital use rises, visits to national parks fall off steadily. The average child can name a dozen electronic brands but not one bush or tree standing outside the window. Against its sunlit glare he must close the blinds on the rest of the world to see the screen more clearly.

Socrates: I suppose, then, that he'd need time to get adjusted before he could see things in the world above. At first, he'd see shadows most easily, then images of men and other things in water, then the things themselves. Of these, he'd be able to study the things in the sky and the sky itself mere easily at night, looking at the light of the stars and the moon, than during the day, looking at the sun and the light of the sun. And at this point he would infer and conclude that the sun provides the seasons and the years, governs everything in the visible world, and is in some way the cause of all the things that he used to see.

According to Richard Louv, author of Last Child in the Woods, *an increasing number of children suffer from Nature Deficit Disorder, a pattern of anxiety, depression, and various physical symptoms, including obesity, because of spending too much time indoors and online. Children raised this way often fear the natural world as messy, dirty, unpredictable, and uncontrollable, and seldom know where their food or water come from.*

Socrates: What about when he reminds himself of his first dwelling place, his fellow prisoners, and what passed for wisdom there? Don't you think that he'd count himself happy for the change and pity the others? And if there had been any honors, praises, or prizes among them for the one who was sharpest at identifying the shadows as they passed by and who best remembered which usually came earlier, which later, and which simultaneously, and who could thus best divine the future, do you think that our man would desire these rewards or envy those among the prisoners who were honored and held power? Instead, wouldn't he feel, with Homer, that he'd much prefer to "work the earth as a serf to another, one without possessions" (Odyssey, xi.489-90), and go through any sufferings, rather than share their opinions and live as they do?

In 2012, a 17-year-old in Wisconsin took home a prize for texting a 149-character message in 39 seconds. Dancing with the Stars rose to the world's most popular television program in 2006 and 2007 and made the Top 10 list in 17 countries. Trying to guess Apple's latest innovations has become an industry in and of itself. Many readers of the online tabloid Huffington Post amuse themselves by leaving mean online comments ("trolling") under stories about celebrity slips and mishaps.

Socrates: Consider this too. If this man went down into the cave again and sat down in his same seat, wouldn't his eyes—coming suddenly out of the sun like that—be filled with darkness?

Glaucon: They certainly would.

Socrates: And before his eyes had recovered—and the adjustment would not be quick—while his vision was still dim, if he had to compete again with the perpetual prisoners in recognizing the shadows, wouldn't he invite ridicule? Wouldn't it be said of him that he'd returned from his upward journey with his eyesight ruined and that it isn't worthwhile even to try to travel upward? And, as for anyone who tried to free them and lead them upward, if they could somehow get their hands on him, wouldn't they kill him?

ExxonMobil fights climate change legislation by deploying more than forty front companies posing as legitimate businesses and citizens' groups to cast doubt on authentic science and accuse advocates for cooling the planet of being anti-business. Shock jocks like Rush Limbaugh, Sean Hannity, and Bill O'Reilly regularly spew hateful labels at environmentalists and activists.

Socrates: In the knowable realm, the form of the good is the last thing to be seen, and it is reached only with difficulty. Once one has seen it, however, one must conclude that it is the cause of all that is correct and beautiful in anything, that it produces both light and its source in the visible realm, and that in the intelligible realm it controls and provides truth and understanding, so that anyone who is to act sensibly in private or public must see it.

"Ecologically considered, it is not primarily our verbal statements that are "true" or "false," but rather the kind of relations that we sustain with the rest of nature. A human community that lives in a mutually beneficial relation with the surrounding earth is a community, we might say, that lives in truth. A civilization that relentlessly destroys the living land it inhabits is not well acquainted with truth, regardless of how many supposed facts it has amassed regarding the calculable properties of its world."[4]

Socrates: What about what happens when someone turns from divine study to the evils of human life? Do you think it's surprising, since his sight is still dim, and he hasn't yet become accustomed to the darkness around him, that he behaves awkwardly and appears completely ridiculous if he's compelled, either in the courts or elsewhere, to contend about the shadows of justice or the statues of which they are the shadows and to dispute about the way these things are understood by people who have never seen justice itself?

Glaucon: That's not surprising at all.

Climate scientists are forced to defend themselves against charges that their science is invented. Van Jones is asked to step down as adviser to President Obama. No one else in government seems aware that the displacement of millions of climate refugees and the destruction of thousands of species in a mass extinction constitutes a planet-wide injustice.

Socrates: No it isn't. But anyone with any understanding would remember that the eyes may be confused in two ways and from two causes, namely, when they've come from the light into the darkness and when they've come from the darkness into the light. Realizing that the same applies to the soul, when someone sees a soul disturbed and unable to see something, he won't laugh mindlessly, but he'll take into consideration whether it has come from a brighter life and is dimmed through not having yet become accustomed to the dark or whether it has come from greater ignorance into greater light and is dazzled by the increased brilliance. Then he'll declare the first soul happy in its experience and life, and he'll pity the latter–but even if he chose to make fun of it, at least he'd be less ridiculous than if he laughed at a soul that has come from the light above.

At a Bay Area presentation of the latest version of Al Gore's "Inconvenient Truth" slideshow, the presenter replies to the suggestion that ecotherapists be on hand to guide people through the terror and paralysis brought up by a steady stream of dire news by affirming that "rational people" will use the facts to advocate for the best course of action: taxing the oil companies.

Socrates: Education isn't what some people declare it to be, namely, putting knowledge into souls that lack it, like putting sight into blind eyes... The power to learn is present in everyone's soul and the instrument with which each learns is like an eye that cannot be turned around from darkness to light without turning the whole body. This instrument cannot be turned around from that which is coming into being without turning the whole soul until it is able to study that which is and the brightest thing that is, namely, the one we call the good. Isn't that right?

Glaucon: Yes.

Socrates: Then education is the craft concerned with doing this very thing, this turning around, and with how the soul can most easily and effectively be made to do it. It isn't the craft of putting sight into the soul. Education takes for granted that sight is there but that it isn't turned the right way or looking where it ought to look, and it tries to redirect it appropriately.

"The Great Turning" is activist and Systems Theory expert Joanna Macy's term from moving from a growth-oriented industrial model of society to that of a life-sustaining civilization.[5]

Socrates: Now, it looks as though the other so-called virtues of the soul are akin to those of the body, for they really aren't there beforehand but are added later by habit and practice. However, the virtue of reason seems to belong above all to something more divine, which never loses its power but is either useful and beneficial or useless and harmful, depending on the way it is turned. Or have you never noticed this about people who are said to be vicious but clever, how keen the vision of their little souls is and how sharply it distinguishes the things it is turned towards? This shows that its sight isn't inferior but rather is forced to serve evil ends, so that the sharper it sees the more evil it accomplishes.

Glaucon: Absolutely.

In 2008, financiers and accountants allowing computer models to make their decisions become easy prey to casino capitalists who prey on the world economy and its investors. As families go under, large banks receive record bailout amounts from the U.S. federal government. Its chief advisers are bankers.

Socrates: However, if a nature of this sort had been hammered at from childhood and freed from the bonds of kinship with becoming, which have been fastened to it by feasting, greed, and other such pleasures and which, like leaden weights, pull its vision downwards–if, being rid of these, it turned to look at true things, then I say that the same soul of the same person would see these most sharply, just as it now does the things it is presently turned towards.

In one month in the U.S., 26.4% of young people between 12 and 20 use alcohol[6], with 17.4% binge drinking. Numerous studies have correlated alcohol and substance abuse with hours spent online. Teens dropping out of high school or refusing to advance to college are heard declaring that they don't want to be corporate sell-outs like their parents.

Socrates: And what about the uneducated who have no experience of truth? Isn't it likely–indeed, doesn't it follow necessarily from what was said before–that they will never adequately govern a city? But neither would those who've been allowed to spend their whole lives being educated. The former would fail because they don't have a single goal at which all their actions, public and private, inevitably aim; the latter would fail because they'd refuse to act, thinking that they had settled while still alive in the faraway Isles of the Blessed.

As of 2011, a year of record ecological decline, the most popular online games included titles like Sacra Terra, Mysteryville, Farmville, The Treasures of Montezuma, Gardenscapes, Ranch Rush, and Paradise Quest. A young couple immersed in Farmville allowed their young child to die of neglect and starvation.

Socrates: It is our task as founders, then, to compel the best natures to reach the study we said before is the most important, namely, to make the ascent and see the good. But when they've made it and looked sufficiently, we mustn't allow them to do what they're allowed to do today.

Glaucon: What's that?

Socrates: To stay there and refuse to go down again to the prisoners in the cave and share their labors and honors, whether they are of less worth or greater.

Like those who protested the telephone and the telegraph, pockets of people give up email and Internet access, throw away their cellphones, and retreat from confronting squarely the dilemmas of digital life. Many go off the grid. Their voices fade from a public discourse to which they no longer contribute anything valuable.

Ascending from Underworld to Earthrise

From within the cave, with its flickering lights and shadows, it is difficult to visualize a bigger picture. Digitization, climate crisis, expiring economies, continual war, mass extinction: what is going on?

A look back through history discloses four grand periods standing out above the flux: the pre-agricultural/indigenous, ancient history and feudalism, the Industrial and Scientific Revolutions, and a fourth that began on the day before Christmas, 1968, when astronauts aboard Apollo 8 transmitted back home the image of Earth rising above the lunar horizon.

Each of these periods resonates thematically with a collective worldview gathered around an archetypal image: Mother Nature, the Heavenly City, the Big Machine, and Earthrise. Each of these images in turn displays a phenomenological thrust or direction: center (the cosmos starts here), vertical (heaven up, earth down), horizontal (spread out and explore), and web-like (everything interdependent). We can, then, speak of four *eradigms*, collective worldviews that carry an archetypal core powerful enough to sway entire eras and populations.

Each eradigm holds sway until the collective consciousness it permeates begins to move beyond it. When that happens, the eradigm shows gaps, stirs doubts, and breaks down, with "breakdown" being an especially apt turn of phrase for a ponderous and increasingly clunky "Big Machine" whose linear techniques and atomistic approaches cannot hope to grasp the ecological or social complexities of life on a crowded, ailing planet.

I have come to believe that the turbulence we face today as our environmental, political, spiritual, and psychological debts all come due at once signals the weardown of the Big Machine and the ascendancy of Earthrise, whose central symbol, our planet seen as a whole, Joseph Campbell described as "the mythic image of our time." Mother Nature emphasized tribalism, localism, and immersion in non-human nature; the Heavenly City, hierarchy, dualism, and priestly authority; and the Big Machine, technics, parts, and materials. Eradigm Earthrise emphasizes network, depth, ecology, embodied spirituality, cultural diversity, and inclusive participation. It is a synchronicity and not a coincidence that so many ecological and environmental movements sprang forth, like the Internet, before and after Apollo 8's launch in 1968. Sometimes we require a higher view of things.

Through Socrates, Plato says education—in this case education for an archetypal theme shift from isolated e-cave to deep web—is not like putting sight into blind eyes: soul and body must be *turned to reality* by a power of good greater than either. Humanity is poised to make a Great Turning that eradigmatic history suggests is inevitable. The question is whether we will turn in time to save ourselves: whether our cave-darkened eyes can stand the light of the world around and within us.

As we turn, we must ponder the invention of new forms of education, inspiration, community, culture, and leadership of the kind that put us back into our senses and bodies, minds and souls, for as Socrates foresaw telling the newly awakened, "Thus, for you and for us, the city will be governed, not like the majority of cities nowadays, by people who fight over shadows and struggle against one another in order to rule–as if that were a great good–but by people who are awake rather than dreaming."

Notes
1. All *Republic* excerpts are from Plato, 1997.
2. Campbell, 2008
3. Turkle, 2011
4. Abrams, 1997
5. See: http://www.joannamacy.net/thegreatturning.html
6. From https://www.drugabuse.gov/drugs-abuse/alcohol

Bibliography
Abram, David. *The Spell of the Sensuous*. Vintage, 1997.

Campbell, Joseph. *The Hero with a Thousand Faces*. New World Library, 2008.

Plato. *Plato: Complete Works*. Edited by John M. Cooper and D. S. Hutchinson. Hackett Publishing Co., 1997.

Turkle, Sherry. *Alone together: Why We Expect More from Technology and Less from Each Other*. New York: Basic Books, 2011.

Craig Chalquist, Ph.D., *is department chair of East-West Psychology at the California Institute of Integral Studies in San Francisco and adjunct faculty at Pacifica Graduate Institute, where he teaches ecopsychology. He is Executive Editor of the* Journal of Holistic Psychology *and the author of several books, including those of the* Animate California Trilogy *and* Terrapsychology: Reengaging the Soul of Place, *editor of* Rebearths: Conversations with a World Ensouled, *and co-editor of* Ecotherapy: Healing with Nature in Mind. *His website is www.Chalquist.com.*

Online Social Networking

The Digital Face of Relational Psychodynamics

By

Aaron Balick

It's one of the simplest of words in the English language; four letters, one syllable. It comes with a nifty blue icon too, a thumbs up. I'm referring to the 'like' button on your Facebook page. It is operated with deceptively simple ease, just a click of a mouse, and yet it really packs a punch. You see, the 'like' button may be the simplest way yet to deploy one of the most important things that one individual can give to another: recognition. The function of intersubjective recognition can be traced right back to infant/mother interaction and is one of the most important psychodynamic functions in the lifelong development of the person.

Given the vital function that recognition serves for our psychological and emotional health, the ease of its deployment across an online social network provokes important questions for depth psychologists. For one, is the clicking of the like button, and the variety of other ways that recognition is deployed across social networks, too easy? And secondly, what might be the consequences of seeking to sate our deep motivations to relate to one another in this particular fashion?

The ways in which online social networks are constructed create a heady and profound psychological brew that belies the simplicity of their interfaces and the ease in which one engages with them. Such a concoction can be seen as a sort of recipe for a highly compelling (some might say addictive) form of social interaction. The first and most important ingredient of this mixture is the basic human motivation to relate to others. This motivation, however, is a tricky one: it can be complex and problematic and not always easy to swallow. In order to really get it into the shape we need for easy and fast consumption, we need a few more ingredients.

To our first ingredient of relational motivation we add generous proportions of ease and convenience, alongside liberal helpings of distraction and instant satisfaction. Next, we mix in volatile extracts of voyeurism and exhibitionism (they go so well together) and a dash of puerile curiosity to taste. The aim is to create just the right flavor combination of bitter and sweet to have you coming back for more. Blend the mixture well, and allow it to rise. Pat down and divide up into little balls that can be taken with you – the best social network is the one that is always near by and easily accessed.

The first version of the World Wide Web, now referred to as Web 1.0, lacked most of these interactive elements. Though it was pioneering in its public accessibility, its architecture was relatively static and was limited to a series of linked, content-heavy web pages. With the exception of computer hobbyists, this version of the Web wasn't so great at linking members of the general public to each other. When it later evolved into Web 2.0, the glitzier interactive version of its former self, the world changed with it. The shift to Web 2.0 enabled an ease of interactivity and human-to-human connectivity for the general public (think Friendster, Friends Reunited, MySpace, YouTube, *Second Life*, and now Twitter and Facebook). The World Wide Web was no longer a static entity, but one upon which regular people could interact with each other with on a daily basis.

The consequences of these developments have been massive, bringing to fuller fruition Marshall McLuhan's prescient description of media through which, he argues, "we have extended our central nervous system itself into a global embrace."[1] This global embrace is as wide reaching as it is compelling since it combines the extension of our own relational selves through a system of interactivity designed to engage our most addictive vulnerabilities as well. Perhaps Nicholas Carr author of *The Shallows: How the Internet is Changing the Way We Think, Read and Remember* puts it best:

if, knowing what we know today about the brain's plasticity, you were to set out to invent a medium that would rewire our mental circuits as quickly and thoroughly as possible, you would probably end up designing something that looks and works a lot like the Internet. It's not just that we tend to use the Net regularly, even obsessively. It's that the Net delivers precisely the kind of sensory and cognitive stimuli- repetitive, intensive, interactive, addictive – that we have been shown to result in strong and rapid alterations in brain circuits and functions . . . the Net may well be the single most powerful mind-altering technology that has ever come into general use.[2]

As I have argued in my book, *The Psychodynamics of Social Networking*[3], the fuel for this utterly compelling development in our modern social lives is recognition. It seems simple because we all know what recognition is, but the way recognition operates is rather more complex. Recognition is a two- way process ideally resulting in an intersubjective state that Jessica Benjamin calls "mutual recognition."[4] When online social networking is boiled down to its bare essentials, what do you get but a very efficient and simple technology for deploying recognition? The trouble is, mutual recognition is neither simply deployed nor simply received.

It's Developmental

Benjamin comes from the tradition of Relational Psychoanalysis, a further development of Object Relations Theory that has been gaining ground across a variety of psychotherapeutic modalities since the publication of the original work of Greenberg and Mitchell in 1983, *Object Relations in Psychoanalytic Theory*.[5] Today, Relational Psychoanalysis has been influenced by a whole variety of disciplines outside traditional psychoanalysis, including fields as diverse as attachment theory, feminism, post-modernism, and continental philosophy; it is a modern and cutting edge iteration of psychoanalysis, reviving a theory and discipline that many have proclaimed anachronistic; this version is anything but. It is not a school of psychoanalysis in its own right, but rather an over arching perspective which can be widely applied a variety of psychotherapeutic disciplines.

Relational Psychoanalysis, like Object Relations, sees the motivation to relate as absolutely central to human experience and the meanings that individuals make of their lives. Its difference lies in the fact that it is fundamentally an intersubjective theory; it conceives of human psychological development not just in relation to the infant (as subject) developing in a world of objects (with an emphasis on the infant's inner world), but rather developing in a world of subjects (other people, particularly the primary caregiver, with a mind of her own). For Benjamin:

> The development of the capacity for mutual recognition can be conceived as a separate trajectory from the internalization of object relations. The subject gradually becomes able to recognize the other person's subjectivity, developing a capacity for attunement and tolerance of difference.[6]

The capacity to manage sameness and difference is a fundamental developmental achievement in relational psychoanalysis, and continues to be a challenge throughout life. However, the nature of the individual's upbringing will have a large part in that person's ability to tolerate difference. For example, does the mother or primary caretaker really wish to recognise the growing infant as a subject in his own right, or does she see him as an extension of herself? The way in which a subject makes their way through early relational challenges will deeply influence both their selfhood and relational patterns as an adult.

The work of British psychoanalyst Donald Winnicott occupies an important position in relational thinking due to his concepts of "good enough mothering" and the "facilitating environment." His famous statement that there is no such thing as a baby[7] is a fundamentally intersubjective statement, indicating the mother/infant relationship is an important co-constructed space. His further development of the concept of the "false self" that the infant creates to meet the needs of his mother (where she is unable to meet his "difference") is another helpful tool in understanding the dynamics of recognition. The false self (and similarly "the persona" in Jung)* develops in the direction of interpersonal or social compliance.

The infant seeks to be authentically recognised by her primary caretakers, but also seeks and finds enjoyment in the discovery of the subjectivity of the other. The continued operation of seeking and being sought continues throughout life and presents us with some of our greatest challenges and greatest pleasures. The pleasures result from those moments of authentic mutual recognition whereas the difficulties revolve around managing narcissistic self-states (of the self and/ or the other) and the function of the false self catching most of the attention (recognition) at the expense of the true self; a series of events that leads to a feeling of alienation form the self, or a sense of being fraudulent. Both Winnicott[8] and Jung[9] share similarities in the perspective that neither the false self nor the persona is deemed pathological per se; it is only when the individual identifies

---

* The first chapter of my book (Balick, 2014: pp 1 - 25) is entitled "Psychodynamics." In this chapter I go into great detail on the similarities between Jung and Winnicott's theories on false self and persona.

with the false self or persona as the whole self that the her or she runs into problems.[10]

Seeking and Being Sought Online

I have written elsewhere[11] that these days a lot of the seeking is now occurring online. In my paper "TMI in the transference LOL: psychoanalytic reflections on Google, social networking, and virtual impingement" I tell a story about how a patient found some information about me in a Google search that fundamentally changed the nature of our therapy together. I came to understand these virtual events that shift the nature of a relationship as "virtual impingements." A virtual impingement is defined as "any event that happens in relation to a person by way of the virtual world, which is experienced as an intrusion on the self."[12] We can assume that impingements of this sort occur online all the time between individuals in and out of therapy. Those fortunate enough to experience them while in therapy have the opportunity to explore them at a deeper level. I wrote my book *The Psychodynamics of Social Networking* as a result of this important clinical experience and the desire to extrapolate my learning from that towards a wider cultural application.

It is important to see the world of online social networking as the *sine qua non* of our online relational selves. It is an arena where the desire to seek and be sought is in full throttle. As online social networks are outward facing, they call upon our "outward facing" facilities the ego, that is, the false self or persona. Both of these concepts are closely related as they refer to the mask we use to operate in the public realm. It is important, however, not to get caught up in the word "false." We all develop a false self in relation to our strengths and unique capacities as individuals, so it is not "false" at all, but as real as any other part of ourselves. It is, however, deployed with the aim of social compliance and is therefore not a fully free expression of our authentic selves (which is itself a complex and problematic concept).

When the psychodynamic functions of false/true self and the motivation for mutual recognition are combined with the ease, convenience and architecture of the online social network, you can see how the social network is replete with opportunities and challenges. In one sense, recognition is so easily acquired over the social network (Look! He "liked" my comment; Great she followed me!) that much of it may accrete to the persona or false self at the expense of other parts of the fuller self. Does the true or "real" self get neglected in this transaction? Benjamin (draws our attention to the importance of real authentic recognition:

Recognition is so central to human existence as to often escape notice
. . . it appears to us in so many guises that it is seldom grasped as an
overarching concept . . . to recognize is to affirm, validate, acknowledge,
know, accept, understand, empathize, take in, tolerate, appreciate, see,
identify with, find familiar . . . love.[13]

A cursory glance at Benjamin's verbs above will show you just how closely
these psychic needs align with the functions of your favourite social network.
The "like" button on Facebook alone can be used to recognize, affirm, validate,
acknowledge, know, accept, understand, appreciate, or find familiar with. A few
comments on a wall will fill in the details for the rest. While these functions no
doubt do a job, they also beg the question of whether or not the simplicity and
ease of delivering such sought after ego needs "fill the jar" as it were, of fully
rounded psychological health. Additionally, the ease with which mis-recognition
can occur over the social network also has to be taken into account. With such
dispatch can we deliver virtual impingement too.

The Role of Mental Health Professionals

Mental health professionals have a complex role in relation to the fast
moving online world of social networking. On the one hand it is imperative
that they come to understand the nature of the online social network as a fully
psychological phenomenon that needs theorizing and understanding more fully.
While there is currently a great deal of research in the field on this subject, most
of it is largely quantitative or survey based and does not adequately address the
deep psychodynamic meaning-making that is so central to our experience of
social networking: more qualitative work is needed in this area.

Research like this is particularly important for children and younger people,
those that Palfrey and Gasser call "Digital Natives"[14]—those who have grown up
fully saturated in digital culture and generally do not make a distinction between
online and offline lives. It is the online arena where these young people will
be seeking much recognition, and we have yet to fully learn the way in which
recognition deployed on social networks fully operates.

Another challenge facing mental health professionals is their own use of
online social networks, and how their presence and accessibility in the virtual
world has consequences for their own personal lives, and the lives of their clients.
Where many psychotherapists were once wary of being publicly available through
online social networks, as these networks have become more and more a regular
part of everyday life many more are joining in; early career psychotherapists
and trainees are likely to be coming into the field already fully loaded as digital

citizens. What does our availability and accessibility as therapists existing online mean to present and future clients? How does one deal with a virtual impingement when it is instigated (purposefully or not) by a therapist towards his or her client? These questions bear serious thinking by mental health professionals.

The computer scientist Melvin Kranzberg famously stated that "Technology is neither good nor bad, nor is it neutral."[15] Sherry Turkle pithily informs us that, "Technology proposes itself as the architect of our intimacies."[16] The combination of these two statements makes an important synergy. It puts into perspective the nature of an online world that has an architecture and for this reason is not neutral. Yet this architecture mediates our intimacies. In many ways, the more virtual we become, the more dependent we are on this architecture. We retain, however, the free will with which to choose how we interact across this architecture. In her article, "Internet Interaction," Kourash Dini describes the multitude of ways in which patients utilise the Internet:

> Patients can use the Internet for purposes that actualize or accentuate either adaptive or pathological functioning. Because of the nature of Internet interaction, users can be secretive or deceiving, exhibitionistic or voyeuristic, to a degree and in ways never before possible. For example, the simultaneous increase of shame and of modes for tension regulation around it can lead to conflictual feelings and, often, dissociative defenses. A need of community has always existed, but as the nature of community is changing, the Internet may lend a capacity to distorted defenses and methods of relating in ways with which we, as therapists, are familiar.[17]

I don't think that Dini is being hyperbolic here when she states that the very nature of community is changing. In reference to Kranzberg's statement,[18] this change is neither good nor bad, but it is equally not neutral. Psychotherapists and the role of psychotherapy in today's society cannot avoid the issue from the comfort of the consultation room, which is rightly in many ways, cut off from the high-speed world of online relating. Though readers of this chapter are presumably more familiar with online dynamics than the wider field is likely to be, there is no doubt great mileage to be had in thoughtfully applying developmental psychodynamics to the ways in which we operate and think about our subjectivities within the online world.

Conclusion

John Naughton compares the development of the Internet (and particularly Web 2.0) to the Gutenberg press and notes that within the first twenty years of the press's invention, society would never have guessed that it would challenge the authority of the Catholic church, trigger the Protestant reformation, facilitate the rise of the modern scientific enterprise and create entire new social classes.[19] We too are within the first twenty years of an invention that is bound to challenge aspects of familiar cultural life that we cannot even begin to understand:

> Anyone hoping that the turbulence wrought by the Internet will eventually subside, and that things will eventually level out, is doomed to disappointment. The complexity of our emerging media ecosystem, together with the 'permissionless innovation' that is facilitated by the Internet, make a return to stability is an unlikely prospect. Instead, our future will be one that is characterized by ongoing disruptive innovation. The good news is that we will adjust to this new realty, just as we have always done in the past. Humans are an adaptive species, and we are good at building tools that help us to cope with changing circumstances.[20]

I concur with Naughton's hope in the faith in the adaptive nature of the human species in the face of unknowable change. Psychoanalysis emerged at the frontier of the great unknown of the human unconscious and Freud stood at the precipice and looked forward with great anticipation. He delayed the publication of his first major work of psychoanalysis *The Interpretation of Dreams* (completed in 1899) to 1900 because he wanted its date of publication to be at the start of the gleaming new century. Few would have guessed that Freud would have been the Gutenberg of the unconscious, fundamentally changing the way the 20th century West would understand itself, its individuals, and its culture.

Few now would think that the insights of a man born in the middle of the 19th century might have something to tell us about a technology that, to him, would have been unfathomable. However, psychoanalysis was born in the face of the unfathomable; and Freud's heirs are up to the task.

Notes

1 Marshall McLuhan, *Understanding Media: The Extensions of Man* (Boston, MA: McGraw-Hill, 1964), p. 19.

2 Nicholas Carr, *The Shallows: How the Internet is Changing the Way We Think, Read and Remember* (New York, NY: W. W. Norton, 2010), pp. 115-116.

3 Aaron Balick, *The Psychodynamics of Social Networking: Connected Up Instantaneous Culture and the Self* (London, England: Karnac, 2014).

4 Jessica Benjamin, *The Bonds of Love: Psychoanalysis, Feminism, and the Problem of Domination* (New York, NY: Pantheon, 1988).

5 Jay Greenberg and Stephen A. Mitchell, *Object Relations in Psychoanalytic Theory* (Cambridge, MA: Harvard University Press, 1983).

6 Jessica Benjamin, "An Outline of Intersubjectivity: The Development of Recognition." Psychoanalytic Psychology (7S, 1990): 33-46.

7 D. W. Winnicott, *The Child, the Family and the Outside World* (London, England: Penguin, 1964).

8 D. W. Winnicott, "Ego Distortion in Terms of True and False Self" in *The Maturational Processes and the Facilitating Environment: Studies in the Theory of Emotional Development*, edited by J. Southerland. (London, England: The Hogarth Press, 1982), 140-152.

9 C. G. Jung, "Two Essays on Analytical Psychology," trans. R. F. C. Hull (Princeton, NJ: Princeton University Press, 1966).

10 Balick, *The Psychodynamics of Social Networking*.

11 Aaron Balick, "TMI in the Transference LOL: Psychoanalytic Reflections on Google, Social Networking, and 'Virtual Impingement,' " *Psychoanalysis, Culture and Society* 17(2, 2012), 120-136.

12 Balick, "TMI in the Transference LOL," 125.

13 Benjamin, *The Bonds of Love*, 15-16.

14 John Palfrey and Urs Gasser, *Born Digital: Understanding the First Generation of Digital Natives* (New York, NY: Basic Books, 2008).

15 Melvin Kranzberg, "Technology and History: Kranzberg's Laws," Technology and Culture. 27(3, 1986): 544 – 560.

16 Sherry Turkle, *Alone Together: Why We Expect More from Technology and Less from Each Other* (New York: NY, Basic Books, 2011), 1.

17 Kourosh Dini, "Internet Interaction: The Effects on Patients' Lives and Analytic Process," Journal of the American Psychoanalytic Association 59 (4, 2009): 982

18 Kranzberg, "Technology and History".

19 John Naughton, *From Gutenberg to Zuckerberg: What You Really Need to Know about the Internet* (London, England: Quercus, 2012), 13.

20 Naughton, *From Gutenberg to Zuckerberg*, 182.

Bibliography

Balick, A. (2012). "TMI in the Transference LOL: Psychoanalytic Reflections on Google, Social Networking, and 'Virtual Impingement.' Psychoanalysis, Culture and Society 17(2): pp. 120 – 136.

Balick, A. (2014). *The Psychodynamics of Social Networking: Connected up Instantaneous Culture and the Self*. London: Karnac.

Benjamin, J. (1988). *The Bonds of Love: Psychoanalysis, Feminism, and the Problem of Domination*. New York: Pantheon.

Benjamin, J. (1990) "An Outline of Intersubjectivity: The Development of Recognition". Psychoanalytic Psychology 7S:33–46.

Carr, N. (2010). *The Shallows: How the Internet is Changing the Way we Think, Read and Remember*. New York, NY: W. W. Norton and Co.

Dini, K. (2009). "Internet Interaction: The Effects on Patients' Lives and Analytic Process." Journal of the American Psychoanalytic Association. 59 (4). 979 – 988.

Greenberg, J. and Mitchell, S. A. (1983). *Object Relations in Psychoanalytic Theory*. Cambridge, MA: Harvard University Press.

Jung, C. G. (1966). *Two Essays on Analytical Psychology*. R. F. C. Hull (Trans.). Princeton, NJ: Princeton University Press.

Kranzberg, M. (1986). "Technology and History: Kranzberg's laws". Technology and Culture. 27(3). 544–560.

Naughton, J. (2012). *From Gutenberg to Zuckerberg; What you Really Need to Know about the Internet*. London: Quercus.

Palfrey, J. And Gasser U. (2008). *Born Digital; Understanding the First Generation of Digital Natives*. New York: Basic Books.

Turkle, S. (2011). *Alone Together: Why We Expect More from Technology and Less from Each Other*. New York, NY: Basic Books.

Winnicott, D. W. (1964). *The Child, the Family and the Outside World*. London: Penguin.

Winnicott, D. W. (1982). "Ego Distortion in Terms of True and False Self. The Maturational Processes and the Facilitating Environment: Studies in the theory of Emotional Development." Ed. J. Southerland. London: The Hogarth Press. 140-152.

* *A version of this chapter entitled "The Real Motivation Behind Social Networking" first appeared in* TILT *Magazine: Therapeutic Innovations in Light of Technology, Winter 2013: Volume 3, Issue 2*

Aaron Balick, Ph.D., *is a UKCP registered psychotherapist, supervisor, and social networking and media consultant working in London. Dr. Balick holds the post of honorary senior lecturer at the Centre for Psychoanalytic Studies at the University of Essex. He has a special interest in relational psychoanalysis and psychotherapy and is a founding member and chair of The Relational School, UK. In addition to his academic and clinical work, Aaron is a media spokesperson for the UKCP, a media consultant and a blogger and mental health writer for a variety of print and online publications. Aaron is the author of two books,* The Psychodynamics of Social Networking: Connected-Up Instantaneous Culture and the Self *(2014, Karnac) and the children's book,* Keep your Cool: How to Deal with Life's Worries and Stress *(2013, Hachette).*

The Universe is Only This Big

Brian Michael Tracy

Sometimes I think the universe
is only this big –

big enough to hide behind
a plush, blue velvet curtain

of dream, visible only where
the crushed and faded fabric

has become threadbare –
where darkness comes through

as light; and where the hem
tattered and torn, disturbs the floor

Brian Michael Tracy is the author of 3 books of poetry. Learn more about Brian's work at www.BrianMichaelTracy.com

Terminal Talk

Reflections on Thinking and Saying in the Digital World

By
Robert D. Romanyshyn

Introduction

This essay is divided into two parts. Part One contains my initial reflections on my first ever webinar talk. Encouraged by my colleagues to whom I had sent these remarks to continue to amplify them, Part Two explores other aspects of the experience of thinking and saying in the digital world.

Part One

As I settled into my post webinar moment, I had the uncanny experience of not feeling quite at home in that space. The uncanny quality of that time was also colored by a mood of sorrow, bathed in an atmosphere of sadness for what seemed to have been lost, left behind or forgotten.

From the work I have been doing regarding technology and its shadows as well as the relation between the technological mind and its style of discourse that creates and sustains its reality, I am familiar with the Gap between that world and its ways of saying and thinking and the quotidian world of embodied life recovered by the tradition of phenomenology, especially the work of Merleau-Ponty.[1,2] Working within that Gap I have become aware that in the Gap when it shows itself as itself Orpheus appears. Orpheus is the eponymous poet, the poet of the gap according to Baudelaire, the only poet whom Plato welcomed back into the Polis, and, as I have argued, the mythic- archetypal figure who is the ground of Jung's psychology[3]. In the age of technology Orpheus is also the shadow figure who, lingering on the Margins of the cyber world, reminds us of what has been forgotten. His songs awaken us, as they were said to do in Plato's time, to the Gap between the human and the divine and call to us to cultivate the human world beneath earth and sky and to dwell poetically in the world. In the uncanny mood of the Gap, Orpheus is near. The eponymous poet enters through loss.

So, after this webinar experience, I waited and tried to listen to what the poet might be asking us to remember in the polis of digital space.

Where is the sky in the digital world? Where is the earth, the flesh of nature? Where is the depth of this space? Its vertically has been usurped by the horizontality of an infinite expanse that eclipses or nearly so the human scale of time and space. And where is the other, the community of others when we meet at and through the terminal, where each and all of us now have a terminal identity, an image presence on a screen that has no haptic sense, a space where we are quite specifically out of touch with each other, a disembodied image, which not weighted with flesh can float free and be anywhere in the digital world, a spectacle of a disembodied self? Can I kiss you in the terminal world? In the words of e. e. Cummings:

> (While you and I have lips and voices which
>   are for kissing and to sing with
> who cares if some one-eyed son of a bitch
> invents an instrument to measure Spring with...)[4]

Are we as Gods in this space, creators of ourselves, makers of a new kind of being that makes a spectacle of itself, a being which has sundered the erotic bonds of the sensual flesh and the sensuous world with all its appeals and seductions, its temptations to linger and to find in the moment the splendor of the simple, the miracle in the mundane?

Are we as Gods who, now floating free outside the envelope of time, an enveloping, a cradling of the present within a past that lingers, haunts, and casts its presence in the present, and a future that bewitches and beguiles the present moment and companions it forward, tempted to imagine, to dream that we are immortal beings, eternal and beyond death?

How do I think, say, and teach in this new world where without the sheltering canopy of time each instant on the screen feels like a command to keep moving, to keep the illusion of self creation in place, a tyranny of immediacy in which the next moment is but what follows this moment, where any and every tomorrow is but what follows today, an endless loop of repetition?

And how do I think, say, and teach in this new world where there is no flesh, where the erotic field of fleshy engagement between self and other, a fleshy entanglement with all its ambiguities and mess, with all its spoken and unspoken gestured desires and appeals, where all the follies and absurdities of trying to say what one means and to mean what one says is nakedly there impregnating the other, where the lies of a hidden mind betray themselves on the face? What are words spoken at the terminal when they are no longer inscribed within the gestures of the flesh? Words of mind unhinged from flesh are tricky, but the body never lies. Did Descartes tell the first lie of this new world: 'I think therefore I am'? What is truth in the digital world, when even the images on the screen can be photo shopped?

I am in new territory here, perhaps not unlike but certainly amplified, as were those like Galileo who was drawn into the Gap between the medieval world and its ways of thinking, saying and teaching and the modern world of science:

Galileo's Telescope

He pointed his telescope at the stars inviting the assembled
    schoolmen to look.
The moon, he said, had craters on it.
Too shocked by such blasphemy that corrupted its perfection,
they refused his invitation.
With their beliefs held firmly in place,
they retreated to their books and plotted their revenge
as their world crumbled into oblivion.[5]

Did those Aristotelian schoolmen experience Galileo's new world as uncanny? How could he proclaim that all objects fall equally fast when the evidence of their senses told them differently? Were there some who in the face of what was approaching chanted repeatedly their mantras while they sought the old ways and tumbled with their world into oblivion? And were there others who with a sense of sorrow tried to preserve while transforming what they once knew? Freud reminds us that the repetition compulsion is an organic rhythm of soul, one of its pulsations in the face of trauma and change, a beat of soul trying to master its anxiety.

The new territory that we now inhabit comes toward us and announces itself as uncanny and in the mood of sorrow that colors the uncanny we are obliged to remember what is passing away in order to imagine another possibility. We are called to imagine a tomorrow that is not just the repetition of today, a tomorrow that re-collects what was and carries it forward into what might be, a creative engagement with time, a gathering up and carrying forward of a living history.

To return then to the question: how do we think, say and teach in the digital world? Attending to the uncanny, being a witness for it, having the courage to stay with the mood of sorrow, we cross over an abyss and linger on a bridge that spans the gap between what was and what might be. We move forward by moving backward. We begin to think, say and teach by remembering not to forget. And we begin to think, say and teach out of the mood of sorrow by being in the mood for *what might be*, the subjunctive mood of thinking, saying and teaching that is contrary to facts regarded as fixed and inevitable and open to what is a wish, a hope, a regret, a possibility and perhaps even a dream. A subjunctive mode of existence, which is a primary feature for me of a poetic sensibility!

In this mood then I try to begin to find my way into thinking, saying and teaching in the space-time of the webinar. I begin *to try on* thinking, saying and teaching *as if* I were a self in space-less space and timeless time, *as if* I were experiencing for a moment floating in digital space without the weight of flesh, an astronaut in this new landscape of weightless existence, *as if* I were immortal—a glimpse of what it might be like to be eternal—like a god.

And yet, and yet, perhaps to give the power of the illusion that this digital world holds its due, all of that above is tempered by the awareness that I am not such a being. And, with that realization that this possibility is a dream of soul comes also the acknowledgement of what is lost and being lost is found again. Strange as it then might be, if one is in the mood for it then might the power of the illusion become an awakened Eros for what was lost and has been found? In the words of T. S. Eliot:

> We shall not cease from exploration
> And the end of all our exploring
> Will be to arrive where we started
> And know the place for the first time.[6]

A Momentary Pause Between Reflections

I have lived in the world of the academy for fifty-one years first as a graduate student and then as a professor and writer. In that long span of time I have deeply appreciated that world as a space to pause and reflect on the tradition of one's discipline and through one's thinking and writing and teaching be in service to the ancestors and the unfinished business of their work. Seminars conducted in that space were fleshy affairs, a back and forth, give and take embodied thinking and saying where a gesture of emphasis, for example, had blood in it and sometimes even fury. One was impregnated as it were by the animated presence of the others, and inspired by the anima of embodied words, by the word being made flesh among us. In the digital world a seminar becomes a webinar and the space-time of thinking and saying are radically changed.

In Part Two I add some further reflections on that change. Before I begin, however, a word of caution. My reflections are not in service to nostalgia. We cannot dis-invent the digital world. But we can, and I would add must, not forget that the erotic bond between the sensual-sensuous flesh of embodiment and the sensuous-sensual flesh of the world is the signature that makes us most fully human. From that first moment when our species rose up on two legs and casts its eyes toward the horizon we have been born to see and bound to behold. How do we make a stand within the digital world? The continuing challenge is how to take up and preserve that bond between flesh and world while transforming it.

Part Two

Reflecting back upon my first webinar moment and re-collecting those first reflections I was drawn deeper into the experience. Being in that landscape I felt as if I had crossed a border into a new country, an unfamiliar place with its own customs and rituals with which I was unfamiliar. It is not the case that I am unpracticed in crossing borders, having spent more than forty years working in the landscape of dreams, learning ways to navigate in that place and most importantly learning how to respect the ways of thinking and saying of the dream world when crossing back into the world of being awake. This work has taught me that the primary challenge in this border crossing is not one of translation but of learning to value differences and avoid judging one world by the ways of thinking and saying that are native to the other world. I have also learned, especially from my work with actors, that building the dream back into the body is another way of working the dream that differs from interpreting its meanings. Indeed, I have come to prefer dream enactment to dream interpretation. The wisdom of the body seems to me a better guide than the ideas of mind. Regardless of what a dream might mean, regardless of whether one approaches a dream as a Freudian, Jungian, Existential-Phenomenologist or otherwise, every dream is a nightly humiliation of the ego mind. As such the dreaming soul humbles the ego mind, bringing it down to flesh, soaking and nourishing it in the humus or soil of nature.

As I am writing these reflections, I become aware that the webinar that has inspired them, *Conversations Between a Psychologist and a Poet*[7], is guiding them toward these remarks about the poet and the dream, which is the topic of the second seminar. It forces me to wonder who is the writer here? Am I writing these remarks or are they being written through me? Or, are the terms of either/ or inadequate to the issue, and is it closer to the experience of writing that would keep soul in mind to say that in the creative moment one is neither the writer as author nor the writer as agent in service to something other, to that which asks to be said and not left unsaid. This is in fact the key theme of how I have attempted to frame the issue of research from soul's point of view. The work that one does is as much a work that has chosen one as it is a work that one chooses, a *chiasm* between being an active author of a work and the receptive agent for the unfinished business in the work.[8] In the digital world does this issue arise?

Be that as it may, in this descent of the spirited mind soaring high with its ideas, the dream makes sense of the dreamer before the dreamer even tries to make sense of the dream. If one knows even a bit of alchemy and is somewhat familiar with its images, then one knows that alchemy was an attempt to understand the spirit–matter tension without splitting it. Might we say, then, that the dreamer is an alchemist of the night, an alchemist who is worked upon in darkness and who in the dark light of soul seeks to free the gold from it leadenness—that is to dissolve the fixed and coagulated beliefs of the ego mind? Moreover, Jung has suggested that quantum physics is a contemporary version of alchemy, a way of knowing that also is seated within that a same tension of spirit-matter.[9,10] I would also add here that Rilke is an Orphic poet and as such his poetry is a dreaming alchemy. As with the dream, then, might we ask who writes the poem?

In addition to the border crossings I have done between the dreaming soul and the waking mind, I am not a virgin in the digital world of technology. Eighteen months ago I bought a cell phone and at this moment I am typing these words on my computer and will e-mail this essay to a colleague. But, about 15 years ago when I began to sit at the computer I discovered that the pace of my thinking quickened and its directionality moved less like a spiral curling back upon itself and more like a straight line. The arrows on the page that went this way and that way from one idea to another, the messy inserts squeezed between words, and the margins outside of which the strange ideas that seemed at first glance unrelated to one's thinking had their place were now erased from the computer screen. The digital world was not only less messy it was also very efficient. The seduction of efficiency and the way it 'saved' time, a phrase that I find to be quite strange and which makes me wonder where we might deposit the time we save, was overwhelming. It slowly eroded the virtues of patience and slowness while writing on paper with a pencil and the pleasures I had taken for granted of chewing on a pencil waiting upon the right word, attending to the full engagement of the hand holding the pencil and making its marks upon the page. The webinar experience awakened the sense of sorrow over these lost virtues and pleasures.

Every experience one has is always layered with a complex history through which the sense of an experience first reveals—and conceals—itself. So my first webinar experience was filtered through the question of technology, which is the work that has been central to me as a psychologist. Working on the margins between phenomenology and Jungian-Archetypal psychology, I have approached technology as a cultural-historical symptom and dream.[11] Tracing the origins of our technological world view back to the 15th century development of linear perspective art, I showed how that cultural-historical invention became a convention, a habit of mind, that laid the foundations for the Cartesian split between mind and body and mind and nature. In establishing the procedures for portraying the three-dimensional world on a two-dimensional canvas, an artist becomes a Spectator who in looking at the world through a window was to focus his fixed gaze upon and take the measure of the world as Spectacle and the body as a Specimen. It is no accident that in that way of configuring subjectivity, embodiment and world the first modern text book in anatomy was written, or that the sound of time announced by the peal of church bells was soon to be watch-ed, or that the world was to be gridded and mapped for exploration and exploitation. We are the inheritors of that way of mapping the world. Has that window, which early on was actually a geometric grid, become the computer screen?

The webinar begins and I see my two colleagues on the screen. Seeing them I am initially reminded of a recent Skype session with my two-year old grandson. Because he lives so far away this technology is welcomed and yet what is absent in this kind of presence lingers as a longing and a loss. I see and hear him and he sees and hears me but we are out of touch. There is, as I suggested in Part One, no haptic sense on the screen and in this recent Skype session I saw how for the first time he seemed to recognize this absence. As 'he' withdrew his hand, which he had just extended toward 'me' to offer a taste of what 'he' was eating, 'he' looked puzzled that 'I' had not taken a small bite of what 'he' had offered. The puzzled look on his face was an expression of a metaphysical question: 'Where was grandpa?'

Very early on children learn the difference between engaging with persons in the flesh and the images on a TV screen, which are not persons with whom one can be in touch. But there I was in Skype space, a strange presence who is neither there with him in the flesh nor like his friend Thomas Train on the TV screen. In this liminal space between flesh and TV images I am a conundrum, grandpa present in his absence and absent in his presence. Recalling this event I realized that in this gap there was for me (and for him?) a mood of longing and loss.

In addition to my two colleagues, I also see an image of myself on the screen and this experience unsettles me. Sitting in my study speaking with my two colleagues I feel myself centered in my body, my subjectivity anchored in this space. At the same time, over there on the screen I see an image of myself who also is speaking with my two colleagues. But I do not feel myself centered there in my body. That image is not a photograph of me because it is 'I' who is speaking. It is also not a film of me that I am watching. The puzzle lies in the experience that the image of me who is speaking over there on the screen and the 'I' who is speaking over here while in my study are speaking simultaneously.

This experience opens another metaphysical conundrum like it did for my grandson, which makes me wonder if pre-digital people like myself and post-digital people like my grandson are two species of our genus. It also makes me wonder if the meeting of two such species might be as 'philosophers' drawn together across thresholds of puzzlement. A long time ago the two remaining species of our genus, Neanderthal and Cro-Magnon, encountered each other and we know the sad outcome of that meeting. Only one species survived!

But I digress, so to return to the reflection, the experience of an 'I' who speaks over there and over here simultaneously is uncanny. It does not qualify as an experience of splitting because I am not an object over there in the digital world for a subject over here in the world of my study. Nor am I, in the words of Merleau-Ponty quite like what he means by flesh, his term for human embodiment, by which he means one who sees because he is seeable.[12] Between, for example, the hand that touches the hand that is touched, the touching hand and the touched hand cross back and forth. Each slips into the other and only with a focused intention does one sense which is which before the slippage between them eludes the grasping mind. Flesh, then, describes an embodied subjectivity that can be for itself also an object. As such, we are neither just free floating minds that are pure subjectivity nor objects reducible to complicated mechanisms. The grammar of language captures this paradox. Embodied human subjectivity is a first person perspective that can take a third person perspective on itself: The 'I' who can speak about observing the eye is not the eye being observed.

So, in this digital world of terminal talk are we perhaps a bit closer but not quite flesh in Merleau-Ponty's terms? Neither subject nor object, nor subject-object chiasm, who am 'I' in this digital world? And where is the 'I' who 'I' am? Is that image over there that disconnects me from my subjectivity over here, a kind of spooky double of myself, a ghostly *doppelganger* who haunts that space over there, a figure of myth and fairy tale of whom it is said that when one encounters such a figure it can be a harbinger of one's death. These thoughts lead me to wonder about the issue of life and death in the digital world. What does it mean to live and what does it mean that we all owe life a death in this digital space and time? There are those like Ray Kurzweil[13] who predicts that with our current abilities in genetic and computer technologies we are fast approaching a singularity where the constraints of our embodiment will be transcended. In short, according to Kurzweil, one day soon we will shed our biological lives for an existence in the digital cloud. Of, course the consequence is clear. Death will be erased. In this regard, as I suggest in *The Frankenstein Prophecies*, an unfinished manuscript and a play in process, Ray Kurzweil is a symptomatic appearance of Victor Frankenstein, and a prophetic amplification of the Spectator Mind on steroids. But will death be eclipsed? And for whom? Are we as beings of flesh destined to go the way of the Neanderthals? Is the transcendence of death the death of who we are? Are we perhaps the last or penultimate generation?

As I continue to linger with the webinar moment, I am also aware that the presence of the audience is also uncanny. They are invisible. Their presence registers as an absence and in their absence they haunt the digital space as a presence. Live theater is like that. The audience is, at least in traditional forms of theater, invisible as the actors play their parts on the other side of an invisible fourth wall. Might we wonder then if the digital space of a webinar is a kind of theater? This, for me, is one of the intriguing questions raised by the webinar experience.

As I reflect on this question, I recall that there are forms of post-modern theater in which that fourth wall is deliberately broken. Are these forms of theater inspired by a desire to break the window that has separated the Spectator Mind from the world, and to make the play an embodied engagement of the characters with the audience? Perhaps such experiments open a space where the characters are real but subtle presences who as such stretch our boundaries of the real and its empirical identification with what can be measured. Beyond our addiction to an empirical sensibility, which equates the real with what is sensible and/or can be inferred from the sensible and can be measured, these experiments move us in the direction of a poetic realism and the cultivation of a poetic sensibility, which recalls the Aristotelian idea of the *nous poietikos* that Von Franz[14] describes as the creative intelligence that dwells in nature and the cosmos. Indeed, the webinar, "Conversations between a Psychologist and a Poet," is one of series of experiments I have been attempting regarding a language for psychology that would be responsive to the shadows of the technological world. They are experiments to recover ways of thinking and speaking that cultivate a poetic sensibility and the flesh of embodied and enacted words. Indeed, in transforming *The Frankenstein Prophecies* into a play the theater group with which I am working breaks the fourth wall. The play begins in the entrance to the theater. It begins before the play itself begins on the stage. The people in the audience become visible participants with the characters of the play. The walls between the fictional and the factual become permeable membranes.

If we might regard the digital space of webinar as a kind of theater, then perhaps the experiments with breaking the invisible fourth wall that separates the visible fictional domain of characters from the invisible domain of the audience are attempts to remind us of what has been forgotten: thinking and saying as the embodiment and enactment of the living word. In my many years as a psychotherapist I have come to appreciate how the symptom is a tension between reminding us of something that is too vital to forget and forgetting it because it is too painful to remember. In this context perhaps the digital world is a symptomatic expression of what has been marginalized and exiled to the shadows of the technological mind. Taken up as such perhaps this might be a collective therapeutic response to the digital world, a new world where grandparents who remember what is too vital to forget can meet grandchildren who imagine what still might be.

Postscript

As I was reading over these musings on webinar work, three more came to mind. I note them here in the spirit of inviting conversation.

The first one is the theme of the Gap about which I spoke above. The Gap is the core of the therapy relationship. It is a pregnant void that is also the container for the embodied complex gestural field. Patient and therapist are drawn into the gap between what is and what might be regarding the patient's suffering. When the field is not embodied—like it is not at the computer terminal; when the field is structured by the therapist's intentions to be useful, meaningful, or helpful, he/she distances him/her self from the immediacy of the encounter between two embodied beings whose gestures carry a complex history, whose symptomatic incarnations are the locus of a loss, the habitat where the figures of soul dwell waiting to tell their tales. Then the relational dynamic between the two is one of power. But when those intentions are let go of then the relation becomes one of being with and in the presence of the other in a field of possibilities. Eros not Power! Eros with all its chaos, ambiguities and fluidity! Can deep psychotherapy be done on Skype?

Second, if the digital landscape is disembodied, and if it is the embodied gestural field that holds the emotional, affective and feeling dimension of human encounters, then where is a place for a mood of sorrow in the digital world? Is the manic pace of the digital world where one can be on call 24/7 a defense against loss, a screen against sorrow? Moreover if the soul's way of finding something is by losing it, if loss is the alchemy that dissolves the ego's literal attachments to others/things and transforms them into their symbolic gold, does the digital world contribute to the soul's exile by the disembodied technological mind, and does it do so by fostering a kind of thinking that erodes the capacity for symbolic thinking? As a psychotherapist I wonder then if the ubiquitous borderline patient is the symptomatic reminder of that loss, for one of the primary features of the borderline personality is the lack for symbolic thinking.

Regarding Eros, we might also wonder if pornography, as one of the largest money- makers on the World Wide Web, is also a symptomatic cry of wounded Eros in the digital world.

Third, fascination, the glitter of the new and the expectations engendered by what is even on the way as newer, distract us from the call of the uncanny. Technological civilization married to capitalist greed would keep us busy and entertained, and would fill the gap with appetites that remain unsatisfied, with a hunger that starves the capacities of memory and imagination.

In a recent conversation with my good friend and colleague Michael Sipiora, he posed this question: 'Why is the media full of stories about Bill Cosby's admittedly horrible exploits while Ebola spreads and ISIS beheads?'

In reply, I suggested that the technological world knows the value and necessity of margins and monsters and uses it to distract us from reflection about the uncanny character of the technological world. As distraction it says to us, "The monster on the margins is not us." We are in the center (or depending on the issue could be. We could be one of the next rich ones, for example). Distracted, the center is strengthened.

Distracted, we never begin to ask what the monster on the margins might say to us. We become deaf to the possibility that the voice from the margins might carry what is hidden in the uncanny. We go on texting and typing, tweeting and Skyping, linking and Facebooking, becoming zombiefied, stupefied and hypnotized. Indeed, this motif lies at the heart of Mary Shelley's *Frankenstein*. Her story is a primer at the early stages of the technological world for how to create a monster. Madison Ave has amplified that primer!

Closing Time

As I read over these remarks one final time before I hit the send button, I realize that the term *reflections* feels premature. The remarks are more like explorations of a wanderer in the digital ocean, ruminations of a kind of ancient mariner whose only compass has been the port from which he has set sail as a guide to where he might be going. In this context, the voyage is not finished.

Notes

1 Maurice Merleau-Ponty, *The Phenomenology of Perception*
2 Merleau-Ponty, *The Visible and The Invisible*
3 Robert D. Romanyshyn, "'Anyway why did it have to be the Death of the Poet?'
4 e. e. Cummings, *100 selected poems, 59.*
5 Romanyshyn, *Leaning Toward the Poet: Eavesdropping on the Poetry of Everyday Life.*
6 T. S. Eliot, "Four Quartets," 59.
7 Online series produced by Depth Insights, Depth Psychology Alliance, April 2015.
8 Romanyshyn, *The Wounded Researcher.*
9 Jung, *Alchemical Studies.*
10 Jung, "Psychology and Alchemy."
11 Romanyshyn, *Technology as Symptom and Dream.*
12 Romanyshyn, "The Body in Psychotherapy."
13 Ray Kurzweil, *The Singularity Is Near.*
14 Marie-Louise von Franz, *Alchemy,* 186.

Bibliography

Cummings, e. e. *100 selected poems.* New York: Grove Weidenfeld, 1959.

Eliot, T. S. *Four Quartets.* New York: A Harvest Book, 1943.

Jung, Carl Gustav. *Alchemical Studies,* trans. R. F. C. Hull (Princeton, NJ: Princeton University Press, 1967).

Jung, Carl Gustav. *Psychology and Alchemy,* trans. R. F. C. Hull. Princeton, NJ: Princeton University Press, 1968.

Kurzweil, Ray. *The Singularity Is Near.* New York: Penguin Books, 2006.

Merleau-Ponty, Maurice. *The Phenomenology of Perception* Translated by Colin Smith. London: Routledge &Kegan Paul, 1962.

Merleau-Ponty, Maurice. *The Visible and The Invisible,* trans. Alphonso Lingis. Evanston: Northwestern University Press, 1968.

Romanyshyn, Robert D. *Technology as Symptom and Dream.* London, New York: Routledge, 1989/2006.

Romanyshyn, Robert D. "'Anyway why did it have to be the Death of the Poet?': The Orphic Roots of Jung's Psychology," *Orpheus, Spring 71: A Journal of Archetype and Culture* (2004): 55-87.

Romanyshyn, Robert D. *The Wounded Researcher.* New Orleans, Louisiana: Spring Journal Books, 2007.

Romanyshyn, Robert D. "The Body in Psychotherapy: Contributions of Merleau-Ponty," in *Body, Mind and Healing After Jung*. Edited by Raya Jones. London and New York: Routledge, 2011, 41-61.

Romanyshyn, Robert D. *Leaning Toward the Poet: Eavesdropping on the Poetry of Everyday Life*. Bloomington, IN: iUniverse, 2014.

von Franz, Marie-Louise. *Alchemy*. Toronto: Inner City Books, 1980.

Robert D. Romanyshyn is an Emeritus Professor of Psychology at Pacifica Graduate Institute. The author of seven books he has contributed articles to edited volumes, published essays in psychology, philosophy and education journals, has done radio, television and on line interviews and has made a film about his journey to the Antarctic. He is currently working on The Frankenstein Prophecies: The Untold Tale in Mary Shelley's Story—Eight Questions and Replies, *and* On Becoming and Un-Becoming a Psychologist: A Memoir of An Ambivalent Love Story.

Electronic Dance Music and the Indomitable Imagination

By
Jason Butler

The laptop computer has quickly become ubiquitous in the world of electronic dance music. Usurping the place once unquestionably afforded to the turntable, laptops have, like many technological advancements, exponentially expanded the realm of what is possible. Instead of blending one record into another record, DJs now have the capability of simultaneously sampling minute fragments from a multitude of songs, seamlessly mashing together a classic Michael Jackson hit with a bassline and beat that they created just hours before the show, chopping up vocal samples to make sounds that have never been heard before, forming an abstract impression, a glitch-filled polyrhythm that has broad appeal to a culture infused with technology. These cut up samples, the distortion of vocals into a kind of techno-speak, are exemplary voices of the technologized imagination—an aesthetic expression of a mind that has moved through the onslaught of technology and come out the other side with an unmistakable need to dance. Mimetic to the fragmentary feeling-tone and frenetic pace of the urban atmosphere, the synthetic synthesis of electronic dance music calls out to the carpel-tunnel wrists and arms, the knotted shoulders, and the bleary eyes of the cubicle prisoner, inviting the compressed, disengaged body to become the dancing body.

Electronic dance music (EDM) is generally played out of massive sound systems equipped to pump thousands of sonic watts through the body of the listener. Thundering, deep, and completely enveloping—it is as if the profound intensification displayed by EDM is the response to a call made by a culture that has grown weary of what Romanyshyn[1] has called the "reality of the objective body, the body as a technical function." Stepping onto the dance the floor, the dancer is immediately overtaken by a field of bass—chests thump and bones rattle as the caverns of one's body fill with a magnitude of sound. Carried by the perfectly syncopated beats, each dancer is invited to cut through the thick crust of the objective body, a body that one *has*, accessing instead the dancing body, a body that one *is*, a body that is claimed by the music, a claim that dislocates the pervasive nag of tedium and hardened responsivity endemic to the technologized world.

EDM, as the designation itself reveals, is a gathering in which the technological world meets with the multifarious worlds of dance and music. Seen alchemically, the name reveals a complex amalgam of different spirits. Afforded primary placement, ensuring clear differentiation from the more traditional analog forms of music, the first word "electronic" fills the imagination with images of modernity, of gadgets, of screens, of being plugged in, connected, but connected in a way that stands in radical difference from our collective history—connected through the medium of technology, which, according to Romanyshyn[2], inherently distances, even disincarnates. The second word "dance" calls to mind body, sweat, immediacy, emotion, connection through the flesh, timelessness, universality, celebration, and ritual. The third word "music" ties the first two together, binding them as integral partners in a marriage of old and new.

Although quintessential features thought to span most, if not the entirety, of human existence, the particular expressions of dance and music are contingent on the cultural-historical situation in which these phenomena take place. Educational theorist Diana Senechal[3] described the cultural context of the United States as a culture dominated by noise. What was a thrilling action movie 20 years ago is now a cinematic relic filled with far too much dialogue and hardly enough frenetic chases, stunts, and special effects. Advertisers have found myriad more ways to penetrate into one's experience with their product, polluting the environment with countless visual and auditory appeals. Facebook fills the mind with status updates that have little relevance for one's life. Overstimulation prevails. With this context in mind, it is tempting to not only place but reduce the world of electronic dance music to this constellation of expanding extremities of arousal. One might argue for a return to simplicity, to the roots of music, the warmth of analog, unplugged, organic.

This is a familiar response to many manifestations of the burgeoning digital revolution. The overwhelming expansiveness and speed of the digital world carries with it this pull to pull back, a move which echoes Heidegger's[4] sentiment: "We can affirm the unavoidable use of technical devices, and also deny them the right to dominate us, and so to warp, confuse, and lay waste our nature."

This paper is an attempt to offer an example of just such a response. I believe the tension between affirmation and domination is held well in the aesthetic display of the dancing body, a universal image of the indomitable quality of embodied imagination and affective expression. Even in the most wretched times of human cruelty, dance has found its way into the lives of the oppressed individuals, casting a circle of ritual space from which individuals may have an experience of reprieve from the onslaught of demands placed upon them, an affirmation of a freedom that cannot be taken.

Whereas human domination is still a central and inescapable concern even in so-called first world countries, there is a far more subtle form of slavery operating vis-à-vis the unexamined relationship to technology. As a culture, we have yet to differentiate our individuality from the technological device. Enmeshed, even merged, with our devices, we start to imagine ourselves through technological fantasies. While within the grip of this fantasy, the intricate mystery of psychological life is imagined as a network of bioelectrical impulses. The human being becomes an advanced microprocessor, and the task of psychology becomes the installation of better software, an upgrade that re-turns the patient to his or her tasks as a productive member of society.

Perhaps EDM and the events it inspires are a homeopathic treatment of our digital sickness. Like cures like. The ones and zeros of the office computer's binary speak are the same ones and zeros of the track that has thousands ecstatically dancing, thrashing, celebrating life. Just as practitioners of Indian Tantra ritualistically consume the substances that evoke and symbolically represent the passions that keep them bound to an existence marked by suffering (sex, alcohol, parched grain, meat, fish), electronic music, takes the very thing that binds body to chair and uses it in such a way to evoke profound expressions of freedom through the ritual of dance.

Western alchemy, similar to Indian Tantra in a variety of ways, has offered a comparable perspective in relation to the composition of the philosopher's stone—the *magnum opus* of the alchemical tradition. According to Thomas

Vaughan[5] of the 17th century, "the first matter of the stone is the very same with the first matter of all things." The alchemical beginning, the *prima materia*, permeates the appearance of nature, and that which is all around, available at any moment, is the quintessential ingredient in crafting the highly coveted philosopher's stone, achievement of which is described analogically as turning lead to gold or more abstractly as the perfect union of spirit and matter, the pinnacle of psycho-spiritual attainment.

Technology as Prima Materia

We are thrown into a world where technological fluency is mandatory professionally, socially, even romantically. Many authors, particularly those who have been influenced by Heidegger, have highlighted the great loss that has arrived by way of technological advancement. Like fine print on the back of a contract, or an invisible component buried in the packaging of each new gadget, hidden losses accompany each new technological acquisition. Loss of time, human relatedness, and personal touch are the sea in which each of us now swim, so hidden through ubiquity that it takes a kind of thinking that sees through the socially-constructed world, what Heidegger[6] called meditative thinking, to even notice that something has been lost.

However, when technology meets a community of dance we find access to those very things that have been lost by way of technology: time stretches like one song moving seamlessly into the next, boundaries around relatedness dissolve as the room warms with the collective heat emitted from a mass of moving bodies, personal touch becomes evident in the smiling eyes of those dancing near, in the way a dancer's hips interpret the song, in the surprising twists taken by the hands of the DJ. Isolation dissolves and body expands, responding without cognitive mediation to the composition of sounds pouring out through the speakers. The distance that technology creates, the way in which "the *telos* of technology's dream … is toward abandonment of the body, toward disincarnation,"[7] is worked through by the immediacy and intensity of the dancer's sensate experience. The pulsing waves of bass wash away the dissociated stare of the technologized body. And here, in all the pieces of our fragmented being, we find that freedom is a verb expressed most poignantly through the archetypal undulations of the dancing body.

And by what means does this shift from our controlled contraction and daily grind to uninhibited expression arrive? Poet Yeats makes an appeal:

Faeries, come take me out of this dull world,
For I would ride with you upon the wind,
Run on the top of the dishevelled tide,
And dance upon the mountains like a flame.[8]

Mary Oliver offers another image:

"Doesn't the wind, turning in circles, invent the dance?"[9]

Of course the *ecstasis* of dance, the shift from the dull world of technical drudgery to a joyous embodiment, is contingent on Faeries and Wind. These images, epitomes of the irrational, are the archetypal counterparts to the controlled, predictable, precision that has come to be expected by those who live in the cloud of instant information and comfort on demand. The technologized psyche abhors delay, discontinuity, system failure. In a world that values controlled predictability, these features erupt like symptoms—technological breakdown as a kind of cultural neuroses. And following Jung, we can read the neurotic symptom as "an attempt of the self-regulating psychic system to restore the balance."[10]

The Necessity of Alchemical Death

Confrontation with the repressed, the shadow of technology, is essential to the alchemical turn of poison to elixir. This move into the shadow was described as the first process of the alchemical opus, the nigredo, or blackening. The operations associated with nigredo, namely mortification and putrification, indicate that the raw material of the beginning must first suffer death and then undergo a process akin to a slow grinding with mortar and pestle. The ground substance must then sit so that it may ferment and rot into a blackness that is blacker than black.[11]

Without nigredo the psyche remains virginal, naïve to its terrain, an "unworked innocence,"[12] the sinless, stainless, purity, which lacks the heat and flexibility that comes from working the material. The virgin white is pre-black, a participation mystique, or unconscious identification with a particular experience. This virginal white, like Persephone in the field of flowers, requires the death and putrification of nigredo, the pull of Hades into the soul's underworld, a psychic space well-depicted in Eliot's "East Coker":

I said to my soul, be still, and wait without hope
For hope would be hope for the wrong thing; wait without love
For love would be love of the wrong thing; there is yet faith
But the faith and the love and the hope are all in the waiting.

Wait without thought, for you are not ready for thought:
So the darkness shall be the light, and the stillness the dancing.[13]

Eliot describes finding the dance in stillness, which when read with a literal eye sounds like a far cry from the sensory tumult of electronic dance music and the hyperstimulating environments in which it is played. It could be argued that it would be more effective to prescribe a regiment of meditation and yoga postures as cure for our "hurry sickness,"[14] treating the symptom with its opposite. However, these moves keep the individual in a dialectic of compensation, coping instead of transmuting. As Kugelmann[15] argued, such strategies can quickly become part of a monstrous attempt to become more adapted to a way of life that grows increasingly more inhumane.

Electronic dance music offers a venue for turning towards and confronting the symptomatic expressions of technology head on, an opportunity to craft an expression of embodied freedom out of the digital deluge, "to sit on the rim of the well of darkness and fish for fallen light with patience."[16] In dancing toward and within the source of the symptom we carve out some space for the soul of technology to meet the analog warmth of the human body, a demonstration of our fundamentally aesthetic nature and an unmistakable expression of the indomitable imagination.

Notes
1 Robert Romanyshyn, *Technology as 'Symptom and Dream*, 17.
2 Ibid.
3 Diana Senechal, *Republic of Noise: The Loss of Solitude in Schools and Culture.*
4 Martin Heidegger, "Memorial Address," in *Discourse on Thinking*, 54.
5 Mark Haeffner, *Dictionary of Alchemy: From Maria Prophetessa to Isaac Newton*, 211.
6 Martin Heidegger, *Discourse on Thinking*.
7 Robert Romanyshyn, *Technology as Symptom and Dream*, 20.
8 William Butler Yeats, *The Land Of Heart's Desire, The Hour Glass and Rosa Alchemica*, 13.
9 Mary Oliver, *Why I wake early: New poems*, 33.
10 Carl Gustav Jung, *Analytical Psychology*, 138.
11 James Hillman, "The Seduction of Black," *Spring* 61.
12 James Hillman, "Silver and the White Earth." *Spring 47*, 24.
13 Thomas Stearns Eliot, *Four quartets*, 28.
14 Leonard Schwartzburd and David Ulmer, "The Treatment of Time Pathologies," in *Heart and mind: Practice of cardiac psychology*, 331.
15 Robert Kugelmann, *Stress: The Nature of Engineered Grief.*
16 Pablo Neruda, *The Sea and the Bells*, 83.

Bibliography
Eliot, Thomas Stearns. *Four Quartets*. Orlando, FL: Houghton Mifflin Harcourt, 1943/1971.

Haeffner, Mark, *Dictionary of Alchemy: From Maria Prophetessa to Isaac Newton* (2nd ed.). New York, NY: Aeon Books, 2004.

Heidegger, Martin. *Discourse on Thinking*. New York, NY: Harper and Row, 1966.

Hillman, James, "The Seduction of Black," *Spring* 61, 1997.

Hillman, James. "Silver and the White Earth." *Spring 47*, 1980.

Jung, Carl Gustav. *Analytical Psychology*. New York, NY: Routledge, 1935/2014.

Kugelmann, Robert. *Stress: The Nature of Engineered Grief*. Westport, CT.: Preager, 1992.

Neruda, Pablo. *The Sea and the Bells*, trans. William O'Daly. Port Townsend, WA: Copper Canyon Press, 2002.

Oliver, Mary. *Why I wake early: New poems*. Boston, MA: Beacon Press, 2005.

Romanyshyn, Robert. *Technology as Symptom and Dream*. New York, NY: Routledge, 1992.

Schwartzburd, Leonard and Ulmer, David, "The Treatment of Time Pathologies," in *Heart and mind: Practice of Cardiac Psychology*. Washington, D.C.: American Psychological Association, 1996.

Senechal, Diana. *Republic of Noise: The Loss of Solitude in Schools and Culture*. Lanham, MD: Rowman & Littlefield Education, 2011.

Yeats, William Butler. *The Land Of Heart's Desire, The Hour Glass and Rosa Alchemica*. New York, NY: Echo Library, 1889/2010.

Jason Butler, Ph.D., *is a licensed clinical psychologist and core faculty in the Holistic Counseling department at John F. Kennedy University. He has a psychotherapy practice in Oakland, California where he sees adults and couples. He received his doctorate in Clinical Psychology from Pacifica Graduate Institute and his master's degree in Transpersonal Psychology from Saybrook University.*

His writing and research interests include archetypal psychotherapy, dreams, depth psychological research methods, technology and the body, and aesthetic modes of relating to psychopathology. He has recently published a book, entitled Archetypal Psychotherapy: The Clinical Legacy of James Hillman, *in the Routledge series on Research in Analytical Psychology and Jungian Studies.*

His most significant passion, however, resides in the pursuit of the perfect blend of tomato, cilantro, onion, and pepper in the dish we all know and love as salsa.

Paintbrush Ramblings

By
Andrés Ocazionez

The pixilated *Atariesque* creatures that populate this book have a story, or more specifically, an evolution. This short essay will attempt to examine the germinal point of their evolution, that delicate beginning when they came to be valued as worthy of life and nurturance and through which they became intertwined with my idea of creativity in psychological becoming (see *Coupling 159*).

Coupling 159

Yes, sad as it sounds, these creatures had to be taken in and adopted. To be totally fair, however, their origin was not so much sad as it was marginal. That is to say, the first of these creatures were literally born in the *margins* of my notepads, of my working time, and of my immediate daily interests.

As a candidate in training at the C. G. Jung Institute, Zürich, and in my doctoral research at Universidad Complutense de Madrid, my interests consisted in trying to understand and articulate the psychology-making process in other training candidates, in myself, in culture, and in theory: a serious, rigorous, dedicated task. After many hours of reading and quoting a range of serious, rigorous, dedicated authors, I ritualistically drowned my free time in the endless text, sound, and image streams of Twitter, YouTube, Facebook, Soundcloud, Spotify, and any and all manner of remotely interesting podcasts I could find. Apparent mindlessness, after hours and periphery: this is the region from where the first creatures popped out their heads (see figures below).

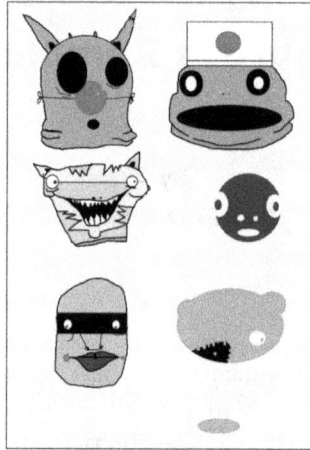

Assorted Cephalea 1 | 5

It was at some point in 2012 that they first appeared to me in a little group of three or four. They arrived expectantly, eager to make a deal: one by one I was to give them some sort of embodiment and *that*, at the same time, would be my gain. By giving materiality to something—*anything*—perhaps I wouldn't feel like a parasitically passive receptor of whatever wave of information passed over me within the margins of my time. The specific tool used to shape these creatures had to be at hand, and the closest one to me was *Paintbrush* (also known as "Paint," "MS Paint," or "Microsoft Paint"), the simple graphics drawing program developed by Microsoft in the 1980's and included in all versions of Microsoft Windows. So we kept our deal. To date, the small cluster of creatures has now grown to over two hundred.

If I were asked about the origin of these creatures, I would be tempted to claim that they are images from the unconscious, the term *unconscious* carrying with it, perhaps, the idea of an author or well of creativity hidden someplace within me. But the way these creatures were configured (as morphological citations from many and various floating discourses) has helped me realize that, as I recently read on *9gag*, a social media site that allows users to upload visual content, "You're not deep, you're not an intellectual, you're not an artist, you're not a critic, you're not a poet, you just have Internet access"[1]—and, we might add, *Microsoft Paintbrush* software.

Encrypted in the creatures' apparently simple deal was a call for the whole notion of marginality itself to be taken in and adopted. This stampede of life was by no means bubbling up from a supposed deep creative periphery of my conscious sphere. Jungian analyst Wolfgang Giegerich would argue that:

> Soul truths do not come from and have never been inside. They are precisely not born in private individuals ("in their unconscious") and are not distinctly spontaneous. Their authentic home is traditions, what always already has been said, believed, and done in the realm of "sharedness." Even "spontaneous" dreams and visions of individual persons, such as in initiations, followed long-established cultural patterns and merely activated them for the individual.[2]

Or as the same author reminds us, "The life of the mind moves out of the human world and settles in the world of things. The things become the masters and man slowly becomes of secondary importance. . . . The place where the action is, the place where the essential decisions happen has passed from man (reason, way of thinking, morality, instinct) to technology."[3]

The presence of these proliferating creatures was, by means of their living insistence, stating that the life of the mind is truly lived and celebrated *out there* in the logosphere webbed around every aspect of our existence (see *Cableados 155*).

Cableados 155

By the time the creature population had grown to over a hundred, I started to wonder about the creative act, and specifically about originality and influence. The essayist and novelist Jonathan Lethem, in his insightful essay *The Ecstasy of Influence*—a written collage stitching together fragments from authors such as Roland Barthes, Mark Twain, and Ralph Waldo Emerson—reminds us that:

> Any text is woven entirely with citations, references, echoes, cultural languages, which cut across it through and through in a vast stereophony. The citations that go to make up a text are anonymous, untraceable, and yet already read; they are quotations without inverted commas. The kernel, the soul – let us go further and say the substance, the bulk, the actual and valuable material of all human utterances is plagiarism. For substantially all ideas are secondhand, consciously and unconsciously drawn from a million outside sources ... There is not a thread that is not a twist of these two strands. By necessity, by proclivity, and by delight we all quote.[4]

Taking in the marginality of these creatures also implied reconsidering my stance towards the psychology making process. In my doctoral dissertation I inquired into the conditions of psychological becoming. I had taken for granted that some form of creativity was called for, but my idea of the specific way in which this creativity worked was still predicated on the notion of the personal unconscious as a hidden creative author. I assumed that the psychologist's creativity merely consisted in the specific style in which he or she dealt with the results of what had "spontaneously" emerged. Indeed, as a "depth" psychologist, I believed that this faculty was—and was supposed to remain—completely unknown; that is, unconscious.

The presentation, form, prose and style of C. G. Jung's currently celebrated *Red Book* is paradigmatic of this latter stance. The *Red Book's* wealth of creative art and dialogue is supposedly Jung's "confrontation with the unconscious." He referred it a stampede, writing that it "burst forth from the unconscious and at first swamped me. It was the *prima materia* of my lifetime work."[5]

But, again, could this *materia* be all that *prima*? As Sonu Shamdasani the historian and editor of the *Red Book*, notes in his introduction: "From an evidential standpoint, given the breadth of his learning, Jung's own material would not have been a particularly convincing example of his thesis that images from the collective unconscious spontaneously emerged without prior acquaintance."[6] Or as Giegerich declares in his review of the *Red Book*, "The vast mythological knowledge amassed by Jung through his reading is translated into 'spontaneously' emerging (but methodically induced) fantasy experiences."[7] Might this not be the specific way by which Jung, perhaps unwittingly, veiled the carpentry of his psychological creativity that later, through an argumentative contortion, "appeared" as spontaneous emergence? (see Apambichado 160).

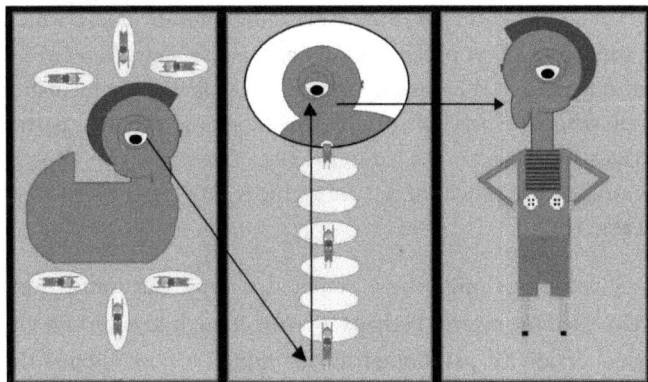

Apambichado 160

From this point of view, these creatures, as the creative work of this psychologist, do not have to be regarded as the spontaneous, privileged, numinous emergence of an artist or a visionary (*shivers*), but rather as the very human and mundane creative process through which I try to articulate that *intimacy* which is at the same time an *externality*. A key word to have in mind here is the neologism *extimity* (externality + intimacy) as has been introduced and elaborated by psychoanalysts Jacques Lacan and Jacques-Alain Miller. The morphology of each one of these drawings arrives as the conjunction of "depth and surface," "inner and outer," "private and public," and, by the same token, at a conception of psychological creation that is not inaccessible either by being located beyond or buried within.

We often seem to forget that this same discipline has at least participated in opening the gates and giving form to the innumerable hybrids, freaks, and mutants that populate our contemporary reality. As Shamdasani reminds us, psychology from the beginning of the nineteenth century was the scenario where:

> Textbooks, Principles, Outlines, Introductions, Compendiums, and Almanacs of psychology poured forth. Journals, Laboratories, Professorships, Courses, Societies, Associations, and Institutes of psychology were set up. A horde of witnesses was called forth and interrogated: the Madman, the Primitive, the Genius, the Degenerate, the Imbecile, the Medium, the Infant and last but not least, the White Rat. New characters entered the social stage: the Schizophrenic, the Narcissistic, the Manic-Depressive, the Anal-Retentive, the Oral-Sadistic, and all the "verts"—the Invert, Pervert, Introvert and Extravert.[8]

Unwittingly or not, psychology *is* creative. As Shamdasani also indicates:

> If there is one thing that psychology and psychotherapy have demonstrated in the twentieth century, it is the malleability of individuals, who have been willing to adopt psychological concepts to view their lives (and that of others). . . . What is important to note is that the formation of different schools of psychology and psychotherapy, with their particular languages and dialects, has led to the rise of archipelagoes of warring communities and subcultures. . . . Psychic reality is par excellence, the fabricated real.[9]

These illustrations might be a pixilated, sloppy, cartoonish wakeup call that I have created for myself. Perhaps it is not enough to entertain ideas *about* psychological creativity, psychological becoming, or psychology's thought of its own becoming. By drawing, talking about, and bringing these characters to life, I start to act upon "my own" psychological creativity or with psychological creativity at its own. It may be, in our times, that the ability to fragment, shuffle, and creatively rearrange our very own medium is the long awaited successor to introspection or interpretation—our very own native doodle.

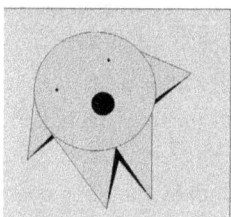   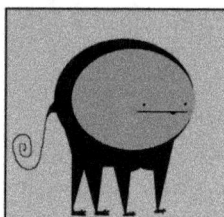   

Esterlina 0 I   Micorey 0 I   Buenas, Malas, Regulares

As the whole architectury that I have been trying to enact stands in an *in-between*, perhaps another big moment in the creatures' "adoption process" is happening *now* as you, reader, read these lines. In our individuality and shared logosphere, we silently *bring them in*. If you are seeing them and reading these lines, then that means that they have made it through. It might be that psychology's creativity stands at the point where psychologists are able to feel inspired, touched and affected. It is at that point of contact, in that *in-between*, that soul truths actually take place. And since this is also true for psychology, the discipline of soul-making, then consequently at least an important part of the *creative psychologist in me* that will (maybe) be able to teach, help, or inspire would not be my personal property but psychology's own. These creatures would then be the pixilated manifesto for the crucial role that resonances, quotations and influences play in psychology's capacity for being soulful, alive, and creative. So on behalf of a population of over two hundred bred creatures (and of many more to come) I have to thank you for your attention.

Billburr120

Billburr32

Billburr 88

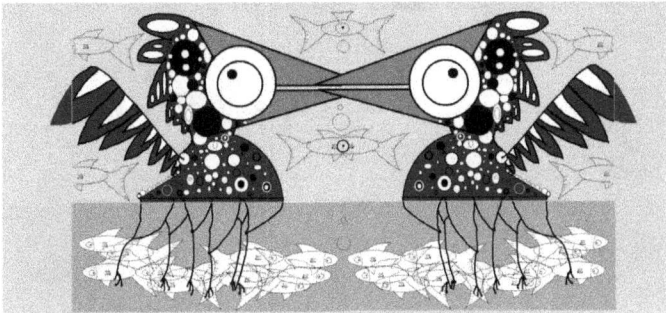

Billburr114

Notes

1 9gag Facebook page, Retrieved from https://www.facebook.com/9gag
2 Wolfgang Giegerich, *What is Soul?*, 2012, 117.
3 Wolfgang Giegerich, *Technology and the Soul: From the Nuclear Bomb to the World Wide Web*, 2007, 197.
4 Jonathan Lethem, "The Ecstasy of Influence," *Harper's Magazine*, 59.
5 Carl Gustav Jung, *Memories, Dreams, Reflections*, 199.
6 Sonu Shamdasani, introduction to *The Red Book. Liber Novus* by Carl Gustav Jung, 220a f.
7 Giegerich, *What is Soul?*, 117.
8 Shamdasani, *Jung and the Making of Modern Psychology: The Dream of a Science*, 3-4.
9 Ibid, 11.

Bibliography

Giegerich, Wolfgang. *Technology and the Soul: From the Nuclear Bomb to the World Wide Web*. New Orleans, LA: Spring Journal, 2007.

Giegerich, Wolfgang. *What is Soul?* New Orleans, LA: Spring Journal, 2012.

Jung, Carl Gustav. *Memories, Dreams, Reflections*. New York, NY: Vintage, 1965.

Jung, Carl Gustav. *The Red Book. Liber Novus*. Edited by Sonu Shamdasani. New York and London: Norton, 2009.

Lethem, Jonathan. "The Ecstasy of Influence." *Harper's Magazine*, Feb 2007: 59.

Shamdasani, Sonu. *Jung and the Making of Modern Psychology: The Dream of a Science*. Cambridge, England: Cambridge UP, 2003.

Andrés Ocazionez, Ph.D., (AGAP) *is a psychotherapist and Jungian analyst with a private practice in Berlin. Andrés is a graduate from the C. G. Jung Institute Zürich and has received a cum laude recognition for his thesis,* The Psychology of Analytical Training, *presented in the Faculty of Philosophy of Universidad Complutense de Madrid. His main concerns orbit around psychological creativity, psychological becoming, depth-psychological epistemology, and the possibilities and challenges of technological tools in the practice of psychotherapy. Andrés also works with sculpture, poetry and digital illustration. Andrés dances like a lobotomized person but continues trying to catch up with rhythm… a mysterious phenomenon for him (this has been endearing and even inspirational to some).*

Virtual Hyperrealities

Redefining the Real World for the Hungry Imagination Through Digital Media

By
Priscilla Hobbs

Introduction

Let's face it: We are living in a material world, and I am a material girl. I, like so many others of my 1980s generation—those whose childhoods are defined by that decade—have grown up surrounded by synergized brands that extend to a variety of different commodities. Our toys had television tie-ins: *He-Man, Transformers, My Little Pony*. Our sugared cereals were a quest for a hidden toy. Our talking teddy bears read us stories at night. And we spent many hours bashing bricks with our fists. No, we weren't kung fu fighters (though we wanted to be). We were the first generation to be raised with Atari, Nintendo, or Sega gaming consoles in our home. We didn't have to go to the arcade, and we didn't have to play outside to expand our imaginations. Our levels of social status were defined by whether we owned the golden cartridge for *The Legend of Zelda* or how quickly we could defeat Bowser and rescue the princess in *Super Mario Brothers*.

We even defined ourselves by which console we owned. The Cola Wars became the Console Wars as we debated which was better: Nintendo or Sega. Game consoles consoled us from cultural stressors we didn't know were bothering us.[1] As the Internet entered into the consumer market, it should come as no surprise that we translated that love for the virtual worlds from our consoles into the computer environments of MMORPGs, or *massively multi-player online role playing games*[2], and Facebook and similar social media websites. With the level of quasi-real-time interaction the computer provides, many of us find a sense of home in these realms.

I have no memory of my living room without a video gaming console. My family's first system was an Atari 2600. Or was it a 3600? Try as I might, at the advanced age of four years old, mastering the joystick and certain games were difficult for me. But somewhere along the way, I received a Nintendo for Christmas and set out, as Mario, to rescue Princess Toadstool by conquering the vicious *goombas* and *koopas* that could kill me with a single touch. Despite countless hours of practice, I never was too good at adventure or role-playing games. My forté is the puzzle game, specifically *Tetris* and the arranging of different blocks to create rows. Four rows created at once made a Tetris. And this talent (preference?) for puzzle games held true until I entered adulthood. Like the video games of my youth, I grew with the technology, improving and getting more skillful with each new kind of controller (though I still suck at *Super Mario Brothers*).

The Internet has become a central figure in the American household. Though traditionally accessed through a computer and a phone line, new technologies bring it ever closer to us, such as the smartphone, e-reader, or tablet. It no longer provides only information, but also communication and entertainment. The Internet *consoles* us in a similar way that our consoles did. Because of the prevalence of the Internet in our lives, Americans (and subsequently most of the rest of the entire world) are constantly redefining community through online channels that connect us instantly with other people of like interests around the world. Where we once connected through newsgroups and chat rooms, now we connect through games that create a virtual world. *Something* about these virtual worlds is comforting. They are more real than real—they are *hyperreal*—so much so, that these games can ask us to pay subscription rates or buy upgrades (a costume for your character for ninety-nine cents!) with real money earned outside of the digital spectrum to enhance our virtual experience.

Hyperreality and consumption go hand-in-hand, making new forms of online gameplay the logical evolution of the marriage between video games and the Internet. The American "Dream" is founded on principles of consumption, but the preference for simulation and play in post-World War II/post-modern America means that we are consuming hyperreality at growing rates.[3] The Internet simply makes it easier by giving us environments that reflect our innermost dreams and desires. These environments can be customized within some set parameters to suit any player. The virtual gamespace becomes mine. I suggest that this need to possess and consume the virtual reflects a hunger in America.[4] Some might claim that it is a hunger for community, and others may say it's a hunger to have better control over their world.

"That Was an Heroic Effort"[5]

If there's any complaint an adult will make about video games, it's that kids aren't getting outside anymore and playing. But, in the mind of a gamer, they *are* getting outside...sort of. That outside is in the safety of their air-conditioned homes; that outside is just as real as the real outside, and it is far more fun. Perhaps there are more friends in the gamespace, or perhaps the quest is more attractive than a game of make-believe. The gamer's relationship to the imaginal is of a different caliber than the traditional relationship to the Land of Make-Believe. Even though the images are provided by the game designer, the quests do penetrate into the gamer's psyche. Video games come with a sense of accomplishment, whether it's in defeating the Boss or in finding the buried treasure, or all of the little treasures along the way.

The American fascination with prefabricated mythologies, or stories we can reenact that follow a plot and rules set by an outside creator or designer, began in the 1960s with medieval war games inspired by the popularity of J. R. R. Tolkien's *The Lord of the Rings*.[6] Like prefabricated houses, these stories are manufactured with all of their components already put together, and the player has a limited ability to customize the parts to meet his or her tastes within set parameters. Two enthusiasts of these kinds of games, Dave Arneson and Gary Gygax, came together in the mid-1970s to write *Dungeons and Dragons*, establishing the tradition of prefabricated mythologies and gaming. A criticism of prefabricated myth is that we are essentially limiting ourselves to a specific sphere created by a few. But since we're having so much fun doing it, should we really care?

A prefabricated myth gives the player a few different options when getting started. First, I have to pick my character, or avatar. Am I a ranger? A wizard? A necromancer? Then, I may have the option of choosing a few characteristics of my character. Male or female? What color of costume? Is there a special power-up or weapon? The choice of character may establish what story gameplay will follow, or whether all characters may follow the same plot.

Though the story is established by the game designers, it is still up to us to figure out how our heroic gestures are accomplished. The measure of success of any of these games varies. It could be how many points we have, or many times we die, or how many bonus items you find in a single play-through. Unlike a *Choose Your Own Adventure* novel, there is a set beginning and there is an established end, with the exception of games whose focus is more about the environment than it is about the play, such as *Minecraft* or *Second Life*, whose adventures center around exploring a fully customizable world and less on fulfilling quests.[7]

The personality of one's avatar is an unconscious version of oneself. It allows a player to become—to identify with—a person who is nothing like the person she is in real life (or *IRL*, as gamers call it). For example, there are stories, like the one shared by a friend of mine:

> When I first began playing *WoW* [*World of Warcraft*], several years ago, it seemed like some veteran bully or another was constantly interfering with my questing. And talk about anonymous: when you're on opposing sides in *WoW*, provided you're not one of the super-nerds who have cracked the code, you can't understand each other's chats anyway. What you CAN understand, however, is sign language. You can dance, smile, laugh, wave. So, I came across this person at about the same level as me, opposite side, working on the same quest. He turned around like he was about to attack me, and I sat down and waved. He paused, then resumed his quest, attacking something else. From behind him, I started shooting at the same things he was, but after he had shot them at least once, so they would still be his kill for the quest. When he was finished, he stuck around and waited for everything to reset, and then did the same thing for me. It was kind of amazing. That whole "do unto others" mantra…

Some players approach their gameplay as though the people with whom they are playing are not humans, just other digital beings, and therefore are not subject to the same kind of moral courtesies we extend other human beings IRL—as though the veil of anonymity permits us to shut down our humanity. Gamers have a tendency to self-police. Players who constantly impede on the gameplay and enjoyment of other players, called "trolls," may get ostracized and possibly banned from the game.

The new technologies have given the games more depth—depth of visuals, not depth of story. The stories of these games are still as complex as they always were. Without the complex, immersive story to draw us in, we cannot become one with the game, or merge our consciousness fully through the game controller and into the screen, identifying ourselves with the avatar before us.

Here's how it works:

Video games turn us each into some kind of hero. There's the hero we expect, the savior, who is tasked with some mission or series of missions to rescue something or someone from an evil bad guy, known as the boss. This hero completes a mission, defeats a level boss (the big boss' goon/subordinate), and gains some kind of reward or experience that then allows the player to advance to the next level. Perhaps you advance—or perhaps you die—in which case, woe to you who forgot to save the game before entering the battle!

There's another kind of hero, one who is seemingly un-heroic. This hero is tasked with building a city or some other community, or maybe this hero is taking care of a virtual pet. Every day the player comes back to the game to harvest products (such as virtual crops or other natural resources) to be redeemed for coins, to build improvements, and to send an update to her friends to see if they can donate anything to help the virtual space grow. Some days will yield a big success—you can finally build that stone castle you've been coveting. Other days will be routine days of waiting for something to be built or to grow. The more the player has in the virtual space, the more virtual money that is earned in the game to buy other virtual improvements. And so on. Anything to keep you logging in every day. This becomes a cycle akin to addiction. The game rewards us for certain behaviors, and, in response, we desire more reward. A recent example of this is the popular Facebook and mobile app game, *Candy Crush Saga*, which fuels addiction by allowing the player to purchase additional turns or power-ups. The BBC reported in December 2013 that the game "is estimated to make £610,000 ($1,000,000) per day from its users."[8]

The hero is one of the oldest archetypes in the world.[9] We, as human beings, love the hero, because the hero ensures that our world continues to function as normal or even a little improved. Or perhaps the hero inspires us to become heroes ourselves. Video games allow us to become the hero without the commitment of a life-changing journey. We play the game, succeed through to the end, and *voila!*—a hero. If the character dies during gameplay, we can always go back to the last save point and try again. Many earlier games punished a lack of skill by sending the gameplay all the way back to the beginning of the game if the character died, but modern games are a little more friendly about second chances—an appropriate response from a cultural environment afraid of coming to an apocalyptic end. Exceptions to this death/save dichotomy are those games made under the Lego brand by Traveller's Tales, in which death is a simple formality of falling to pieces, only to come together again and continue the adventure as though nothing had happened (minus 2000 studs, coins made from a single Lego dot, but a quick player can recover them before they disappear). Video games teach us that the hero's journey is not plagued by problems of mortality; that we can achieve some kind of greatness without any painful sacrifice. And if we can achieve greatness without sacrifice, then this should apply IRL as well, right? The rules of social convention and natural law do not apply to the rules of gaming convention.

But then, what motivation should we have to try to succeed in the real world when we can always succeed in the gaming world? For, even though the gaming world is constructed by someone else, and even though that "someone else" wrote a plot for us to follow that allows little room for change, we still have to control our avatar across the chasm, kill the bad guys, and find the missing treasure. We still make the sacrifices of the hero, even if only in the gaming space. By engaging in the archetype of the hero through the myth of the game, even virtually, we can be taught the same lessons without physical sacrifice.

Hyperreality Gets A Second Life

"Hyperreality" is a term used by post-modernist philosophers, such as Jean Baudrillard and Umberto Eco, to describe the phenomenon surrounding the moment when a *simulacra*, or simulated signifier, is perceived as being more real (genuine, authentic) than the thing or event it is simulating. The simulacra is an idealized, perhaps romanticized, version of the thing or event, which makes it more attractive than the original. Baudrillard identifies three orders of simulacra:

> (1) simulacra that are natural, naturalist, founded on the image or imitation and counterfeit, that are humorous, optimistic, and that aim for the restriction or the idea institution of nature made in God's image; (2) simulacra that are productive, productivist, founded on energy, force, its materialization by the machine and in the whole system of production – a Promethian aim of a continuous globalization and expansion, or an indefinite liberation of energy... ; (3) simulacra of simulation, founded on information, the model, the cybernetic game – total operationality, hyperreality, aim of total control.[10]

The first two categories are the realms of the utopian dream and science fiction, respectively. These simulacra replicate phenomena that we can directly experience or that we can construct. The third category, that of hyperreality, replicates simulation itself. Hyperrealistic environments are constructed from ideal images—this is the way that we can bring our dreams into the concrete reality of our experience.

A hyperrealistic world operates in a shallow ether. While there may be a "backstage" area to this realm, such as basic programming, maintaining the simulation requires full concentration of resources on the illusion. The effect on the psychology of a people who live within this simulated realm becomes such that even psychic activity (dreams, myths, cultural interrelationships) likewise function in this shallow level, in which there is no genuine desire to tend to the depths of anything, be it an issue or a dream. There is no practicality in this realm, because the simulated environment promotes play; someone else backstage will handle anything that is required. But this isn't a bad thing, as some may contend. We'll get to that in a moment.

I do want to note before moving on that hyperreality isn't unreality.[11] Hyperreality is a reality in which the simulated is perceived as more real than the reality, and constructs a total environment such that the line is blurred between the authenticity of the simulacra and its re-imagining of the real. Unreality, on the other hand, does not attempt to dapple with realism from the outset, and leaves little room for doubt of its motives. Nor is hyperreality fake, because its intention is to draw us in and make us part of its mythos. To be fake, a simulacrum has to distance the observer from it, such that the observer knows it to be fake. Cognitively, we know a hyperrealistic world is not real, but we willingly suspend our reason and yield to the environment. A prime example of a successful hyperrealistic world is Disneyland. Though one can cognitively recognize that the Disneyland environment isn't real, the Imagineers applied such attention to detail that the environment is absolute. A stroll down Main Street, U.S.A., feels like a stroll through a small town, while Frontierland encapsulates us in the Old West— sensations recreated for the game *Kinect: Disneyland Adventures*, which allows us to experience the "Disney Magic" at home. From the comfort of our home, *Kinect: Disneyland Adventure* allows us to experience Disneyland with simulated environments and attractions. The Kinect technology for Xbox 360 and Xbox One (similar simulators exist on other platforms) allows us to engage kinetically with the virtual space, bringing the physical body into the dream-world.

We allow ourselves to be captivated by hyperreality. What simulation constructs is a parallel universe, and this is the realm of dream and fantasy. Baudrillard offers a cautionary message against this, saying that this destroys both the image and the platform on which the imaginary exists, taking its seduction with it.[12] Indeed the disillusionment Baudrillard is warning about has seeped into the larger society; we are overstimulated with simulation.

Common places have been transformed into hyperreal worlds: malls, movie theaters, restaurants, educational institutions, religious institutions, among several others. Furthermore, we are barraged with the onslaught of advertising, news, and other digital media outlets attempting to "amuse ourselves to death."[13] Virtual hyperreality, then, is our escape from the hyperreality that was originally intended as the escape from reality.

Baudrillard contends that modern, post-war American culture is constructed as an expression of the hyperreal, that Americans have developed a preference for the simulacra, and this promotes a worldview that is grounded in hyperreality, i.e., is fundamentally ungrounded, consumptive, expansive—and frustratingly fascinating.

What does this mean? It means that we have a preference for the simulated environments of the hyperreal. Hyperreality feeds our images of American myth; specifically, it feeds the illusion of America as a utopia and the myth of Manifest Destiny by tapping into American romanticism and pulling the signifiers out of the realm of reality and putting them into the intangible realm of simulation and technology to create the image of the perfect world. Since the end of the Great War (WWI), we have constructed environments that allowed us to actually *be* in the image we are trying to create: the suburban boom, Disneyland, themed restaurants and shopping centers. Because this vision of a perfect world of abundance and harmony is so strong, such constructed environments suggest little to no room for change, which provides reassurance from the perceived chaos of reality. Without perceived change, hyperreality constructs an immortal world, a long-standing myth in the civilized world.

New Game or Continue Game?

How many times have you heard this?

I was bored one night and stumbled across this really cool new website that …

or

I was curious to see what all the fuss was about, so I created a free account …

or

I'm low on funds this month, and I have to choose between my WoW [World of Warcraft] *subscription and my cell phone bill. Of course, I choose the WOW subscription. I don't want to leave my guild in the lurch!*

or

We met on the Internet!

The Internet is our virtual playground. "Virtual reality" describes computer-simulated environments, real or imaginary, that replicate real world experiences. It's as though we're actually *there*. Virtual hyperreality, however, marries hyperreality with our consumptive behaviors. Americans like to consume; we've been consuming since the first European colonists landed on the East Coast. At first we were consuming the land, spreading Democracy and Christianity under the guise of Manifest Destiny. As technology progressed, we started consuming stuff. Cheap stuff. And before long, we started consuming fake stuff. Americans have a hunger that cannot be satiated easily. As our expanding waistlines and growing credit card balances prove, the more we eat, the more we crave. The more we crave, the more we replicate. The more we replicate, the more we eat. And so on, and so on.

So we play. Play allows us to get in touch with the imaginal. As Johann Huizinga, a sociologist of play, tells us, that play

> is a function of the living, but is not susceptible of exact definition either logically, biologically, or aesthetically. The play-concept must always remain distinct from all the other forms of thought in which we express the structure of mental and social life. Hence we shall have to confine ourselves to describing the main characteristics of play.[14]

I, and the rest of those 1980s kids I mentioned in the introduction, play by recreating their (our) childhood, which helps us embrace dreams and emotions that have gotten buried by the responsibilities of adulthood. Video games provided the first forays into a virtual hyperrealistic sphere, creating for the consumer a place where the laws of physics and social conventions are irrelevant; a space where we could live out our fantasies of being the hero by actually controlling the hero's adventure, not just passively engaging with it through the imagination. Any of us can break the bricks and rescue the princess, or we can ninja-kick our way to the Boss, or we can find the buried treasure.

And then there are MMORPGs, those massively multi-player online role playing games, that bring many players into the same virtual realm. Each player assumes an avatar and navigates the same playing field as the other avatars, coming into conflict or compromise depending on the player. Unlike other video games, the MMO world exists even when I'm are not currently playing. Adventures continue to happen. Other players continue to level-up. Treasures are found and bosses are defeated. All while I am asleep—in the game world that is. Hopefully, I didn't have my eyes set on that gold statue, because M@sterTrixxxx666 got to it first, but if I can find him (or her?), I can fight for that gold statue. Perhaps I'll succeed, perhaps I won't. But my opponent needs to go. If only we could dispose of our real world opponents so easily!

For most players, distinguishing between the real world and the gaming world isn't a problem. Playing the game is fun, just a mode of entertainment, a way to unwind. For other players, it's not quite that easy because they have given themselves over to the game. These players are the ones who, after what feels like a couple hours of game play, realize that they've spent the entire day playing the game—where did the time go? And there are players who schedule their day around their game play. They have a 10 o'clock date with their guild on *World of Warcraft*, so everything that needs doing better be done by then or it's not getting done. And there are players who never leave the game world. "Never" is a strong term. They do leave the game world from time to time, but they have put so much of themselves into the game that the gaming and material worlds have flipped. In the gaming world, these people come alive, but in the real world, they feel they are social outsiders; they find belonging and acceptance in the game world.

100 Gold Coins = 1 Up[15]

The video game world has influenced our real world in that it has encouraged everything to become more interactive. Since the redux of the console wars in the late 1990s that saw newer, prettier game-scapes on newer, prettier consoles such as the Playstation, and since the introduction of the Internet into the consumer home in the 1990s, the real world has become progressively more like a video game world. Just as the hyperreal worlds of the 1950s and 1960s influenced the real world by bringing our Cold War consumerist fantasies to life in three-dimensional environments (Disneyland for instance), so have the virtual hyperreal worlds of the 2000s brought a new wave of dreams and fantasies to life in three-dimensional environments. In a literal way, these dreams are brought to life through Cosplay ("costume play," the dressing as a character, thing, or idea from a fictional work for purposes of role-playing in a non-game environment) and other fan outlets.

But, more importantly, we see the influence of video games impacting the level of interactivity we now experience with our technology. Computers and cellphones compete for our affection with apps and widgets, designed to conveniently give us information, or so we are led to believe. Erik Davis notes,

> Information technology tweaks our perceptions, communicates our picture of the world to one another, and constructs remarkable and sometimes insidious forms of control over the cultural stories that shape our sense of the world. The moment we invent a significant new device for communication—talking drums, papyrus scrolls, printed books, crystal sets, computers, pagers—we partially reconstruct the self

and its world, creating new opportunities (and new traps) for thought, perception, and social experience.[16]

A computer built in the 2000s must be full of shiny sounds and visuals, not just functional. Cell phones are now "smart" as they strive to keep up with tablets. Through decisions one makes about one's phone settings or app use, these devices get to know you. Figure us out. Soon they become your closest friends.[17] Sure, we think we are using our smart phones to play games, text or e-mail our friends, or share retro-style photographs with our social networks, but these are just distractions from the main point or issue. What we are really doing is giving our smart phone our attention, nurturing it like a newborn baby, massaging its screen and feeding it our data. In reality, our phones, our computers, our cars with their talking GPS systems—these are all toys. Or they can be seen as tools of our hero quests, just as magical as the wand or sword our avatar uses in battle. By combining music, graphics, and story, video games penetrate into our most inner dreams and fantasies by creating an immersive experience.

Conclusion

There are different types of virtual hyperrealities just as there are different types of personalities. One personality may prefer a first person shooter, another the world of the MMORPG, and still another the creativity that comes from building your own farm from a few virtual seeds.

The children of the 1980s were replaced by the children of the 1990s, many of whom know of no life without the Internet. For them, the Internet provides all of the answers, and it is the only way to communicate with friends and family. The prevalence of the Internet ensures that our world will become increasingly like a video game. The lines between the hyperreal and the real will become increasingly blurred. We have already seen how the Internet can build new sense of community or interpersonal relationships. Perhaps the video games heroes of the future will be tasked with saving *us* from the overabundance of hyperreality.

Notes

1 For a cultural text exploring some stressors in America, take a listen to Billy Joel's "We Didn't Start the Fire".

2 This category of games, as the name suggests, is played online by a community of players, each playing his or her own quest while interacting with each other to build a virtual community of shared experience and resources.

3 In January 2013, Facebook reported "1 billion users; 604 million mobile users; More than 42 million pages and 9 million apps" ("Do you know What's up?"). This is a

significant jump from the 1 million users at the end of 2004 ("Number of active users at Facebook over the years") Similarly, World of Warcraft, which recently appears to have "lost its WoW factor," currently claims 9.1 million users (Bedigan).

4 The focus of this essay is on American culture, though many of the same claims could be applied to others. They are a discussion for another paper and will not be explored here.

5 A phrase often repeated throughout the console game *Gauntlet: Dark Legacy* (2001).

6 Daniel Mackay, *The Fantasy Role-Playing Game: A New Performing Art* (Jefferson: McFarland, 2001), 15.

7 For example, some tech-savvy professors have experimented with using *Second Life* to create a virtual classroom to construct a stronger sense of community among the students than typically offered by Blackboard or other "traditional" online classrooms.

8 "What is the appeal of Candy Crush Saga?" *BBC.com*, last modified December 17, 2013, http://www.bbc.com/news/magazine-25334716

9 For an in-depth discussion of the hero as archetype, see Joseph Campbell's *The Hero with a Thousand Faces.*

10 Jean Baudrillard, *Simulacra and Simulation*, trans. Sheila Faria Glaser (Ann Arbor: University of Michigan Press, 1994), 121.

11 Priscilla Hobbs, "Towards a Happily Ever After: Disneyland and Imagineering the American Dream" (Ph.D. dissertation, Pacifica Graduate Institute, 2012), 94.

12 Jean Baudrillard, *Simulacra and Simulation*, trans. Sheila Faria Glaser (Ann Arbor: University of Michigan Press, 1994), 106.

13 Neil Postman, Amusing Ourselves to Death: Public Discourse in the Age of Show Business (New York: Penguin, 2005).

14 Johan Huizinga, Homo Ludens: A Study of the Play Element in Culture (Boston: Beacon, 1955), 7.

15 A reference to a reward system in the Super Mario games.

16 Erik Davis, TechGnosis: Myth, Magic and Mysticism in the Age of Information (New York: Harmony, 1998), 4.

17 See the 2013 film, *Her*, from director Spike Jonze, Annapurna Pictures, U.S.A.

Bibliography

Baudrillard Jean. *Simulacra and Simulation*. Trans. Sheila Faria Glaser. Ann Arbor: University of Michigan Press, 1994.

Bedigian, Louis. "World of Warcraft Has Lost its 'WoW' Factor." *Forbes.com*. Last modified May 10, 2012. http://www.forbes.com/sites/benzingainsights/2012/05/10/world-of-warcraft-has-lost-its-wow-factor/

Campbell, Joseph. *The Hero with a Thousand Faces*. 2nd ed. New York: Bollingen, 1968.

Davis, Erik. *TechGnosis: Myth, Magic and Mysticism in the Age of Information*. New York: Harmony, 1998.

"Do you know What's up? Check out these 2013 Social Media Statistics." *Facebook.com*. Last modified January 27, 2013. https://www.facebook.com/notes/up-creative-inc/do-you-know-whats-up-check-out-these-2013-social-media-statistics/470970089631080

Eco, Umberto. "Travels in Hyperreality." *Travels in Hyperreality: Essays*. Translated by William Weaver. San Diego: Harcourt, 1986. 1-58.

Hobbs, Priscilla. "Towards a Happily Ever After: Disneyland and Imagineering the American Dream." Ph.D. diss, Pacifica Graduate Institute, 2012.

Huizinga, Johan. *Homo Ludens: A Study of the Play Element in Culture*. Boston: Beacon, 1955.

Mackay, Daniel. *The Fantasy Role-Playing Game: A new Performing Art.* Jefferson: McFarland & Co., 2001.

"Number of active users at Facebook over the years." *Yahoo News.* Last modified May 1, 2013. http://news.yahoo.com/number-active-users-facebook-over-230449748.html

Postman, Neil. *Amusing Ourselves to Death: Public Discourse in the Age of Show Business.* New York: Penguin, 2005.

"What is the appeal of Candy Crush Saga?" *BBC.com.* Last modified December 17, 2013. http://www.bbc.com/news/magazine-25334716

Priscilla Hobbs, Ph.D., earned her doctorate in Mythological Studies from Pacifica Graduate Institute and is the author of Walt's Utopia: Disneyland and American Mythmaking. *Articles she has published or presented at conferences concentrate popular culture as a modern, living mythological system, including:* "The Tri-Wizard Cup: Alchemy and Transformation in Harry Potter," "The Wizarding World of Harry Potter: From Book to Embodied Myth," "Rewriting Fairy Tales: Disney's Silly Symphonies and the Great Depression," *and* "Every Pony Has a Story: Revisions of Greco-Roman Mythology in My Little Pony: Friendship is Magic." *Dr. Hobbs is constantly looking critically at the relationship between popular culture and cultural identity, with current research focusing on theme parks, Disney studies, and American studies.*

Be the Story, Change the Story

Engaging Gender-based Archetypes in Online Science Fiction and Fantasy Fandom

By

Lola McCrary

In the absence of an effective general mythology, each of us has [our] own private, unrecognized, rudimentary, yet secretly potent pantheon of dream. The latest incarnation of Oedipus, the continued romance of Beauty and the Beast, stands this afternoon on the corner of Forty-second Street and Fifth Avenue, waiting for the traffic light to change.

—Joseph Campbell[1]

The main motifs of the myths are the same, and they have always been the same. If you want to find your own mythology, the key is with what society do you associate? Every mythology has grown up in a certain society in a bounded field. Then they come into collision and relationship, and they amalgamate, and you get a more complex mythology.

—Joseph Campbell[2]

These quotations show that at both the beginning and the end of a career spanning nearly forty years American mythologist Joseph Campbell emphasized that myths need to change as society changes, or run the risk of becoming meaningless, and possibly harmful, to new generations and new cultural amalgams. One cultural shift Campbell discussed with Bill Moyers in the interviews leading up to the PBS series, *The Power of Myth*, was how technology changes the mythic landscape. He mentioned that airplanes and other machines have entered dreams, and that a relationship with a mechanical worldview was showing up in contemporary stories. Then he spoke about the personal computer he used in the late 1980s:

> I have had a revelation from my computer about mythology. You buy certain software, and there is a whole set of signals that lead to the achievement of your aim. If you begin fooling around with signals that belong to another system of software, they just don't work.... If a person is really involved in a [mythic system] and really building his life on it, he better stay with the software that he has got. But a chap like myself, who likes to play around with the software—well, I can run around.[3]

Campbell died in 1987, shortly after these interviews with Moyers were completed, and prior to online social networking and widespread use of personal computers. Yet even his limited use of that new technology led him to think about computers and their relationship to mythic imagery.

In part because of personal computers and the Internet, there have been amazing changes since Campbell's death in how stories are generated and experienced. Fact and imagination are increasingly accessible to more of the population. When I wondered what is at the corner of Forty-second Street and Fifth Avenue in New York City (mentioned by Campbell in the "Beauty and the Beast" quotation at the beginning of this essay), I used current technology— Google Maps—to discover that it is the location of the New York Public Library. When Campbell was researching and writing *The Hero with a Thousand Faces* in the 1940s, the public library was the "technology" many used to access stories (most books were too expensive for many people, especially at the end of the Great Depression). When Campbell commented on changing stories in 1949, motion pictures were less than fifty years old. Radio programming in the United States was about twenty years old (at that time radio included the telling of stories that would later become TV series), and broadcast television was in its infancy. Sixty-plus years after Campbell's indirect reference to the New York Library, I read lots of fiction, but today mostly I buy ebooks. If I use my local public library, I check their online catalog for the books I want, request them, and pick them up when I get email telling me they are ready. Many e-readers allow people to preview books for free before buying, or borrow ebooks from the library. I watch broadcast TV on the Internet. As a grad student, I did the majority of my research on my laptop at home, using the online databases, articles, and books available on my university's website. When I wanted to locate the correct sources of the quotations from Campbell above, I used Google to get the book they came from, then Amazon's "search inside" feature to find the page numbers. Beginning with the printing press making books more available, then the development of public libraries, new technology historically changed the availability of story.

Not all stories are mythic, but Campbell recognized that most of us become acquainted with mythic themes and metaphors via various story mediums such as art, the written word, video, music, dance, or oral traditions. The availability of the World Wide Web changes not only access to stories and myths in all these forms, but contributes to new forms of story creation. However, it is also changing response to these stories through almost immediate online criticism or comments in social media, and through the availability of online fandoms. Before I explore how social media is affecting story, I will discuss the relationship between myth, archetype, and their relationship to story.

The Images and the Archetypes

Campbell's work on the enduring themes of ever changing stories was based in part on the theories of analytical psychologist, C. G. Jung. By 1945 (shortly before Campbell published *The Hero with a Thousand Faces*), Jung drew a clear distinction between his concept of archetypes, and archetypal images. The archetypes of the collective unconscious, he said, exist outside space and time as patterns which human consciousness can identity through repetitive cross-cultural images that span thousands of years. The images are not the archetypes: the patterns existing outside space and time cannot be fully known, and therefore also cannot be fully exhausted as a source of human expression of new realities. Archetypes take form in human consciousness through images and symbols, most often present in dreams, stories, myths, and active imagination. Jung said, "The archetype is essentially an unconscious content that is altered by becoming conscious and by being perceived, and it takes its color from the individual consciousness in which it happens to appear."[4] Archetypal images are human creations or manifestations we interact with in our world of space and time.

Jung, as did Campbell, took advantage of technology to increase awareness of his work. Steamship passage (instead of sailing boats) in the early 20th century enabled Jung to travel to the United States to give lectures and meet other psychologists. Later in his career, tapes and films made of him answering questions contributed to his renown.[5] In 1959, shortly before his death, Jung agreed to a BBC TV interview of his life and work.[6] Recently, technology has allowed full color reproductions of the art and text in Jung's *The Red Book*, previously viewed only by very few scholars after Jung's death.[7] This book contained a personal exploration of myth and archetype in Jung's unconscious. Much of the art Jung used to explore myths and archetypes in *The Red Book* can be seen online in Google images.

In *Aion*, Jung comments, "The archetypes most clearly characteristic from the empirical point of view are those which have the most frequent and most disturbing influence on the ego. Those are the shadow, the anima, and the animus."[8] By "ego" Jung means each person's conscious perception of self. While Jung's concept of the shadow states that it exists in all forms of human activity, this essay will focus on Jung's gender-based archetypes typified by the anima (feminine principle) and animus (masculine principle) he mentions above. The context for this exploration of gender-based archetypes will be the changing story in the "bounded field" of contemporary online science fiction and fantasy (sf/f) fandom.

Since story is a broad topic, I will offer two types of stories to frame this exploration. After defining sf/f, I will discuss why this online fan community provides an interesting context for examining contemporary views of gender-based archetypes, and how this fandom is attempting to change the stories exploring and expressing these archetypes.

Gender-based Stories: Power-over and Power-to

All cultures tell stories about appropriate roles and attitudes for men and women. In addition to the attitudes toward gender roles that our families use to shape us, cultural stories are an additional influence that shape our sense of self. Today many of these cultural stories come through technology: movies, TV shows, and the Internet. Their influence matures side by side with individual personality factors that may inspire us to try to change the stories we hear about what is possible individually and culturally. As well as these family and cultural influences, Jung, and many of his students, claim that the gender-based archetypes of the anima and animus determine the course of our relationships with others. There are also theorists such as Jung, Campbell, and contemporary scholar Craig Chalquist, who suggest that each of us is born with a mythic theme (often gender-based) that influences—consciously or unconsciously—the story that we live. While there are complex theories about the influence of gender-based stories, subject to constant reexamination in a variety of popular psychology movements and in academic disciplines, I want to use a more organic perspective from the s/sf culture that revolves around story.

It is important to note that when I talk about stories, I am not speaking only of fiction and tall tales. The stories cultures and families tell their members seem, to them, to be based on an agreed-upon view of reality: they are seen not as fiction, but as truth. Yet any student of history, anthropology, religion, or sociology knows that what we tell each other about who we are changes from culture to culture and age to age. Cultural attitudes that this generation in the United States now regards as fiction may have been seen by our grandparents as truth—for example, what makes up a family; or not—most cultural historians agree that the idealized families in American 1950s TV shows probably rarely existed even then. New versions of Oedipus and Beauty and the Beast evolve around us in increasingly complex ways.

It is also important to note that a "culture" can be as small as a family, or as large as a country, religion, or race, and that each of us needs to make conscious the stories of the specific and various cultures (Campbell's bounded fields) in which we exist over the course of our lifetimes. Then we may possibly be more able to decide whether to live that story or change it.

For this examination I wish to suggest two broad categories of culturally based stories—often, but not exclusively, talking about gender roles. The first is stories about "power-over": Who has power over individuals or subsets in a culture? Is it parents? Husbands? Wives? The government? Owners? The military? A church or religious group? An employer? Power-over stories try to limit choices individuals can make by invoking an authority who decides if the choice is acceptable in the culture.

The second type is stories about "power-to": What do I as an individual, or part of a group, have the power to do? Can I make choices about who I can partner with or marry? About when, or if, I bear or raise children? About the occupations or interests I can pursue? About what aspects of my culture(s) I can criticize? About when and how I choose to die? About what my body should look like, and what gender I identify as?

Obviously stories about power-over and power-to intersect, but there is value in considering them separately. If I manage to move out of the stories about who has power over me, I may still find myself constrained by other stories about what I have the power to do.

Please note while this article is concerned with gender-based stories I am aware that I am not addressing here the additional very real and limiting factors of race, income, or the influence of illness on how we make choices about the stories we want to live.

My contention is that contemporary online sf/f fandom frequently and consistently questions the existing cultural stories about who has power-over and power-to (and their exploration often does include the influence of race, income levels, and illness). Questioning existing stories is not limited to the culture of sf/f fandom, of course, but this bounded field does place inquiries in broad cultural contexts, speculating about how new stories told about individual and cultural identity can begin to change our sense of self. But none of those individual selves exist in a vacuum. Even if I create a new story for myself about power-over and power-to, how others relate to me is often conditioned by the stories of power-over and power-to that they have consciously or unconsciously accepted as true. Women discovered this during World War II when they took on jobs in United States factories while men were in the armed forces. After the war American culture took time to recover from the fact that many women didn't want to give those jobs up to go back to lower paying jobs, or to the "story" that their correct role was to be homemakers and wives. Whether I like it or not, my choices are often constrained by the stories others believe. Early science fiction storyteller Mary Shelley found this to be true nearly two hundred years ago.

An Early Sf/f Storyteller

Sf/f stories are sometimes referred to as speculative fiction. Traditionally these genres not only speculate about what science can do, but about how changes in science also change culture and nature. Contemporary fantasy writing—while often seen by those outside these fandoms as about elves, unicorns, and return-to-nature utopias—instead confronts mythic themes head-on, speculating about the differences between what we long for and what we have.

One of the earliest speculative fiction novels, first published in 1818, was by Mary Wollstonecraft Godwin Shelley. The writing and publication of *Frankenstein; Or, the Modern Prometheus* anticipated issues about story and gender that exist throughout the two centuries after her time. Born in England in 1797, Mary was a third generation radical who grew up during the Industrial Revolution when technology was quickly and substantively changing culture.[*] Her mother was an early feminist writer who lived her ideals about education for girls, women's involvement in political affairs, and intimacy based on love rather than just in married relationships. She died of childbed fever eleven days after Mary's birth, leaving her daughter her name, her writings, and a father who

---

[*] Learn more about Mary Shelley at via the DISCovering Authors series, viaGale Student Resources, 2003, at http://bit.ly/2dmlSCF

was convinced that his wife's life should be celebrated with truth rather than the discretion society then required. Her father, William Godwin, was one of the fathers of anarchist writing, believing that people had to end monarchies through political involvement, replacing them with governments honoring the equality of all its citizens. William Godwin's parents were non-conformist Calvinists (his father a minister) in England—a radical position for the time, if a conservative one. Brought up in his parents' faith, Godwin rejected religious institutions in favor of reason. He believed his daughter Mary had a birthright of intellect, and raised her with exposure to the most modern ideas of the time, encouraging her to be her mother's daughter and to think for herself. [9]

As her mother and father before her, Mary Shelley wrote stories. *Frankenstein* was her first published book. Some consider it the first modern science fiction novel. Not only does Shelley reference a mythic theme in her title, but some accounts of the creation of the novel by Shelley say the story coalesced as the result of a waking dream. Begun when she was eighteen years old, writing in the early 1800s, this novel considered how science can cause unforeseen, and possibly disastrous, results when it tries to co-opt life's existing patterns. Shelley first published her book anonymously, since women at that time rarely published anything but romantic fiction.

In studying Mary Shelley's early life, I noticed some interesting synchronicities between her birth and the birth of her first novel. A few weeks before she was born in 1797, a new comet appeared in the sky in England, discovered by Caroline Herschel, the assistant to the British King's Astronomer. (In 1835 Herschel was one of the first two women elected to honorary membership of the Royal Astronomical Society).[*] The Godwins thought the comet a good omen for the forthcoming baby.[**] At the same time, the fire in the sky that August was overshadowed by the England's strongest summer storm in recent memory. Almost nineteen years later, in 1816 in a mansion called Diodati ("facts of God"—a loose translation) on Lake Geneva in Switzerland, Mary Godwin (she was not at this time married to Percy Shelley although she was pregnant with his child) gathered with her family of choice and some friends to wait out the fire in the sky of a severe lightning storm. This was in "the year without a summer" due to the effects of worldwide volcanic activity. In that place, on a real dark and stormy night much like the nights around her birth, Mary conceived her story about a monster made of dead human parts brought back to life by electricity. Instead of writing a romance between a new Beauty and the Beast, she was a Beauty writing about the dangers of science giving birth to a Beast.

---

[*]   Learn about Caroline Herschel at http://womenshistory.about.com/od/scienceastronomy/p/herschel.htm

[**] See *Romantic Outlaws: The Extraordinary Lives of Mary Wollstonecraft & Mary Shelley,* by Charlotte Gordon

Mary Shelley, following in her parents' footsteps, attempted to change her society's stories about what it meant to be female by living the progressive values of her parents. Regency and Victorian England were not yet ready to accept Mary's choices, and she struggled most of her life.

Like this early female role model, women authors today continue to fight to not be seen as second-class writers of speculative fiction. In the 20th century, some women used male pen names (such as Andre Norton and James Tiptree, Jr.) or their initials (such as C. L. Moore and C. J. Cherryh) in an effort to have their work published and read. Cultural stereotypes about the feminine prevented many from seeing the worth of women writing on "masculine" topics such as science and technology. Today removal of gender bias in online sf/f fandom is easier because it's possible to have a gender-free anonymous user name. However, it's also more difficult for published authors since the Internet makes uncovering details about almost anyone easier than it used to be. It is unlikely that today award-winning writer James Tiptree, Jr. (real name, Alice B. Sheldon) would be able to conceal her gender for ten years. When her identity was speculated about after she won her awards a male author said in writing that she couldn't possibly be female because of the high quality of her work.

The Development of Sf/f Fandom

As interest in speculative fiction grew in the early 20th century, writers, publishers, and fans of sf/f developed the custom of gathering at least once a year. One formal and ongoing gathering of sf/f writers and fans, known as Worldcon, began in 1939. There has been a Worldcon every year since (excluding the years during World War II). Worldcons are fan organized, with non-profit groups bidding for future sites of Worldcon. The location changes every year. Worldcon in 2014 had 10,826 members, up from 6,300 members in 2012.* The first Worldcon had 200 members.

From 1955 to the present, each Worldcon included a nomination process and award voted by members for the best English works in sf/f for the previous year. The prize is called the Hugo Award (after Hugo Gernsback, an early sf/f publisher), and many consider it the most prestigious award in sf/f.

Worldcon is not the only fan organized sf/f convention. Most regions in the United States, and many regions in other countries have annual conventions (commonly called cons). *Locus* magazine lists 13 literary conventions upcoming worldwide in 2015 in addition to Worldcon. Their website does not list cons for sf/f sub-genres such as media, comics, or music, which increases the total number of annual cons significantly.

---

*   More details at http://www.gencon.com/press/2014recordattendance

Until the 1960s most published sf/f was by men.[9] Women, however, were involved in fandom from the beginning. In 2000, after nearly 20 years of study and participation in sf/s fandom, Camille Bacon-Smith published *Science Fiction Culture*. Bacon-Smith is a published writer of sf/f, with a Ph.D. in folklore and folklife. This fascinating book examines 20th century sf/f fandom, including the historical role of women and other minority groups. In her introduction she draws an interesting conclusion about the society of fandom, and about the writers of sf/f:

> A journalist who wants to know what the future will look like usually asks a science fiction writer. Hard science fiction, as the industry calls the subgenre most grounded in the physical sciences, looks at present science, extrapolates scientific development into the future, and then speculates on how society will reconfigure itself to cope (or not cope) with the technology that science has created. In the process, the genre often finds itself chasing its own extrapolations as they become the present reality.... So when the ethnographer asks the question, "What does postmodern culture look like?", the obvious place to find the answer is the science fiction community."[10]

She acknowledges that fan cultures exist around other genres, but believes that sf/f fandom is among the oldest, and therefore is "where the forms begin" for other fandoms.11 Covering only early online fandom such as Usenet, her book predates some of the most prevalent social networking sites, the development of ebooks, and the expansion of self-publishing, all of which I will show have contributed to changing stories about power-over and power-to in online fandom.

Sf/f fandom has always attracted an eclectic group of people with a long-standing culture of inclusiveness. Atheists, pagans, scientists, libertarians, democrats, all gender identities, all races, people of every sexual orientation, those in monogamous relationships, those in polyamorous relationships, all socialize, discuss, wonder, and party together. As online fandom developed, ideas shared on the Internet inspired discussion on many social themes, most of which were also explored in the genre's creations.

Even with a self-proclaimed culture of progressive inclusiveness, many women feel they still struggle to overcome anti-female bias in sf/f. Looking over lists of guests of honor and toastmasters at Worldcons, as well as the Hugo Award winners, the percentage of male guests and winners to female guests and winners is high even up to the present, although Worldcon 2012 may have started some new trends. This was the first year I could find that women won in three of the four major writing categories (including the first Hugo awarded to a trans woman). One woman was nominated for three Hugos, and another for four (both won one Hugo). Women continued to be represented in these four writing awards in 2013 (nine women nominated, with one woman winning) and 2014 (eight women nominated winning two out of the four awards). But until 2014 a woman had never won the Hugo for best professional artist, and only a few women were ever nominated. Discussions online and during conventions continue about just how inclusive fandom really is, about who has power-over, and who has power-to in this story-based society. These discussions have become more acrimonious the past few years with some people (mostly men) claiming that nominations and awards are not given based on quality, but on an anti-male left wing liberal agenda in fandom*

Online Sf/f Fandom

As the 20th century progressed, science fiction often became science fact. Many sf/f fans helped develop computer technology. Computer-based communication grew from contact within scientific and engineering enclaves in the early 1970s to commercial and private use of these networks, resulting in the fast expansion of email and Usenet in the early 1990s.

Online science fiction fandom grew with it. Usenet made possible newsgroups centered around interests, including sf/f fandom. Google's archived Usenet groups show initial posts from rec.arts.sf.written and rec.arts.sf.fandom in October 1991. These newsgroups, with email and posts, were the precursor to social networking on the World Wide Web. Groups of sf/f fans who met in person at cons and stayed in contact on Usenet now continue, in the second decade of the 21st century, to communicate online as well as at conventions. The anonymity of online handles (usernames) from the earliest days continues to make a difference in stories about power-over and power-to. Often you have no idea what gender someone is. Their ideas can be evaluated based on what they say, not on the writer's gender. In fact, many Usenet communities adopted a set of genderless pronouns to further this trend.

But gender bias continues in sf/f fandom, as in other groups in our culture. In early 2013 an author's self-published story called *Spots the Space Marine* was removed from sale by Amazon Kindle due to on a trademark claim on the term "space marine" by Games Workshop. After attempting to deal with it herself, despite a lack of money and time to oppose the claim by Games Workshop to exclusive use of a trope present in sf/f from its earliest days, the author (M. C. A. Hogarth) asked fans to spread the word online about the issue. It went viral

---

* See the blog site of Brad Torgersen at https://bradrtorgersen.wordpress.com/2015/01/07/announcing-sad-puppies-3

in a few days, with big names and little names successfully opposing the effort to co-opt a favorite sf/f trope. Many people on Twitter changed their online identification to "Space Marine *name*" as a taunt, inviting Games Workshop to close down their accounts based on use of the term. Due to the collective efforts of sf/f fandom Games Workshop backed down, and Hogarth's story is still available for purchase on Kindle. But this amazing effort included a number of people I personally saw who assumed both the title character and the author were male. Spots was a middle-aged mom called up due to her military reserve status, and M. C. A. Hogarth is female.

The online world has been, since its earliest days, a safe harbor for people to share their stories about power-over and power-to. For many living in places that would persecute them based on aspects of their identity, it was the only safe place to seek support and help in communities of open-minded people. Since my day job is in a conservative industry, even today I attempt to be anonymous in some online social networks. Many people were dismayed by Google's decision to insist on real names when they established Google+ in 2011. Although we understand it is, in part, an effort to encourage online accountability, many of us choose—for a variety of reasons—not to take part if we cannot remain anonymous. It's very difficult to live and tell your story when you are fired, kicked out of your home, or have your children taken away from you because of choices other people condemn.

A serious example of anti-female bias involving the technology of video games became an online *cause célèbrè* starting in 2013. The controversy also highlights why many people feel safer being anonymous online. It revolved around the first Internet podcast by Anita Sarkeesian (feministfrequency.com) in her series called "Tropes vs Women in Video Games" funded by a Kickstarter campaign. The most recent podcast in the series at the time of this writing was posted on her above-mentioned site in August 2014. Sarkeesian, who has a master's degree in social and political thought from York University, experienced mostly male harassment starting during the Kickstarter campaign, and continuing to this day. In many ways Sarkeesian espouses Artemisian-like values of female self-determination without unwanted male interference, and uses largely online technology to share her message. The shadow response to her work culminated in October 2014 where threats of a mass-murder shooting during her speaking engagement at Utah State University caused the event to be canceled. Her work also became part of an online controversy called Gamergate, which began in August 2014. Women supporting changes in female portrayal in video games were subject to male online harassment that included rape and murder threats, the publication of their home addresses, and efforts to hack their social network sites. Sarkeesian appeared on *The Colbert Report* in October 2014 to talk about her work and the threats to her and other women in Gamergate. Men who supported changes to female roles in video games were vilified by other men, but not threatened with harm to the extent that women were.

Many video games include sf/f themes, and men and women in online fandom were involved in the discussions around Sarkeesian's work and Gamergate. In spite of male criticism, to show that her efforts to change the story about female roles in video games were recognized by those writing the stories, Sarkeesian was presented with the 2014 Game Developers Choice Ambassador Award.

My Involvement in Sf/f Fandom

I began reading science fiction and fantasy in the early 1970s. I started participating in sf/f fandom in about 1985 in the San Francisco Bay area, with occasional trips to cons in other parts of the United States. In 1991, courtesy of a computer scientist boyfriend, I got my first email account and Internet access. I've had both ever since. He was also a sf/f fan and participated in early online fandom, introducing me to it. I imagine that if I looked through the 1992-93 archives for rec.arts.sf.fandom, I would locate posts I made. Most certainly I read those groups. I remember the first time I tentatively sent email to an author who was in one of the groups I was reading. I was thrilled to get a reply from her answering my question. The apparent intimacy of online contact with authors and other fans is addictive and satisfying.

I wish to mention again that storytelling in sf/f takes many forms: the written word, art, the spoken word through drama, comedy, TV, movies, and fan productions, and finally, in music. Music that comes out of sf/f fandom is called "filk." "Filk music" was a typo for "folk music" in an article written in the 1950s and the name stuck. Those who participate in this sub-genre of sf/f fandom are called "filkers." Developments in home productions studios, availability of digital download instead of the need to produce physical CDs, ability to publish videos on YouTube, and social networking to spread the news about new products have radically increased access to this music since 2000. In 2012 a filk CD containing themes addressing stories about women was nominated for a Hugo in the "Best Related Work" category for the first time. There are cons for filk around the world, and several award systems for filk music have been established by fans. I have been involved in filk since my earliest days in fandom, and at least half my extensive music favorites list is filk. Many filkers are students of myth and folklore. Today filkers are among those changing the stories about power-over and power-to in sf/f fandom, and the Internet has contributed to filk's role to help change stories.

For example, in her song "My story is not done" Seanan McGuire offers another perspective on the stories females adopt for themselves:

> So come on all you fox-girls and you ghost-girls
> And you pretty pirates,
> Come on all you wild girls and you lost girls
> And you shrinking violets,
> Come and pay the piper, say you'll leave their war unwon.
> It's only words on paper, and your story is not done.[12]

She suggests that women no longer pay the piper for limited choices such as wife, mother, nurse, or schoolteacher, but instead be willing to embrace longed for self-visions that society may frown on, and pay for those choices with the expensive coin of self-determination. By being the story, the war effort to change the story can sometimes be short-circuited. This song was on McGuire's *Wicked Girls* album, the filk CD nominated for a 2012 Hugo for Best Related Work. Lyrics for her songs are posted on her website, and videos of performances of her songs are available on YouTube.

Aspects of Online Sf/f fandom that intensify Changing Stories

The changes in the online world since 1999 have been tremendous, and strongly impacted online sf/f fandom:

2000: Paypal for more secure online payments

2003: MySpace and increased access to inexpensive, self-installed, home Internet services, and wireless routers

2004: Facebook and the beginning of Wordpress, which provides easy websites and blogging

2005: YouTube

2006: Twitter

2009: Greater availability and publishing of ebooks through Amazon's Kindle and competitors; Kickstarter and the spread of crowdfunding; Wordpress dominated the market share for blogs

2010: Increased availability of mobile devices with access to the Internet, and with apps specifically developed for their users

These innovations resulted in several changes to online sf/f fandom, increasing the influence of story and storytellers:

1) Instant and ongoing contact between authors, artists, musicians and their fans in social networks like Facebook, Twitter, blogs, and email

To contact an author prior to email and posting on social networking sites you sent mail to their publisher, included a return stamped envelope, and hoped it was forwarded to them. If you received a reply, it often took months. You might get additional information about an author from a published interview with them. You might get a chance to be in a large, crowded room with them at a convention, or say hi when you asked them to autograph a book. Today creators of sf/f regularly chat with their fans on Twitter, Facebook or blogs. Most of these forums allow you to cross-post, giving readers a chance to select which social networking site they want to use to follow the author. I no longer need to subscribe to a sf/f magazine to find out publication dates for new books; the authors post them. Authors know within hours of a new book being published how their audience feels about it. Some creators elect to share aspects of their personal as well as professional lives.

It is also important to remember that most creators of sf/f are themselves fans of the genre. One used to meet peers at conventions, or maybe exchange letters or emails. Now creators follow the work of other artists and writers on social networking sites. As a result stories about power-over and power-to experienced by fans and creators can receive responses within the community that go viral in a few days, highlighting—again—how some stories need to change.

The people whose work I follow are no longer remote. Often on a day-to-day basis, I understand their triumphs and struggles in producing the books, art, movies, and music I love. Bacon-Smith commented on this:

> Looking at the social lives of the artists and producers of science fiction, fantasy, and horror, we must abandon the romantic theory of the solitary writer bashing away at the lonely word processor in the middle of the woods. Literature is formed by consensus, not least of those who create it and who now and always share lively social connections, through which they debate the norms of their literary forms in a wide variety of forums, including the literature itself.[13]

2) Easy availability of more sf/f through free online promotions, ebooks, fan fiction, and digital downloads

People like getting free things. They like having questions answered. Before a new work comes out, often the creator will provide background material, or snippets of the work, to interest their fans. Blogs that can be read without a log-in, and digital downloads of free material make supporting someone's work that much more exciting.

Voting for various awards is often now online, making it easier to participate. Supporting members of Worldcon make nominations for the annual Hugo Awards and vote on the final ballot, and can now do so online. In addition, for the cost of the supporting membership (about $45 USD in 2014), digital downloads of much of the nominated works (including in 2012, five novels, 15 pieces of short fiction, digital images from nominated artists, and the entire CD nominated for the Hugo) were made available to members. Digital packets were also provided in 2013 and 2014. Buying the written works nominated would cost much more than the membership. I believe that membership numbers for Worldcon are growing due to the ease of purchasing supporting memberships and participating in the Hugo process online. More people are influencing which stories win awards. Furthermore, from 2011-2014 the Hugo awards ceremony was streamed free online, offering people who could not attend more incentive to pay to participate in the award process. More access to creations online sets up a feedback loop that can change story in a short time.

Ease of access and interaction with creators is only one factor encouraging the growth of online fandom. Many fans like writing in the universes of their favorite works, and sharing that writing with others. Fan fiction (fanfic) goes back to the start of 20th century sf/f fandom. Now fanfic is available—mostly for free—online. Many professional authors started as fanfic writers. Some authors prefer that others not write in their universes. Authors don't read the fanfic available for their stories due to possible plagiarism issues as they continue to publish, but some read (or write) fanfic for other authors. Fans often take stories and change them in fanfic to meet needs they don't see present in the original story. One example is making characters in stories gay, trans, or another race. Fanfic writers do this to provide greater representation of these types of characters in fiction. Because of this an author may take more care to include these types of people in new published works. Fanfic has the possibility of demonstrating that published stories often are not representative of the full spectrum of society, and to change the stories in the bounded field of sf/f fandom.

3) An increasing willingness of authors, artists and musicians to self-publish or self-produce, often using crowdfunding for capital

This is an amazing change. Fans of all kinds have mourned the fact that something they love can't happen—or continue to happen—because no publisher or producer will touch it, or because its creator can't find funding. In the past, some indie musicians might have raised capital for a new CD with pre-orders for signed copies. But crowdfunding takes this idea to a different level.

I have backed crowdfunding projects for books, music, a museum, a sf/f archive, movies, fieldwork in psychology and spirituality, and purchase of lands sacred to Native Americans. After backing projects, I end up with something I will enjoy or value that might otherwise never exist. Several authors who couldn't find a publisher for a sequel they wanted to write ended up with more funding than they would ever have received through an advance. M. C. A Hogarth turned her expertise with several overfunded Kickstarter projects into a manual on how to successfully run a Kickstarter. Many of these people share the creative process, from start to finish, with their backers, providing an interesting view into the nuts and bolts of a successful project.

Rather than the monster-bureaucrats called publishers or movie and TV executives deciding what material might sell, fans can vote with their bank accounts, letting sf/f creators know what pleases them. According to authors, this has already begun to change mainstream publishing. The Amazon Kindle program, for example, has established programs attracting self-published authors with higher royalties. This influences authors to self-publish instead of seeking out a traditional agent and publishing house.

On a less formal basis than sites such as Kickstarter, creators are simply upfront with their fans about what support they will need to make a project happen. One indie musician began a monthly subscription that provides subscribers with first access to his live concert recordings and new music. In return, he had an income that allowed him to pay his bills. The lack of worry makes it easier for him to create more things for us to enjoy. In 2014 a site called patreon.com automated this process, enabling patrons to preauthorize regular donations to creators to support their work.

M. C. A. Hogarth uses another funding path and serializes completed works on her website.[14] She provides one episode per week free, with a donation button. If the donations following a post reach a certain dollar amount, she posts a second episode with another donation button, with the same arrangement for a third episode. Her readers can follow for free or throw in few dollars to read the story more quickly. After the serial is completed, Hogarth frequently runs a Kickstarter to turn it into a print, e-book and/or audiobook. Because she posts the stories before publishing the books, some of her stories have been modified based on comments she receives on a post. In one serial, *Black Blossom*, she hosted meetings between her characters and her readers, letting them ask questions or make comments. The discussions can often take on mythic sensibilities since characters in a story often portray archetypal figures. Those conversation posts— as collaborations with her readers—are among my favorite of her creations.

Along with her art and stories, I get to hear about Hogarth's seven-year-old daughter, and about how her parents escaped from Cuba. She discusses health issues and how she deals with them. She lets us know what the money we pay her provides for her and her family. She supports and publicizes other projects. Despite being a somewhat introverted personality, she has established an intimacy with her audience that nurtures everyone involved, changing the stories about who has power over her work and what she and her audience have the power to achieve together. It was her strong online fan base that contributed to the viral response after the withdrawal from Amazon Kindle of *Spots the Space Marine* mentioned above.

Some of my favorite characters in other authors' stories have Twitter or Tumblr accounts, and interacting with them (not the authors of the stories) is an intriguing experience.

Male and Female Allies

Creators and fans in sf/f are often colleagues and friends using technology to frame and re-frame stories about gender. Google any Hugo nominated creator, or even most traditionally or self-published sf/f authors, and you will find on their social networking sites extensive discussions about the role gender plays in story, and the relationship between story and life. But it has become obvious to me that the re-framing of gender in story in sf/f is moving away from the old masculine and feminine archetypes. Creators and fans are not interested in anima/animus. They are interested in every person having the freedom to escape the old power-over stories in favor of a new power-to be who they are and do what they want to do (unless they are being thoughtless or cruel). Gender is not the defining characteristic of their lives; personality and passion are. Men and women act more as allies for each other (not men being champions for women—they don't see women as *needing* a champion). Anima and animus don't complete each other. People complete each other. The online work on gender in this bounded field holds the potential to modify—even unknowingly—Jung's view of gender-based archetypes.

Jung's Stories about Archetypes

Jung's analytical psychology—founded in the early 1900s—was groundbreaking in its day, much as the creators above are breaking new ground a hundred years later. One aspect of his work was that Jung believed it was the beginning, not the end, of the examination of archetypes, the collective unconscious, and their relationship to the human self. He wanted others to continue and expand his work. Another was that Jung's students, and subsequent colleagues—again beginning in the early 1900s—included a high proportion of women. Two years before his death in 1961, Jung began to plan a book on his work for a popular audience. Jung wrote one section of the book, telling its editor he chose the other four contributors "because of their skill and experience in the particular subjects allocated to them."[15] Three of those four contributors were women. Jung's analytical psychology, over the course of his lifetime, included more female analysts and teachers than existed in all other branches of psychology combined.

As mentioned before, Jung's mature work began around 1945, and included a firm distinction between archetypes and archetypal images. Jung was familiar with the historical antecedents of archetypes that preceded his use and explanations of the term. In an article revised in 1954 called "Psychological Aspects of the Mother Archetype," Jung is clear regarding the difference between archetypes and archetypal images:

> If I have any share in these discoveries, it consists in my having shown that archetypes are not disseminated only by tradition, language, and migration, but that they can re-arise spontaneously at any time, at any place, and without outside influence.
>
> The far-reaching implications of this statement must not be overlooked. For it means that there are present in every person's psyche forms which are unconscious but nevertheless active—living dispositions, ideas in the Platonic sense, that perform and continually influence our thoughts and feelings and actions.
>
> Again and again I encounter the mistaken notion that an archetype is determined in regard to its content, in other words that it is a kind of unconscious idea (if such an expression is admissible). It is necessary to point out once more that archetypes are not determined as regards their content, but only as regards their form and then only to a very limited degree. A primordial image is determined as to its content only when it has become conscious and is therefore filled out with the material of conscious experience. Its form, however, as I have explained elsewhere, might perhaps be compared to the axial system of a crystal, which as it were, pre[-]forms the crystalline structure in the mother liquid, although it has no material existence of its own. This first appears according to the specific way in which the ions and molecules aggregate....The same is true of the archetype. In principle, it can be named and has an invariable nucleus of meaning—but always only in principle, never as regards its concrete manifestation. In the same way, the specific appearance

of the mother image in any given time cannot be deduced from the mother archetype alone, but depends on innumerable other factors.[16]

This long quote is a good summary of the "story" Jung tells about archetypes, and is from his mature work. By the 1950s Jung was regularly including the technology of taped audio and video interviews to portray his work, speaking about many archetypes and images.[17] In whatever format he used Jung of course needed to provide verbiage that described the forms or archetypes he deduced from the images and stories that arise and repeat across human cultures and across time. Since he is seeking to classify archetypes by their repeating content and images in human culture, it is perhaps inevitable that the terminology he chooses to label many archetypes encompasses specific gender roles assigned throughout human culture. The impulse to nurture and care for children is seen as "mother" and the impulse to provide for and protect children as "father," for example.

For Jung the process of individuation—making conscious an increasing amount of unconscious material—involves both males and females integrating the gender-opposite archetypes into their psyches. But the language he used to describe archetypal forms was often based on the prevalent, and historical, gender roles of his time and culture. How archetypes and archetypal images influenced his analytical psychology in the consulting room and the classroom was also influenced by gender roles, despite the inclusion of many women in positions of authority in his work. As Maggy Anthony, in *Valkyries: The Women around Jung*, wrote:

> Apart from this, it may be stated that while the women around Jung were undoubtedly creative, intelligent women, none of them diverged very far from his thought, nor deepened it noticeably. Not one of them ever saw fit [even after his death—my comment] to question any of his assertions about women and the animus concept, nor added any conflicting research of her own...Their observations on the animus would have been particularly valuable, but only if they had taken the liberty first of putting aside Jung's assumption. He himself makes several statements throughout his writings concerning the nebulousness of his basic material on the animus.[18]

Not to mention the value of their new thoughts on the animus in relationship to the anima. Jung died over sixty years ago. There are contemporary depth psychologists and Jungian scholars who continue to examine gender-based archetypes. But academia tends to function slowly, and Jungian analysis can take years. There is an immediacy online that grabs our attention, evoking questions and—often triggering reactive shadow material as well as numinous breakthroughs. Many of the efforts to deal with oppression and repression can be watched online, practically in real time. Online sf/f fandom is one of the places re-examination is happening for those with eyes to see.

I do not wish to minimize the biological differences between those identified at birth as male or female, especially given new scientific insights—often reached through better medical technology since Jung's death. Nor do I wish to deny the importance of gender for those who strongly see themselves as male or female, regardless of the physiological characteristics they were born with. And for some, engagement with the masculine and the feminine, whether human or divine, is a deeply loved part of their psyche.

This is my point: stories we are told, or stories we write for ourselves, can limit us, but can also encourage the numinous. Because of technological development in the last hundred years we have ready access to more stories from more sources. The stories that pull or repel us may change over the course of our lives. But those who, with the best of intentions, intend to free us to be masculine or feminine—even in new, re-examined ways--may be trapping us into new versions of old stories rather than helping us create new stories; a new mythology, that doesn't walk up to an Athena and say, "You can't do that! You're a girl!"

What would happen if one possibility was for the qualities in Jung's "axial system" of the archetypes—the qualities we live our lives by—to no longer be gender-based? I think this is one thing many fans and creators in online sf/f are striving for in the stories they tell: to choose who they are and how they live their lives based on qualities that pull their attention and energy, without having to worry about any gender identifications those qualities have held in the past. They are suggesting that identification with a particular gender should not limit a person to any values, actions, lifestyles, or attributes associated with that gender by anyone, including Jung. People are simply people and should be free to choose whatever works for them that does not have any overt and intentional negative impact on others.

I suggest that continued identification within the depth psychology community of values and perspectives with the masculine or the feminine contains the potential of retarding the growth of those values as *human* values, necessary—in both shadow and light—to our development. I believe it is possible to celebrate human and divine gender without linking artificial attributes of masculine and feminine to a specific gender.

What would that world look like? Whatever our children and grandchildren will see it is likely they will view much of it through an online lens, enacting stories we can barely imagine. In 1949 Joseph Campbell, in the last paragraph of *The Hero with a Thousand Faces*, nailed the urgent need for the immediacy of changing the story by being the story:

> The modern hero, the modern individual who dares to heed the call . . . cannot, indeed must not, wait for his community to cast off its slough of pride, fear, rationalized avarice, and sanctified misunderstanding. "Live," Nietzsche says, "as though the day were here." It is not society that is to guide and save the creative hero, but precisely the reverse. And so every one of us shares the supreme ordeal . . . not in the bright moments of [the] tribe's great victories, but in the silences of [our] personal despair.[19]

I hope the online society of s/sf fandom will keep discussing gender roles until the danger of masculine and feminine archetypes becoming cultural stereotypes is part of the past rather than the future. And I hope they continue to write stories that further this—not necessarily so people become androgynous, but to allow our sense of human values and qualities to become post-gender-based.

Notes

1 Joseph Campbell. *The Hero with a Thousand Faces*. Princeton, NJ: Princeton University Press, 1949, 4

2 Joseph Campbell. *The Power of Myth*. New York: Anchor Books, 1988, 27-28

3 Ibid, 25

4 C. G. Jung. *The Collected Works*. Edited by Herbert Read, Michael Fordham, Gerhardt Adler and William McGuire. Translated by R. F. C. Hull. Vol. 9 Part 1. 20 vols. Princeton, NJ: Princeton University Press, 1981, 5

5. See *The World Within—C. G. Jung in His Own Words* and *A Matter of Heart*, among others

6 J. Freeman. *Carl Jung: Face to Face*. 1 24, 2013. https://www.youtube.com/watch?v=FPGMWF7kU_8

7 Jung. *The Red Book. Liber Novus*. Edited by Sonu Shamdasani. London: Norton, 2009

8 Jung. *The Collected Works*. Edited by Herbert Read, Michael Fordham, Gerhardt Adler and William McGuire. Translated by R. F. C. Hull. Vol. 9 Part 2. 20 vols. Princeton, NJ: Princeton University Press, 1979, 8

9 One list of women who were published in 1939 can be found at http://retrohugowomen.livejournal.com/270.html

10 Camille Bacon-Smith. *Science Fiction Culture*. Philadelphia: University of Pennsylvania Press, 2000, 1

11 Ibid, 5

12 Seanan McGuire. *Seanan McGuire*, 2006. http://www/seananmcguire.com 2006

13 Bacon-Smith. *Science Fiction Culture*. Philadelphia: University of Pennsylvania Press, 2000, 5

14 M. C. A. Hogarth. *M. C. A. Hogarth*. n.d. http://mcahogarth.org

15 Jung, *Man and His Symbols*. New York: Dell Publishing, 1964, vii

16 Jung. *The Collected Works*. Edited by Herbert Read, Michael Fordham, Gerhardt Adler and William McGuire. Translated by R. F. C. Hull. Vol. 9 Part 1. 20 vols. Princeton, NJ: Princeton University Press, 1981, 79-80

17 Jung. *C. G. Jung Speaking: Interviews and Encounters.* Princeton, NJ: Princeton University Press, 1977

18 Anthony Maggy. *Valkyries: The Women Around Jung.* Element Books Ltd, 1991, 107

19 Campbell. *The Hero with a Thousand Faces.* Princeton, NJ: Princeton University Press, 1949,391

Bibliography

Bacon-Smith, Camille. *Science Fiction Culture.* Philadelphia: University of Pennsylvania Press, 2000.

Campbell, Joseph. *The Hero with a Thousand Faces.* Princeton, NJ: Princeton University Press, 1949.

—. *The Power of Myth.* New York: Anchor Books, 1988.

Freeman, John. Carl Jung: Face to Face. 1 24, 2013. Retrieved from https://www.youtube.com/watch?v=FPGMWF7kU_8

M. C. A. Hogarth. *M. C. A. Hogarth.* n.d. Retrieved from http://mcahogarth.org

Jung, C. G. *C. G. Jung Speaking: Interviews and Encounters.* Princeton, NJ: Princeton University Press, 1977.

—. *Man and His Symbols.* New York: Dell Publishing, 1964.

—. *The Collected Works.* Edited by Herbert Read, Michael Fordham, Gerhardt Adler and William McGuire. Translated by R. F. C. Hull. Vol. 9 Part 1. 20 vols. Princeton, NJ: Princeton University Press, 1981.

—. *The Collected Works.* Edited by Herbert Read, Michael Fordham, Gerhardt Adler and William McGuire. Translated by R. F. C. Hull. Vol. 9 Part 2. 20 vols. Princeton, NJ: Princeton University Press, 1979.

—. *The Red Book. Liber Novus.* Edited by Sonu Shamdasani. London: Norton, 2009.

Maggy, Anthony. *Valkyries: The Women Around Jung.* Element Books Ltd, 1991.

McGuire, Seanan. *SeananMcGuire.* 2006. Retrieved from http://www.seananmcguire.com

In elementary school, **Lola McCrary** *read myth and folklore. In high school she read science fiction and fantasy. In college she read theology, philosophy, and history. In graduate school she read C. G. Jung and Joseph Campbell, and began to understand why she read (and reads) all those other things. Her master's degree senior project at JFK University in Concord, CA was on how theorist Ken Wilber didn't understand C. G. Jung. Presently she is looking at genealogy from a depth psychology perspective. She also works at as a first reader, proofreader, and fact checker for both fiction and non-fiction writing. She is on the editorial board of* Immanence: The Journal of Applied Mythology, Legend, and Folklore. *She can be reached at lolamccrary@yahoo.com.*

A Jungian Alice in Social Media Land

Some Reflections on Solastalgia, Kinship Libido, and Tribes Formed on Facebook

By

Sharon Heath

In his essay, *On the Relationship of Analytical Psychology to Poetry*, Jung wrote:

> Therein lies the social significance of art: it is constantly at work educating the spirit of the age, conjuring up the forms in which the age is most lacking. The unsatisfied yearning of the artist reaches back to the primordial image in the unconscious which is best fitted to compensate the inadequacy and one-sidedness of the present.[1]

In my own immersive circumambulation of the brave new world of Facebook, I've discovered that the social media phenomenon has much to tell us about modern mass culture, from issues of soul-alienation and superficiality (as seen in sound bites, "branding," and an overarching worship of Mammon) to an ineluctable push by the collective unconscious to creatively inseminate the spirit of our time with an age-old truth: that we live or die, not only via our own strength and integrity, but also by an inextricable linking of ego to the larger Self and psyche to Other. As we are all learning in this time of climate crisis, that Other includes, not just other humans, but all sentient beings, our mother planet, our cosmos, "the dead" to whom Jung so often refers in his *Red Book*[2], and those myriad others still waiting to be born.

Facebook wasn't an easy sell for me. I started out pretty much a Luddite when it came to the sensation-function intricacies of computers, VCRs, and cell phones. I fretted like crazy over what happens when the pace of technological change overtakes our psychological development and emotional maturity. *Koyaanisqatsi*, the Hopi word for "life out of balance," echoed my own concerns about where we're heading. I'd worked hard to ground my tendencies toward what Jung termed the *puella*, the "eternal girl," and wanted no part of technologies that would lead me farther away from embodiment and a grounded relationship with the world. But the handiness of word processing for writing novels seduced me into the world of PCs and Macs. And my connection with people in the publishing world ultimately lured me into dipping a hesitant toe into Facebook.

Before I knew it, the appeal of its potential for playfulness yanked the depressed child I'd once been into a full-bodied immersion. And what started as a kind of "Marco Polo" in the social media swimming pool turned into a deep-sea-dive into more provocative, moving, and ultimately saltier and live-giving waters.

But playfulness and the appeal of Facebook to the child and adolescent in me was admittedly the first hook. One of the popular givens about Mark Zuckerberg, the 27-year-old creator of what is now a more than 1.3 billion member social network, is that he is a brilliant computer geek who devised Facebook, in part, in an attempt to make friends. (In the 2010 Academy Award-nominated film *The Social Network*, Zuckerberg is portrayed as both consciously manipulative and unconsciously callous, but the undertone of social ineptitude and alienation is hard to miss.) Whether or not those characterizations are completely accurate, it is significant that the word for members of one's chosen circle of Facebook users is "friend."

No one would have accused me of being a math and science whiz as a child, but I was no stranger to an unmet yearning for friends and a deep dread of social isolation. When I was a child, my family moved to new locations approximately every year and a half, with me attending four elementary schools, two junior high schools, and two high schools. The difficulty of breaking into already established cliques of girls ensured that I would become my aged grandfather's constant companion, sitting by his side watching children play outside our window, too bound to sorrow and insecurity to venture out to join them. A particularly powerful dream imaged my childhood state as inhabiting an underground coffin while the house above it burned.

One of my primary desires in applying for analytic training was to make community with souls who were similarly called to doing Psyche's work, particularly as the clinical work we do can be so incredibly lonely. And, in fact, it's been particularly healing to me to come together with other analysts and therapists at conferences and retreats. Over time, I've learned that my early encapsulation belied the cravings of a creative Gemini woman for self-expression, dialogue, and engagement with the world in ever-widening spheres.

I've always been moved by Rilke's exquisite self-portrait in his poem *I Live My Life:* "I am circling around God, around the ancient tower, and I have been circling for a thousand years, and I still don't know if I am a falcon, or a storm, or a great song."[3] As a writer and teacher of the Creativity elective at the C. G. Jung Institute of Los Angeles, I've learned that self-expression, for many of us, can be a crucial vehicle by which to navigate that tower and discover the many facets of ourselves.

Facebook has been dubbed, not unfairly, as an A-ticket to voyeurism, the ultimate narcissistic playground, an exhibitionist's delight, a socially sanctioned way to indulge in the craving to be seen. Its profile page wall is a forum for virtual graffiti that can be understood to echo the psychological functions of actual graffiti in our urban barrios and ghettos. Adolescent taggers may be frustrated artists, but they are often also frustrated and disempowered young souls, unmirrored and unrecognized by family, social institutions, the culture-at-large, and most importantly, within themselves, seeking any way they can to make their mark on the environment, to claim their own little place and sense of belonging on this earth. In an analogous way, Facebookers use their walls to announce themselves, to post their photos, links, videos, and status updates—which are, in turn, open to running commentary and discussion by their own gangs, or chosen friendship lists, or by opposing gangs, though the latter often end up being "un-friended."

Fascinated and curious when I first signed up, I began as more of a voyeur. My first friends were already old hands at the social media game who'd grown beyond My Space and Friendster and were already tweeting madly on Twitter. Their posts ranged from silly to serious, sardonic to mundane. Some of them posted that they'd just had their first cup of morning coffee or participated in one of Facebook's innumerable quizzes or games like Farmville; others put down the latest gaffes of various politicians with quick and caustic wit. One thing I noticed was the facility with which my new friends' minds associated a verbal post, to a YouTube video, to a photography show, to a *Huffington Post* blog. I could feel my own associative capacities speeding up, a process that had already begun in the writing, researching, and Googling necessary to complete my last novel.

Later I was to learn through one of my Facebook friends about U.C.L.A. neuroscientist Gary Small's work on what he sees as a "dramatic shift in how we gather information and communicate" that "has touched off a rapid evolution of the brain." Small contends, "Perhaps not since early man first discovered how to use a tool has the human brain been affected so quickly and so dramatically. As the brain evolves and shifts its focus towards new technological skills, it drifts away from fundamental social skills."[4] According to *Newsweek* writer Janeen Interlandi, Small "puts people into two categories: digital natives and digital immigrants." Small's idea is that the former are better at snap decisions and juggling lots of sensory input, whereas the latter are great at reading facial expressions.

Such speculation in the scientific community brings to mind a distinction made in anthropology between traditional and modern cultures, in which the power differential shifts with modernization from the wise elder to the younger generation's innovations and priorities. In that sense, Mark Zuckerberg and other social media developers are increasingly the culture-shapers of the brave new world in which the baby boomers and beyond find themselves. As Bob Dylan put it in the anthem of the sixties generation, when the cultural fulcrum from elders to the young was reaching its tipping point:

Come mothers and fathers
Throughout the land
And don't criticize
What you can't understand
Your sons and your daughters
Are beyond your command
Your old road is
Rapidly agin'.
Please get out of the new one
If you can't lend your hand
For the times they are a-changin'.[5]

As I began to recognize the largeness of the phenomenon I'd entered into by joining Facebook, my own fulcrum began to shift. When I'd first signed on, I only asked people I already knew to be my Facebook friends; soon I began to respond when strangers asked to "friend" me. Fascinated, amused, or challenged by someone's response to a friend's wall post, I started to reach out to such strangers myself, and within a year my Facebook friend roster moved beyond triple digits.

My tipping point between toe-in-the-water-wader and throwing- introversive-caution-to-the-winds-surfing-enthusiast occurred when I was included in my first "Note," an invitation to participate in a discussion thread that reminded me of the old chat rooms. This one concerned the Quantum Physics theory of multiple universes. I'd recently completed a coming-of-age novel, *The History of My Body*, about a young girl who becomes a quantum physicist, and I was struck by the synchronicity between where researching the rarified world of physics had been taking my science-challenged mind and what I was now reading in various comments on this thread. This was my first intimation that Facebook might be more than what it seemed. I began to more intently explore my friends' walls and to reach out when a stranger posted something particularly seminal and exciting regarding the interface of science, philosophy, and consciousness.

Writing *The History of My Body* had already led me to the Hindu myth of Indra's Net or Web, in which the god Indra's heaven is said to consist of a net of crisscrossing threads, with a jewel suspended from each intersection mirroring every other jewel in the web. Not a bad description of life's interconnectedness itself, and certainly enough of an image of the Internet and world wide web that I've wondered if those two names didn't originate with at least an unconscious reference to Indra. Rooted in the longing for mirroring, Facebook itself can be seen as a cyber version of that Hindu heaven.

I found myself reaching out in particular to those people whose posts mirrored the cutting edge of my own development, ultimately extending to the ones who opened my eyes more fully to our beleaguered planet—ecological scientists and activists. As I engaged with people I might not meet at the Jung Institute or in my own typological neck of the woods, I recalled the wonderful quote attributed to Anais Nin: "Each friend represents a world in us, a world not born until they arrive, and it is only by this meeting that a new world is born."[6]

Opening doors to new worlds can also be culturally advantageous, as anthropologists recognized early on in their discovery of the practice of exogamy amongst indigenous tribes they studied. The brilliant Claude Levi-Strauss offered an "Alliance Theory" of exogamy, suggesting that the ritual marrying between peoples of two or more tribes ensured the economic and cultural flourishing of groups profiting from such exogamous exchange.[7] The same might be applied to the world of beliefs and ideas, with inter-disciplinary dialogue being the best hedge against the stagnation of unexamined beliefs and the hostile stasis of fundamentalism.

The environmental community on Facebook began to exert an increasingly compelling pull on me that was only strengthened with the god-awful crisis initiated by the 2010 Deep Horizon oil spill in the Gulf of Mexico. Many years ago, I'd been profoundly moved by Jung's words in his autobiography, *Memories, Dreams, Reflections:*

> At times, I feel as if I am spread out over the landscape and inside things, and am myself living in every tree, in the splashing of the waves, in the clouds and the animals that come and go, in the procession of the seasons. There is nothing...with which I am not linked.[8]

I, too, had always been a nature lover, but I was born and bred a city girl. My first forays into ecological circles offered a widening outlook to the poetic spirit-soul of me. Imagine my joy in reading this Facebook post by environmental lawyer Carolyn Raffensperger:

> On the high precipice of the heart. No finger holds. No toe holds. It is all dark and then the dark too blooms and sings. The dark feet and the dark wings of fellow travelers hold a net below. This shall not fail.

Carolyn's vantage point is akin to that of environmental entrepreneur Paul Hawken:

> When asked if I am pessimistic or optimistic about the future, my answer is always the same: If you look at the science about what is happening on earth and aren't pessimistic, you don't understand the data. But if you meet the people who are working to restore this earth and the lives of the poor, and you aren't optimistic, you haven't got a pulse.[9]

My own pulse was quickening as Facebook fast became my primary source of news about the Gulf, with environmentalists on the ground reporting what even the *New York Times* failed to publish.

Earlier, I alluded to Rilke's image of circling God. Yeats offered his own image, a far bleaker one, on the heels of World War I in his poem *The Second Coming*, which begins:

Turning and turning in the widening gyre.
The falcon cannot hear the falconer;
Things fall apart; the centre cannot hold;
Mere anarchy is loosed upon the world,
The blood-dimmed tide is loosed, and everywhere
The ceremony of innocence is drowned;

The best lack all conviction, while the worst
Are full of passionate intensity. [1]

The poem ends with the haunting lines, "And what rough beast, its hour come round at last, Slouches towards Bethlehem to be born?"

I know I was not the only one to recall that sorry creature upon viewing the unspeakable photos of pelicans drenched in oil. In 1939, Bertolt Brecht appended a four-line *Motto* to his *Svendborg Poems*:

In the dark times
Will there also be singing?
Yes, there will be singing
About the dark times. [11]

We *are* living in dark times. And when the Deepwater Horizon drilling rig exploded in 2010, the walls of Facebook burst forth with songs, images, videos, links, reflections, and cries of outrage and recognition at our complicity in the unconsciousness that threatens our world. Within my own collection of Facebook friends, a smaller cadre of about 50 people began to coalesce who were able to symbolically link the personal and political, concrete news events with the psychological, spiritual, and creative.

Many ecopsychologists have adopted the term "solastalgia" to describe the helplessness and despair experienced when we register threats to our home environment. [12] We Jungians can understand that phenomenon as an externalized companion piece to the Cartesian rift in the western psyche, as well as the ego-Self alienation that inevitably triggers a conscious suffering of the individuation process. What I've come to discover is that the more than 1.3 billion active users of Facebook include an increasing number of people who are seeking meaning via the empowering experience of creative expression and exchange. As my Facebook connections spread exponentially across web and globe to include young and old, political firebrands of various stripes, artists of every genre, environmental activists, and Jungian lantsmen*, I realized I was being initiated into the collective psyche's use of the forward-leaning and seeming mechanized spirit of our times to plumb the vast Indra's Web of interconnection that unites us all.

Witnessing for some time with horror the decline of newspapers and printed books, I had been blind to the concurrent democratization of the art and act of writing, as well as a union of the opposites of self-reflection and communication,

---

* A Yiddish word for neighbor or "soul kin"

in the evolving world of social media. My Facebook friends' posts are like sonnets, haikus, or mini-novels. And unlike the traditional piece of literature, the best blogs, wall posts, and threads can be seen as invitations to respond, a bridging of inner and outer realities, an innovative reach beyond the persona level of public discourse, exposing shadow and Self alike. Which is say nothing of the links to extraordinary paintings, photos, and music videos regularly offered up as testimony to the creative spirit via the Facebook community.

The topics discussed on the pages of my now nearly 2,000 Facebook friends range from the utterly mundane to science, politics, psychology, philosophy, and the sheer delight of life-affirming humor. The longest comment threads on my profile page have concerned the Gulf Oil tragedy, the mid-term elections, Laurens van der Post and Jung, safely removing bees from walls, the poet Mary Oliver, You Tube songs, cosmetic surgery, favorite parts of London, the concept of the Mitochondrial Eve, the performance art of Laurie Anderson, and friends playfully fantasizing forming girl groups, having slumber parties, and bouncing on the bed. I've come to look at Facebook conversation as a kind of call and response that frequently affirms, occasionally contradicts, sometimes trivializes, but often deepens the common point of reflection. I find myself thinking of those with whom I regularly communicate wall-to-wall as my Facebook tribe, one of millions of tribes singing songs of the dark times back and forth across the Internet and, in the process, constellating little sparks of conscious light.

Jung once commented that the function of the archetypes is to reconnect us with the root condition. One of the root conditions of the human animal relates to kinship libido, the archetype of the tribe, an archetype we need to "get" at the deepest level if we are to recognize and take action regarding our common interests in healing the planet that supports us and generates our individual development and unfolding.

Since the Gulf Oil crisis seemed to have been a trigger for the coming together on Facebook into a larger exogamous tribal structure, I'd like to give you a feel for the kind of discussion thread that can get going on environmental themes. Carolyn Raffensperger opens by posting this status report:

I am speaking this week at a colloquium...But I've heard that the grad students are depressed after being bombarded by climate chaos information. (I'm) reweaving my talk with strands from Rebecca Solnit and Vaclav Havel on activism and hope.

Then Renee Aron Lertzman, psychoanalytic educator and researcher, comments:

Yes, this is something – despair, depression – that is chronic and will only be on the rise. Messages of hope are important, but so are lessons from psychotherapy, such as acknowledgement of the pain, validation, and a sense of compassion.

To which Alison Rose Levy, health writer and journalist, responds:

It becomes depression when it is turned in—in futility. Cherish the anger as energy for movement….(As) individuals we may suffer in facing these realities, and as individuals there is something we can do. Empower the need to participate one by one AND as a community...(We) are all together as part of a biological web that is vibrating with aliveness and resilience and survival potential.

At this point I compliment Alison for identifying, in the empowerment of individuals through active community, a potential Ariadne thread in and through the darkness, to which Casey Hayden, co-author of *Deep in Our Hearts: Nine White Women in the Freedom Movement* objects:

It seems to me that we are the species weaving a web and the rest of creation is caught in it and being extinguished. Where I live the birds, the desert animals and plants, and the water are rapidly passing away, no matter how much we are part of some thread of light in our own minds.

David Eisenberg, director of a center for sustainable construction, jumps in and points out that:

the importance of 'affect' on 'effect' is crucial…I often spend a lot of time thinking about my audience—and my audiences often contain significant numbers of people who don't share the world view held by those commenting here. I'm constantly seeking ways…that can transcend the auto-reject response of those inclined to deny or reject my ideas… I've referred to our work in the building codes realm as "doing heartwork with code officials" by which I mean connecting to the caring nature of their work…There is a very tricky point at which the revelation that they have missed something huge and not been fully carrying out the work of safeguarding the public from hazards attributed to the built environment can drive them back into denial. So I have frequently framed the whole process in terms of having always been doing the best we could with what we knew.

I'd like to offer another flavor of conversational thread to fill out your sense of how Facebook posts can weave up and down, in and out, like the best intimate conversations. It is part of a 19-comment conversational thread generated by my posting of Mary Oliver's poem, *Wild Geese*, which concludes with the words:

> Whoever you are, no matter how lonely,
> the world offers itself to your imagination,
> calls to you like the wild geese, harsh and exciting--
> over and over announcing your place
> in the family of things.[13]

Deborah Jiang-Stein, a writer who was born heroin-addicted to a mother under guard at the Alderson Federal Prison for Women, and who tours women's prisons as a soul-affirming speaker, responds:

> I think I need to read this to the women in prisons next month when I speak; thanks for the reminder of (it). I just read it aloud, imagining 1200 women in khakis listening to this, waiting for those with arms crossed to uncross as I walk amongst them with poetry...Even the guards will listen to this one! I'll let you know. I hope I get a church-kind-of Amen on this.

Carolyn chimes in with a paraphrasing of Persian poet, Hafez: "Deborah, this poem is in your honor":

> The small man
> Builds Prisons
> For Everyone He Knows
>
> But the Wise Woman
> Must Duck
> Under the Moon
> To Throw Keys to the Beautiful and Rowdy Prisoners.

Then Margo Stebbing, artist and entrepreneur, offers:

> Last month I watched: *What I Want My Words to Do for You*, with Eve Ensler at the New Bedford Correctional facility. I was so profoundly moved by this documentary. I love that you are doing this. I will read this poem on the 16th and think of you all, with deep sighs and arms uncrossing.

The feeling tone generated in this thread led me to coin the term "Oliverettes" for the poetry-lovers I was meeting on my wall. They, in turn, were linking to other exogamous threesomes, foursomes, and twenty-somes, who ended up becoming part of my Facebook tribe.

I marvel how these communications mirrored what Sir Laurens van der Post described nearly forty years ago:

> I began to meet people in remote parts of the world and...to receive letters...that made me see these lonely spirits as already members...of a new community which as yet had no institutions to express it. This gave me a new certainty...that of the deeps of the disintegrating pattern of my time, a greater community was in preparation and could not be prevented from coming.[14]

I've already mentioned the Facebook community's multi-layered response to the Gulf crisis. Later, we saw the people-power of social media in generating political change, in particular the toppling of Mubarak in Egypt. As Jerry Fleishman reported in the *Los Angeles Times* in 2011, Egypt's "April 6 youth movement organized protests and plotted strategies through Facebook, to outmaneuver the police."[15] While some, like journalist Malcolm Gladwell, were quick to point out that revolutions occurred long before the Internet, it can hardly be denied that the wide dissemination of information via social media amplified the reach and rapidity of the revolutionary message, with the Facebook page, "We are all Khaled Said,"[16] gaining over 500,000 visitors, an event that echoes the more recent 2015 attack on the French newspaper *Charlie Hebdo.*[17]

Of course, the power of our inventions, like the psyche itself, is as subject to shadow as illumination. Just as the Egyptian revolution may lead to democracy, prolonged chaos, or an oppressively fundamentalist regime, and reactionary sentiments are as likely as progressive ones to be broadcast on walls, Facebook raises important questions about what mayhem might be wrought from this new type of relationship emerging from the collective psyche. Participating in Facebook is similar in more than a few ways to attending a film or a play, requiring a suspension of disbelief that sets aside the convention or frame of what we consider real. Among the challenges posed by social media are serious questions of visibility vs. anonymity and privacy (or what's good for the extraversive goose might not be so hot for the introverted gander). I have had Facebook friends flirt with me, ask me to interpret their dreams, request to become analysands, come to Jung Institute lectures, and, once, even visit me for a weekend, shocking me midway through the experience that I'd invited a stranger into my home, something that would have terrified me, had my daughter done the same thing. (In case you're worrying, it turned out fine; my instinctual read of her trustworthiness and depth proved to be accurate, and she and I continue to build upon that first impulsive connection.) On the other hand, when Rep. Gabrielle Giffords was shot, I had to immediately "unfriend" one ostensible Facebook friend after he responded with an ugly and threatening comment to my post of a *New York Times* gun-control editorial.

While I was disturbed and frightened by his response, I was also inspired by the subsequent comment by Jessica Trupin, the literary agent with whom I'd been connected via Facebook, who pointed out to my soon-to-be-ex-friend:

> The shooter was taken down by a 61-year-old woman who was quick to jam her hand under his gun so he couldn't reload. Three men, age indeterminate, then tackled him and held him down. The congresswoman was likely saved by a 20 year old who ran into a hail of bullets and kept her from bleeding to death right there. Not a single one of them had a gun. I certainly hope your post is a rough and ill-timed parody, but if it's not, you should re-examine your willingness to post something that threatening at a time like this.

I learned from this experience that someone being a friend of a friend is no guarantee of sanity—I'd accepted this man's original friend request because he was friends with one of my favorite *New York Times* columnists—but I'd also been given the privilege of witnessing a very fine communicator respond with a level tone and clear thinking to someone possessed by primitive energies.

Another often-discussed potential pitfall of social media like Facebook is the avoidance of a lived life, in which the substance and veracity of virtual connections are confused with the meaning and animal warmth of embodied relationship that requires work, patience, engagement with the shadow, and a testing of the ideal against the real. The film *Catfish*—which my daughter helped publicize—provocatively tackles the problem of online honesty vs. dishonesty by documenting what happened when a young man fell in love with a Facebook friend, only to discover that she was far from how she'd portrayed herself. Facebook and other web media and games use Avatars as symbolic images and sub-personalities that stand, true or false, for who we are. My own Facebook profile picture recently took the form of a blown-up photo of a Christmas amaryllis I received from a student, but has been at various times in the past a painting of Lord Hanuman embracing Rama, a photo of an Afghani girl handing a flower to an American soldier, and an image from *Lady and the Tramp*.

Facebook not only presents opportunities for avoidance of a lived life, but can also lend itself to addictive drives, malicious gossip, and out and out viciousness like my erstwhile gun enthusiast friend—not to mention the dark side of tribalism itself, with its pull toward fundamentalism, loss of individual integrity, and mass-mindedness.

Facebook tribes can exaggerate our human tendency to preach to the choir and demonize the Other, or, as Anne Lamott puts it, "You can safely assume that you've created God in your own image when it turns out that God hates all the same people you do."[18] I have one whole strand of otherwise quite tolerant Facebook friends who absolutely revile anyone who dares criticize Obama, especially during his first term, and another that consistently vilifies the man as strenuously as the most fervent Tea Partier, even years after his election. Morally neutral, Facebook gives us a chance to witness and indulge in the darkest elements of shadow projection, supported by numerous others who will join us in our paranoia in a *folie a deux* times a thousand.

I also want to emphasize that I am exploring Facebook from the perspective of a mature adult. The perils of Facebook for adolescents could and does fill many books with disturbing questions, ranging from MIT professor Sherry Turkle's notion of "presentation anxiety," in which teenagers exhaust themselves "as they constantly tweak their Facebook profiles for maximum cool," to Dartmouth's Alex Jordan's research that suggests that self-esteem drops as Facebookers compare themselves to others' profiles, which are the social equivalent of "airbrushed photos on the covers of women's magazines."[19] Whatever naiveté we adults demonstrate in this hothouse of social exposure can be multiplied exponentially in younger people who are even less conscious of potential consequences. My daughter has pointed out to me how Facebook has been a regular stomping ground for bullies and that young people run the risk of having youthful mistakes documented for posterity, potentially affecting future professional opportunities. Kids not only hurt each other's feelings with some regularity on Facebook; they can also do considerable self-harm, as in the case of the boy who was suspended from his high school after crudely commenting on his Facebook wall about his teacher's body.[20]

And I don't want to minimize the tendency of social media, like our culture at large, in elevating the trivial to an art form. A quick Google search reveals that there are over 32 million users currently playing Farmville on a daily basis, according to GamesRadar.com. Undoubtedly in reaction to some of the more obvious failings of Facebook—particularly that it was originally designed solely for college students—a whole host of more sophisticated social media have emerged, among them: Shelfari, a social cataloging website, in which participants build virtual bookshelves of books they own or have read and can review and recommend to other friends on the site; Quora, a kind of blend of Facebook and Wikipedia, which describes itself as a "continually improving collection of questions and answers created, edited, and organized by everyone who uses it;" and Para Pachamama, Spirit of the Earth, a shamanically-oriented social medium that bills itself as "a global community network of sharing, exchanging, gathering and informing our world about the Great Shift happening on Earth."

What an odd juxtaposition: shamanism and machines. Indeed, a few of my Jungian colleagues still refuse to receive Institute messages via e-mail; for all I know, they don't own computers. Having referred to *myself* more than a few times as a Luddite, I researched—via Google, of course—where the expression "Luddite" originated. It turns out that in 1779, enraged by mechanization, Ned Ludd was reputed to have smashed two knitting frames, or mechanical knitting machines. I was struck that it was the new-fangled means by which linking, or knitting, occurred that ignited Ned's fury. I can imagine him going mad over the mission-statement of Tim Berners-Lee, originator of the World Wide Web, who said that his quest was to make the web "a place where the whim of a human being and the reasoning of a machine coexist in an ideal, powerful mixture."[21]

Such a co-existence raises a host of questions. Among them: what do we make of the fact that, according to Lisa Barrett of Northeastern University, the amygdala is larger in people with more extensive social networks?[22] Since the amygdala relates to emotion, vision, memory, and fight or flight responses to fear, does the degree of stress we experience increase—not only in response to population explosion, environmental degradation, noise pollution, and the collapse of traditional religious, familial, and social containers—but also as we expand our spheres of social interaction? What happens when we're not so able to filter our social connections, but are inundated with thousands of them via machine? How do we metabolize the speed at which "*these* times they are a-changin'?"

This question takes me back to my own early aversion to computers in general, which I worried were too…well, mechanical. What aspect of evolving humanity does social media select for? Who are we—what incarnations of ourselves— when we're on Facebook? Avatar? Homunculus? Golem? What happens when the youngest generation has a harder time than its predecessors in reading the expressions on a human face? Does mechanization implicitly exclude, or can it ever actually facilitate, soul?

Something in the human psyche, the flower of Nature's capacity to reflect upon Herself, includes the mechanical. What does that mean? In her poem "The Invocation to Kali," May Sarton wrote:

What Hell have we made of the subtle weaving
Of nerve with brain, that all centers tear?
We live in a dark complex of rage and grieving.
The machine grates, grates, whatever we are.[23]

Like many Jungians, I am all-too-aware of the dark complexes of rage and grieving, but what of the synthetic function of the collective unconscious itself? Might the machines we've created bring to the fore an awareness of the *unus mundus* in the spirit of *our* time?

It's been my own habit to counterpose the mechanical against the natural, with machines being objects somehow separate from the bodies that built them and the psyches that first imagined them. If so, then their "unnaturality" is akin to the individuation process itself as *opus contra naturum*, a work that goes against, yet originates in nature.

So, too, our machines—which we are compelled by living reality to see as one of nature's particularly perplexing crops. From the beginning of our evolution, we humans have designed tools to manipulate our environment. For anthropologists, our increasingly sophisticated use of tools has differentiated us from every other species on this planet. Paleoanthropologist Stanley Ambrose has proposed that "our ancestors' technology, hands, brains, and language co-evolved." He speculates that "complex tool-making, which required fine motor skills, problem solving, and task planning, may have influenced the evolution of the frontal lobe, and co-evolved with the gift of grammatical language 300,000 years ago."[24]

Using my Apple MacBook to surf the web, I discovered a machine is defined as a "device," often having many parts, that uses energy to perform some activity by transforming "the direction or magnitude of a force." The original derivation of the word "machine" is from the early Greek "mechos," which suggests, "means, expedient, remedy." We use the word to describe, amongst other things, a rigid person, a political system, and the natural functioning of the human body itself. Among the first *simple* machines that redirected force to make life easier were crude wedges chipped into rocks to form hand axes by early hominids. Anthropologists call the first *complex* machines "prime movers," which use some sort of natural force to perform manual or related work. An early example of this sort of machine was the Persian Wheel, created to convert the flow of water into energy. While, historically, we've defined machines as requiring moving parts, "the advent of electronic technology has led to the development of machines without moving parts —the computer being the most obvious example."[25]

Vernor Vinge is a retired professor of mathematics and computer science and a prize-winning science fiction writer, whose 1993 essay, *The Coming Technological*

Singularity, argues that the creation of superhuman artificial intelligence will mark the point at which "the human era will be ended," in that no current models of reality are sufficient to predict beyond it.[26] He is far from the only technologist foreseeing this, and there is considerable discussion in the field over whether such an evolution would be beneficial, harmful, or an existential threat.

Who knew that we'd be alive in a time when such an event seems even remotely possible? Or that its possibility might be coupled with climate change that threatens far more than our own species? But the Spirit of the Depths tells us that there have been existentially threatening times before us and that there are timeless, existentially transforming elements within our psychological depths and in the universe itself. One of those elements is portrayed in the mythology of the Homunculi, those personifications of patterns of inner organization that devour themselves and give birth to new incarnations as we suffer our way into more fully inhabiting our share of human wholeness, dreaming the dream of our world forward. Might we see the Mark Zuckerbergs of our time being moved, consciously or not, by the ageless, unfolding collective psyche as teleologically as the spirit that animated the alchemists of old, with young men and women noodling away as passionately at new software programs to transform the human adventure as those *fratar* and *soror mystica* at their retorts? Or would the current advances into cyberspace be more accurately amplified by the Golem, an inferior creation mimicking human intelligence but lacking its soul?

A more optimistic point of view of the current arc of human development is articulated by Tom Atlee of the Co-Intelligence Institute, who uses the metaphor of the scientific community to propose a collective intelligence that can mediate the poles of "group think" and "individual cognitive bias" in order to enhance problem solving via an evolving collaborative process, a kind of two-heads-are-better-than-one-and-millions-are-even-better philosophy of human evolution.[27] Mathematical cosmologist Brian Swimme puts forth his own view of evolutionary spirituality in this way (borrowing liberally from Jung in the process):

Humanity is the fruit of fourteen billion years of unbroken evolution, now becoming conscious of itself...When the Bible speaks about God forming us from the dust of the Earth, it's actually true, we did not come into this world—we grew out of it, just like an apple grows from an apple tree. Do you get this? I mean, do you really get this? We are the universe becoming conscious of itself. We are stardust that has begun to contemplate the stars. We have arisen out of the dynamics of the Earth. "Four billion years ago, our planet was molten rock, and now it sings opera."[28]

Of course, through her human sons and daughters, the Earth doesn't just sing opera. She also makes war and poisons Her own environment. Buddhist teacher Thích Nhất Hạnh has been quoted as saying that "it is possible that the next Buddha will not take the form of an individual," but "of a community, a community practicing understanding and loving kindness, a community practicing mindful living. This may be the most important thing we can do for the survival of the earth."[29] From this vantage point, might social media's capacity to bring into our homes the reality of participating in a wider world community bend the machine to serve as a kind of homeopathic remedy for what we've done to our souls and the fabric of the earth with our machines?

Perhaps. But in the final analysis, all the machines in the world can never improve upon the silence at the center of the soul that generates new birth. Virtually every creation myth throughout the ages tells us that new life begins with the void. If we give ourselves over fully to the addictive temptation to wallpaper every inch of inner space with the neon seductions of our machines— our televisions, our iPads, our Facebook—we crush the capacity to make meaning of what our imaginations generate, leaving us wide-open to creating scores of Golems who ham-fistedly trample possibility and the earth who gave birth to us all.

In a beautifully written and well-researched *New Yorker* essay titled "The Information: How the Internet Gets Inside Us," Adam Gopnik poses similar questions in a lively, historical vein. Gopnik characterizes three common attitudes appearing in recent books about the Internet as "the Never-Betters, the Better-Nevers, and the Ever-Wasers," deftly exploring the points of view of those who see the Internet as a godsend, as a curse, or as merely the most current example of human change. He ends up editorializing in a down-to-earth way, "Thoughts are bigger than the things that deliver them. Our contraptions may shape our consciousness, but it is our consciousness that makes our credos, and we mostly live by those."[30] His answer to all the hand-wringing and idealization is to maintain a balance between wired-in activity and our more embodied, related, and reflective lives, keeping the bright new toys of our brave new world in proportion.

A great idea, but when the force of new technology carries the energy of the collective unconscious, balance is not so easy to hold and we are not exactly likely to behave reasonably. Or as the young protagonist of my novel, *The History of My Body*, observes, "God is pretty big, so it figures he has a bigger void than any of us to fill."[31]

I got twenty-two responses when I posted the following words from novelist Jim Harrison's *Dalva* on Facebook: "I remember my grandfather telling me how each of us must live with a full measure of loneliness that is inescapable, and we must not destroy ourselves with our passion to escape this aloneness."[32]

Our human noses are always sniffing for ways to evade the whistling wind of the void and the tension of holding the opposites. Social media like Facebook can serve the master of that avoidance or be a looking glass in which to observe the psyche as it struggles to balance individual integrity and expression with an equally implacable demand for kinship.

In Lewis Carroll's *Alice Through the Looking Glass,* Alice is relieved of the confusion of her adventures by being woken for tea. We have no such *deus ex machina* to save us from our wrestle with our appetites and obsessions, our needs and fears, the predations and transforming potential of *our* machines. I've had such a hefty dose of Facebook in writing this paper that my temptation is to resolve all the issues it raises by quitting it altogether. But I won't. The little girl I once was will be damned if she lies still in that underground coffin while Home burns. Like William Shedd, she knows that "a ship is safe in harbor, but that's not what ships are for."[33]

Oh, and by the way—will you be my friend?

Notes

1 C. G. Jung, (1922/1966.) On the Relation of Analytical Psychology to Poetry. *The Spirit in Man, Art, and Literature.* CW 15. Trans. R. F. C. Hull. Princeton, NJ: Princeton University Press. 82, ¶130.

2 Jung. *The Red Book.* (2009.) Ed. Sonu Shamdasani. Trans. Mark Kyburz, John Peck & Sonu Shamdasani. New York, New York: W. W. Norton.

3 Rainer Maria Rilke, 1899/1995. "I Live my Life." In *News of the universe: Poems of twofold consciousness.* Edited by Robert Bly. San Francisco, CA. Sierra Club Books. 76

4 As cited in Janeen Interlandi, (October 14, 2008.) Reading This Will Change Your Brain. *Newsweek.* http://www.newsweek.com/2008/10/13/reading-this-will-change-your-brain.html

5 Bob Dylan, 1964. "The Times They Are a-Changin'." New York, NY: Columbia Records.

6 Anais Nin, 2011. Knowledge Pk. http://knowledgepkcomquotations/author/Anais+Nin.

7 Claude Levi-Strauss, 1949/2011. See Wikipedia (2011a).

8 Jung, 1989. *Memories, Dreams, Reflections.* Ed. Aniela Jaffe. Trans. Clara Winston & Richard Winston. New York, NY. Vintage. 225-226.

9 Paul Hawken, 2009. "Commencement: Healing or Stealing." University of Portland (Online). http://www.up.edu/commencement/default.aspx?cid=9456

10 Rilke. 1899/1995. "I Live my Life." Stanza 1, followed by Stanza 2

11 Bertolt Brecht, (1939/1997.) *Bertolt Brecht: Poems 1913-1956.* Ed. John Willett & Ralpha Manheim. London, England: Routledge. 320.

12 Glen Albrecht, 2005. Solastalgia, a New Concept in Human Health and Identity. *Philosophy Activism Nature* 3: 41–44.

13 Mary Oliver (1986/2011) "Wild geese." In *Dream work*. Boston, MA: Atlantic Monthly Press.

14 Sir Laurens van der Post, 1977. *Jung and the Story of our Time*. Washington, D.C., New York, NY: Vintage Books, 35.

15 Jerry Fleishman, 2011. *Los Angeles Times*, January 27: http://articles.latimes.com/2011/jan/27/world/la-fg-egypt-youth-20110128

16 Ned Parker, 2011. Revolution in the Age of Internet. *Los Angeles Times*: February 11, http://www.latimes.com/news/nationworld/world/la-fg-egypt-google-20110212,0,7159629.story

17 John D. Sutter, 2015. 'Je suis Charlie,' at least for now. *CNN*, January 11, http://www.cnn.com/2015/01/11/opinion/sutter-je-suis-charlie/index.html

18 Anne Lamott, 1995. *Bird by Bird*. New York, NY: Random House. 22.

19 Sherry Turkle and Alex Jordan are both cited in Libby Copeland, 2011. Doublex: The Anti-social Network. *Slate*, January 26. http://www.slate.com/toolbar.aspx?action=print&id=2282620

20 Jolie O'Dell, 2011. Mashable. http://mashable.com/2011/02/01/facebook-free-speech-high-school/

21 Wikipedia. 2011d. Tim Berners-Lee. *Wikipedia, The Free Encyclopedia*: http://en.wikipedia.org/w/index.php?title=Tim_Berners-Lee&oldid=414741867

22 Landau, Elizabeth. 2010. Do You Have a Brain for Social Networks? CNN Health, December 26. http://pagingdrgupta.blogs.cnn.com/2010/12/26/do-you-have-a-brain-forsocial-networks/

23 May Sarton, 1971. The Invocation to Kali. In *A Grain of Mustard Seed*. New York, NY: W. W. Norton, 19.

24 Stanley Ambrose, Summer 2001. Anthropologist Proposes That Toolmaking and Languages Coevolved. *LAS News*: http://www.las.illinois.edu/alumni/magazine/articles/2001/anthropologist/

25 Wikipedia. 2011b. Machine. *Wikipedia, The Free Encyclopedia*: http://en.wikipedia.org/w/index.php?title=Machine&oldid=414265297

26 Verner Vinge. 1993. The Coming Technological Singularity: How to Survive in the Post-Human Era. http://www.aleph.se/Trans/Global/Singularity/sing.html

27 Tom Atlee, 2011. The Co-Intelligence Institute. http://www.co-intelligence.org/tomatleebio.html

28 Brian Swimme, 1994. *The Universe Story: From the Primordial Flaring Forth to the Ecozoic Era—a Celebration of the Unfolding of the Cosmos*. New York, NY: HarperOne.

29 As cited in Deena Metzger, January 24, 2011. http://parapachamama.blogspot.com/2011/01/companions-on-quest-for-viable-world.html

30 Adam Gopnik, Feb. 14 & 21, 2011. Does the Internet Change How we Think? *The New Yorker*. New York, NY: Conde Nast.

31 Sharon Heath, 2001. *The History of My Body*. Carmel, CA: Genoa House.

32 Jim Harrison, 1991. *Dalva*. New York, NY: Washington Square Press.

33 William Shedd, 2011. ThinkExist.com: http://thinkexist.com/quotes/william_shedd/

Bibliography

Albrecht, Glen. Solastalgia, a New Concept in Human Health and Identity. *Philosophy Activism Nature* 3 (2005.): 41–44.

Ambrose, Stanley. (Summer 2001.) Anthropologist Proposes That Toolmaking and Languages Coevolved. *LAS News*: http://www.las.illinois.edu/alumni/magazine/articles/2001/anthropologist/

Atlee, Tom. (2011) The Co-Intelligence Institute. http://www.co-intelligence.org/tomat-leebio.html

Brecht, Bertolt. (1939/1997.) *Bertolt Brecht: Poems 1913-1956*. Ed. John Willlett & Ralpha Manheim. London, England: Routledge. 320.

Copeland, Libby. 2011. Doublex: The Anti-Social Network. *Slate*, January 26. http://www.slate.com/toolbar.aspx?action=print&id=2282620

Dylan, Bob. 1964. The Times They Are a-Changin'. New York, NY: Columbia Records.

Fleishman, Jerry. (2011.) *Los Angeles Times*, January 27: http://articles.latimes.com/2011/jan/27/world/la-fg-egypt-youth-20110128

Gopnik, Adam. (Feb. 14 & 21, 2011.) Does the Internet Change How We Think? *The New Yorker*. New York, NY: Conde Nast.

Harrison, Jim. (1991.) *Dalva*. New York, NY: Washington Square Press.

Hawken, Paul. (2009.) Commencement: Healing or Stealing. University of Portland (Online). http://www.up.edu/commencement/default.aspx?cid=9456

Heath, Sharon. (2001.) *The History of My Body*. Carmel, CA: Genoa House.

Interlandi, Janeen. (October 14, 2008.) Reading This Will Change Your Brain. *Newsweek*. http://www.newsweek.com/2008/10/13/reading-this-will-change-your-brain.html

Jung, C. G. (1922/1966.) On the Relation of Analytical Psychology to Poetry. *The Spirit in Man, Art, and Literature*. CW 15. Trans. R. F. C. Hull. Princeton, NJ: Princeton University Press. 82.

Jung, C. G. 1989. *Memories, Dreams, Reflections*. Ed. Aniela Jaffe. Trans. Clara Winston & Richard Winston. New York, NY. Vintage. 225-226.

Jung, C. G. *The Red Book*. (2009.) Ed. Sonu Shamdasani. Trans. Mark Kyburz, John Peck & Sonu Shamdasani. New York, New York: W. W. Norton.

Lamott, Anne. (1995.) *Bird by Bird*. New York, NY: Random House. 22.

Landau, Elizabeth. 2010. Do you Have a Brain for Social Networks? CNN Health, December 26. http://pagingdrgupta.blogs.cnn.com/2010/12/26/do-you-have-a-brain-forsocial-networks/

Metzger, Deena. January 24, 2011. http://parapachamama.blogspot.com/2011/01/companions-on-quest-for-viable-world.html

Nin, Anais. 2011. Knowledge Pk. http://knowledgepk.com/quotations/author/Anais+Nin.

O'Dell, Jolie. 2011. Mashable. http://mashable.com/2011/02/01/facebook-free-speech-high-school/

Oliver, Mary. (1986) Wild geese. In *Dream Work*. Boston: Atlantic Monthly Press.

Parker, Ned. (2011.) Revolution in the Age of Internet. *Los Angeles Times*: February 11, http://www.latimes.com/news/nationworld/world/la-fg-egypt-google-20110212,0,7159629.story

Raffi. 2011. The Right to a Future: We Need a New Lexicon for Conveying Climate Collapse. *The Huffington Post*, January 18. http://www.huffingtonpost.com/raffi/raffi-climatechange_b_809353.html

Rilke, Rainer Maria. 1899/1995. I Live my Life. In *News of the universe: Poems of Twofold Consciousness*. Edited by Robert Bly. San Francisco, CA. Sierra Club Books.

Sarton, May. 1971. The Invocation to Kali. In *A Grain of Mustard Seed*. New York, NY: W. W. Norton.

Shedd, William. 2011. ThinkExist.com: http://thinkexist.com/quotes/william_shedd/

Swimme, Brian. 1994. *The Universe Story: From the Primordial Flaring Forth to the Ecozoic Era—a Celebration of the Unfolding of the Cosmos*. New York, NY: HarperOne.

van der Post, Sir Laurens. 1977. *Jung and the Story of our Time*. Washington, D.C., New York, NY: Vintage Books.

Vinge, Verner. 1993. The Coming Technological Singularity: How to Survive in the Post-Human Era. http://www.aleph.se/Trans/Global/Singularity/sing.html

Wikipedia contributors. 2011a. Alliance theory. *Wikipedia, The Free Encyclopedia*: http://en.wikipedia.org/w/index.php?title=Alliance_theory&oldid=414055248

———. 2011b. Machine. *Wikipedia, The Free Encyclopedia*: http://en.wikipedia.org/w/index.php?title=Machine&oldid=414265297

———. 2011c. Precautionary Principle. *Wikipedia, The Free Encyclopedia*: http://en.wikipedia.org/w/index.php?title=Precautionary_principle&oldid=413976900

———. 2011d. Tim Berners-Lee. *Wikipedia, The Free Encyclopedia*: http://en.wikipedia.org/w/index.php?title=Tim_Berners-Lee&oldid=414741867

Wikipedia contributors. 2011e. *Wikipedia, The Free Encyclopedia*, February 17. Accessed February 20, 2011. http://en.wikipedia.org/w/index.php?title=Vernor_Vinge&oldid=414343513.Vinge&oldid=414343513

Yeats, William Butler. 1920/1994. The Second Coming. In *Michael Robartes and the Dancer*. Edited by Thomas Parkinson and Anne Brannen. Ithaca, NY: Cornell University Press.

A version of this essay originally appeared in Jung Journal: Culture & Psyche, 2012, Volume 6, Number 2.

Sharon Heath, M.A., M.F.T,. *is a certified Jungian analyst in private practice and a member of the faculty of the C. G. Jung Institute of Los Angeles. A previous Associate and Manuscript Editor of* Psychological Perspectives, *she guest edited the special issue* The Child Within/The Child Without. *She has written articles for* The Journal of Jungian Theory and Practice, Psychological Perspectives, *and* Jung Journal: Culture & Psyche. *She has blogged for* The Huffington Post *and* TerraSpheres, *and she maintains her own blog at* www.sharonheath.com. *She contributed a chapter, "The Church of Her Body" to the anthology* Marked by Fire: Stories of the Jungian Way. *Her novel,* The History of My Body, *was published by Fisher King/Genoa House in October 2011. Its sequel,* Tizita, *is forthcoming.*

Interplay

Bridging Dynamic Systems
through Video Game Narrative

By

Elizabeth Shepherd

There may be nothing more important than story. The art of story formation is directly linked to the process of meaning-making, and what it is to be human.

Meaning-making takes place intrapsychically within an individual, and also dynamically, as part of larger interpersonal and social systems. Because the individual's conscious and unconscious life is steeped within a historical, cultural, and ancestral context, replete with conceptual paradigms specific to time and place, every intrapsychic process is continuously shaped by interactions with larger emerging systems. The human mind naturally attends to patterns and seeks to create order from incoming information. The organization of this information, in turn, develops and evolves working models of inner and outer experience, giving rise to the natural proclivity toward story formation and engagement with narrative patterns. Just as internal schemas within the individual inform interactions with others and dictate philosophical and logistical lenses for viewing and interpreting experience, they also compel people toward perceiving and formulating story structure as a way of living in, and interacting with, the world in a meaningful way.

The creation of story is an intrinsic, psychological operation, crucial to expression and orientation.[1] The mediums for narrative have grown and shifted over the course of human evolution, and as a result, determine the nature of information integration, and therefore, comprehension of internal and external reality. The video game is among the most contemporary forms, descending from a long line of storytelling modes. From its earliest debuts as cave art and fire-side tales, through the advent of the written word to the modern motion picture, narrative has manifested worldwide in countless forms over thousands of years.[2] At the end of the 19th century, during the boom of industrial sciences, story found a new and vibrant corpus through the advantages of film. Film gave narrative a fresh life and language, whereas before, it existed predominantly in the imagination of the reader, listener, or spectator. Narrative could now be displayed in moving image. With film, authorship amassed increased influence over the audience, and new advancements in storytelling matured with the medium. Technology and modes of storytelling developed together, with the mounting sophistication and implementation of musical scoring, acting techniques, editorial capabilities, and digital enhancements. Out of the fertile bed of digitization also came the video game. Video games ushered in the unique and exciting additional element of interactivity to the narrative tradition, which continues to be of rising interest and enthusiastic study today.

In a general sense, interactivity occurs when there is a reciprocal, cause-and-effect dynamic that exists between two or more variables. Isaac Newton, in his laws of motion, asserted that the action of a variable produces an equal and opposing effect on another variable.[3] Newton was referring to the physics of force and the exchanges that take place within relationships. Applied to narrative and its responsive population, proof of interaction can be seen simply in the emotional responses of a people. When an individual becomes tearful while reading a novel, frightened when watching a movie, or gripped by a verbal account, an interaction is taking place between the story and the participant. This provocative exchange has always existed in the narrative arts; yet with video games, interactivity is prompted to a level of engagement between the player and the played such that the story can only unfold with the mechanical provocations of the individual. In video games, a basic storyline premise is present, yet the course of the narrative and ultimate outcome are determined by, and dependent upon, the player. In such scenarios, a rich dynamic exists that is actively responsive: a game narrative is morphed by the decisions and actions of a player, and alternately, a player is subjected to the physiological responses and emotional reactions incited by the game. Video games reveal that greater degrees of interactivity between the participant and the medium itself foster the emerging experience of story co-creation.

The objective of this essay is to examine the function and effects of interactivity within narrative, explicitly related to video games. The exploration of these topics is focused through a depth psychological lens, with attention to socio-cultural semiotics—the study of the ways in which people socially designate meaning to phenomena and how changes within cultural systems can alter the meaning applied to symbols and metaphor. The Jungian concepts of unconscious and archetypal influences are presented first, as well as an overview of mythic narrative that predominantly incorporates the findings of mythologist, Joseph Campbell.

For this work, several of the video game industry's leading developers and designers were interviewed to give first-hand perspectives on their experiences of facilitating modern day storytelling.[*] Topics pertaining to interactivity, the needs of players, narrative appeal, the promotion of agency, and benefits of play are discussed, as well as the interviewee's opinions regarding the complex nature of gaming, and their predictions of where they see the video game medium heading in the future.

In order to comprehend the significance of video games as a modern storytelling medium and the weight of interactivity, the basic Jungian subjects of ego development and the individuation process should first be examined. In the depth psychological tradition, and specifically according to Carl Jung, a prominent founder of psycho-analytical thought, the human aspect of the psyche is seen as possessing a capacity for and inclination toward growth. Jung referred to the overarching growth process as individuation, wherein an individual's perception of self potentially expands and deepens through revelatory experience[4]. The personal perceiving, thinking, feeling, doing component of the psyche is referred to as the ego, or the known "I." Jung declared that, "we understand the ego as the complex factor to which all conscious contents are related."[5] Further, in addition to conscious content, the ego is also influenced by unconscious factors. Consciousness is comprised of what the ego is aware of, and the unconscious is constructed of differing levels of that which is unknown. It is the aim of the individuation process to integrate unconscious material into the psyche's consciousness, thereby refining the ego's definition of itself within the context of the lived experience.[6] As unconscious content rises to awareness seeking lived expression, it achieves audience with the conscious mind via dreams, reverie, intuitions, callings, and art.

Supplementary to the idea of a personal unconscious that belongs to the individual and contains content specific to that person, Jung believed that the

---

[*] For documentation purposes, each interview referenced in this essay is followed by the interview date in parentheses.

unconscious also holds collective material, accumulated throughout history and universally inherited:

> Everything that will be happens on the basis of what has been, and of what—consciously or unconsciously—still exists as a memory-trace. In so far as no man is born totally new, but continually repeats the stage of development last reached by the species, he contains unconsciously, as an *a priori datum*, the entire psychic structure developed both upwards and downwards by his ancestors in the course of the ages. That is what gives the unconscious its characteristic "historical" aspect, but it is at the same time the *sine qua non* for shaping the future.[7]

The collective unconscious is an intrinsic constituent that is contained within each human being; it both educates and is informed by the personal psyche, but being that it is also reflective of the entire species, it very commonly is seen arising in mass social phenomena as well. Simply put, just as an individual possesses a private unconscious, there exist expanding circles of unconscious strata belonging to social, cultural, and global domains that simultaneously inform the group and the individual. As a single human undergoes a personal, story-making transformation over the course of a life, so too does society as a whole. In this light, narrative—and particularly the trends in storytelling mediums—become telling artifacts of the collective unconscious.

The emergence of new mediums is never accidental, and each mode of storytelling requires different types of engagement with the material. While the content of a given narrative or narrative genre is important because it symptomatically reflects large-scale unconscious information, the medium itself is just as vital because it echoes the demands, desires, and deficits of a particular society through its chosen point of entry into story. As seen with video games, interactivity defines the current stylistic trend in experiencing and forming narrative. Such mediums become popularized when they facilitate the relationship between the public and the narrative in a way that aptly addresses a need, known or unknown. Every era is replete with its own unique techniques for encountering story and meaning-making that effectively channel the collective unconscious voice of that given place and time period.

According to Jung, aspects of the unconscious are autonomous, exerting influences over the individual or group: "Consciousness grows out of an unconscious psyche which is older than it, and which goes on functioning together with it or even in spite of it."[8] Yet the relationship between the conscious and unconscious mind is also dynamic. The network is reciprocal and symbiotic: just as the unconscious mind can hold sway over consciousness (as in dreams or impulses), so too can consciousness impact the unconscious (as when historical changes in groups of people alter cultural expressions or symptoms that then become part of the collective milieu). In all reaches of the conscious/unconscious territory, whether referring to societal expressions or personal dreams, the manifestations of the orienting psyche always involve story.

Often, when regarding unconscious material that has found conscious articulation in the material world, it is evidence of a compensatory function. Jungian analyst Murray Stein declared that compensation operates to balance polarized emphases within the psychic system: "These compensations are tuned precisely to the present moment, and their timing is governed strictly by what consciousness is doing or not doing, by the onesided [sic] attitudes and developments of the ego-consciousness."[9] This theory is applied when observing personal or global trends. Psychologically pathological symptoms within an individual can be seen as literal manifestations of psychic imbalance that, when viewed through this complementary lens, point toward what is being ignored or shut off unconsciously. Likewise, content that materializes on the movie screen or in video games can also be seen as compensatory for what is overtly lacking in a cultural institution. Our stories, and their modes of dissemination, often become the receptacles for unconscious matter to be explored consciously.

Universally applicable and archetypally driven stories can be considered myths, and the study of mythology has revealed how narrative has been used to align human beings in accordance with an existential framework: what it means to be human, and what is worth pursuing in a finite lifetime. Humanistic psychologist Rollo May explained,

> Myths are narrative patterns that give significance to our existence. Whether the meaning of existence is only what we put into life by our own individual fortitude, as Sartre would hold, or whether there is a meaning we need to discover, as Kierkegaard would state, the result is the same: myths are our way of finding this meaning and significance. Myths are like the beams in a house: not exposed to outside view, they are the structure which holds the house together so people can live in it.[10]

The creation of narrative and mythology is tightly woven into the fabric of our psychological history, and this operation finds incarnation in the actions of humankind across the globe. Joseph Campbell wrote,

> Throughout the inhabited world, in all times and under every circumstance, the myths of man have flourished; and they have been

the living inspiration of whatever else may have appeared out of the activities of the human body and mind. It would not be too much to say that myth is the secret opening through which the inexhaustible energies of the cosmos pour into human cultural manifestation. Religions, philosophies, arts, the social forms of primitive and historic man, prime discoveries in science and technology, the very dreams that blister sleep, boil up from the basic, magic ring of myth.[11]

Campbell also emphasized that while stories may change, the underlying mythic composition stays fairly constant. The images and events populating stories, and the mediums through which they find a forum, must shift over time in order to remain organically relevant and responsive to the public. In being malleable to the immediate needs of the conscious and the unconscious mind, mythic narrative actually bridges both spheres, encouraging integration and individuation. To be effective in doing so, a given story or storytelling mode must resonate with the contemporary psyche. This is where video games have come to play.

At the heart of this discussion is the theme of symbiotic relationships. The conscious and unconscious mind, the collective unconscious and society, an audience and mythic narrative all represent synergetic pairs that reflect, compliment, and initiate growth and change within the other. These mirroring elements rely upon a conduit to enable effective communication, and in all of these cases, storytelling mediums can serve as that link. Bridging spheres through open pathways of exchange enables the evolution of each domain and makes possible both transformation and individuation. Video games, as a modern storytelling medium, confect opportunities to continually confront the innermost reaches of our psychic composition. These opportunities are made increasingly available by the heightened degree of interactivity embedded in the gaming format—interactivity that promotes participation in the ongoing dialogue of the collective climate.

Video game storytelling devices and the narratives themselves are brimming with collectively symbolic potency and application. In-game mechanics require decisive action, inherent to the interactive design, and generate choice-oriented impasses that are at once individually familiar and culturally relevant. Video games both uphold and contest social value systems, offer vicarious enactment of repressed human tendencies in a suitably inconsequential environment, and provide compensatory escape from daily doldrums and inequalities. They kindle the public's appetite for possibility and support connection with others and with larger, epic archetypes and motifs.

This digital medium, like all other narrative art forms, depends upon the skillful shepherding of a designated storyteller. In filling that role, game designers incorporate archetypal material to engage and facilitate recognition and projective identification in the player. The public's ensuing ownership over the receptive, narrative fabric gives rise to unprecedented storytelling experience. It is also the charge of the designer to sensitively guide the narrative flow and adjust control between the medium and its audience in order to effectively fit the specific, dynamic situation. With the collective unconscious—ever-present in creative, cultural developments—and the personal unconscious additionally informing each artist's rendition, the video game medium surfaces as a timely manifestation that is as strangely recognizable as it is excitingly novel.

Introduction of Participants

This work was based on information gained from several interview participants in the video game and digital media industries. The participants responded either in writing to personalized questionnaires or via phone interviews. Each interviewee brought his or her own special flair and passion to the project, shedding light upon some of the most hotly-debated areas within the field, such as managing desired levels of authorship in gaming narrative, the needs of the populace that are seen to be fundamental, the ways in which games meet those needs, and the trajectorial aims of video game designers as they move forward into the future. Strong common themes arose, particularly: the importance of the designer approaching the storytelling craft reverently as an emerging art form; the dual nature of the young, digital medium; the potency of interactivity in storytelling; and the encouragement of agency in the player. Before delving into the subject matter further, it is crucial to introduce the voices in this conversation.

Stephen Dinehart is a leading expert in transmedia storytelling, and an award-winning interactive narrative designer, artist, and writer. He is currently Professor of Game Design for the Kansas City Art Institute and head of the independent game developer, NarrWare. Dinehart has teamed efforts with companies such as Warner Brothers, Activision, Zenimax, THQ, and many more, on franchises that include *The Marvel Universe, Batman, Constantine, Lord of the Rings, Dawn of War,* and *Company of Heroes,* to name a few. Early in his career, when originally enrolled at the University of Southern California's School of Cinematic Arts, he was granted a scholarship from Electronic Arts and went on to create the successful indie games *Cloud,* and *Journey of Jin.*

Shane Neville has had experience as a writer, designer, sports film director, and has additionally served as the producer and studio manager at Ubisoft, the third largest independent game publisher in Europe and the United States. Shane has worked at Relic, Longtail Studios, and Electronic Arts. He is also credited for being instrumental in producing the Nokia N-Gage gaming platform. In 2010, Neville started his own independent gaming company, Ninja Robot Dinosaur Entertainment, where he has found great personal pleasure in building hit mobile app games, like *Shellrazer*.

Matt Toner is an experienced veteran in the digital industry, with his many titles ranging from game designer to media producer, professor to entrepreneur. After being integral to the founding and management of We Media Inc., and CanApple New Media, he has gone on to serve as president of the social media company, Zeros 2 Heroes Media, a studio that generates a plethora of entertainment properties including television, film, mobile applications, alternate reality games, and animation. In the academic realm, Toner established and championed the Vancouver Film School's game design stream and has additionally taught game design at Simon Fraser University's School of Interactive Arts and Technology. His most recent success has been in politics. Toner was elected to represent the New Democratic Party in Vancouver, Canada, where he advocates fortification of the local digital job market.

Rick Davidson signed on as an interview participant not only as someone with a lengthy history in the game industry, but also as someone who holds an MA in organizational psychology. He is a prominent game developer, team builder, and consumer researcher. This Renaissance man has provided strategic brand management consulting for large corporations and lectured at the university level. Davidson is the founder and CEO of Inspirado Games, a development company for socially-meaningful games with the vision of making the world a better place. He has directed, produced, and launched numerous console games, and currently focuses on inventing compelling, family-friendly mobile games through PopCap studio.

Armando Troisi is one of the gaming industry's top developers. He has been at the forefront of *machinima* technology expansion (the practice of producing real-time animated films from video game graphic engines) and transmedia storytelling. With a penchant for cinematic drama, he first made his breakthrough at the Canadian-based company, BioWare, where he presided as the lead cinematic designer on the *Mass Effect* series and coordinated efforts across the entire department. *Mass Effect* was extremely well-received, earning Troisi his reputation as an innovator in interactive narrative and a master of blending strengths across different digital mediums. He moved to Microsoft's

343 Industries, where his attention to detail and fervor for fostering collaborative energies landed him as the narrative director of *Halo 4*. The overwhelmingly positive reviews that *Halo 4* received upon its debut point to the care that went into manufacturing compelling characters that engage the players in a provocatively immersive experience.

Lindsay Morgan Lockhart also worked on the *Halo 4* project as a narrative designer. Prior to her contract with 343 industries, she became a seasoned developer in the differing genres of first person shooters (FPS), role-playing games (RPG), massively multiplayer online games (MMO/MMOG), and social games. Some of her notable roles include writing and designing for Sony Online Entertainment on the epic *Everquest 2* and *Legends of Norath: Ethernauts*, and as senior content and lore designer while at Trion Worlds where she fashioned realms for the award-winning, *Rift*. Her unique blend of artistic and technical skills coupled with her savvy ability to integrate interactive components into story gives her an edge when it comes to assembling believable yet fantastic realities.

Nathan Moller joined the narrative design team on *Halo 4* after years of dedication to the digital field. Before specializing in video games, he took part in the New York film and television scene and then moved on to gain accolades for his work with machinima. He has brought his talent to BioWare and 5th Cell Media on projects such as *Mass Effect, Dragon Age: Origins,* and *Star Wars: The Old Republic*.

Brian Reed has an extensive background in video game writing and design for several, top-selling franchises. Additionally, he creates comics full-time, and is well-known for his work with *Ms. Marvel* and several mini-series for Marvel, including *Spider-Man Unlimited* and *New Avengers: Illuminati*. Between his comic and video game involvement, Reed, who passionately promotes meaningful narrative, has a thriving fan-base in the millions.

David Berner is a published author and game designer. He has taught courses at The Art Institute of Seattle. Berner has worked as a writer for indie game companies, and now owns his own publishing company, Broken Relic. He is currently writing for multiple in-production video game projects.

Dusty Everman first began his career in the video game field as a cinematic designer for the action-RPG, *Jade Empire*. Everman rapidly ascended to lead level designer for the *Mass Effect* movement and is now in the process of building downloadable content for the third installment. Notorious for his efficiency in achieving quality results, his comprehension of the systemic life of the game development process continues to land him in top-ranking roles.

Digital Myths: Video Game Storytelling

Video games are ideal for examining narrative from a depth psychological perspective because they are the youngest and most rapidly-growing, popular art form to define this generation. Being only a few decades old, the history of video game expansion is easy to track, and while a detailed breakdown of monumental milestones will not be chronicled here, there are many accounts written on the subject, such as the work by prolific electronic entertainment author, Steven Kent.[12] What should be noted is that from *Pong* to *Call of Duty*, and from *Super Mario Bros* to *Mass Effect,* video games have advanced at a striking pace, both in terms of visual technology and in storytelling sophistication. Out of their signature vector-graphic and 8-bit foundations, video games came thundering into the public attention with a commanding potency.

Not only does the recent birth of this exciting new medium lend opportunities for fertile research, but those responsible for the actualization of this craft are still very much in the present stages of discovery. Journalist and avid video game proponent, Tom Bissell, writes that video games are, "created in a formal vacuum by men and women who still walk among us. There are not many mediums whose Dantes and Homers one can ring up and talk to. With games, one can."[13] Interactive entertainment is no longer the niche pastime it started out as, but can now boast an audience in the millions and a flourishing presence that spans the globe. Matt Toner speaks to this, claiming that video games are becoming a progressively more mainstream activity, and that the constant challenge and charge for developers is to continually re-imagine and re-visualize their craft, in terms of a widening consumer base (October 20, 2012). As more and more people flock to their computers, consoles, and mobile apps, the onus on the designer is to shape products that appeal to masses instead of a select few.

While the video game format is still only in its fledgling stages of potential, and developers are venturing into experimentation (particularly with the advent of indie games), it is becoming apparent that they can be so much more than mere leisure hobbies comprised of pointing and shooting, and ravine jumping. Bissell states, "No longer content with putting better muscles on digital skeletons, game designers have a new imperative—to make gamers *feel* something beyond excitement."[14] This mission stems from the movement of games taking on a cinematic tenor, as many facets from film are gradually being incorporated. Film has a long-standing history of emotionally connecting with people through projective communication;[15] and in borrowing cinematic attributes, video games, at times, posture at assuming a similar role. Award-winning Hollywood screenwriter and media expert, Carolyn Handler Miller, remarks that "the sale of games now brings in more money every year than the ticket sales of movies in the United States."[16] While this account does not take into consideration DVD and downloadable sales, the report alone warrants that games be acknowledged, at least, as an up and coming force to be reckoned with.

Video games set themselves apart from anteceding types of storytelling and cultural engagement. Novels, film, and video games all intentionally utilize narrative, but the relationship between the medium and the individual or the audience in each of these forms is very different. The main categorical division distinguishing the video game from its predecessors is a matter of interactivity. Yes, all modes of storytelling are dynamic and involve interaction, but the extent to which video games require the player's commands and directives to proceed sets them apart from more passive narrative environments governed prominently by authorial guidance. Game mechanics marshal in conscious choice on behalf of the player, and when conscious choice enters the narrative equation it allows for engagement with the story through active participation.

With some games, individuals are presented with intellectual or moral dilemmas necessitating decision and resulting in consequence. Game designers, Katie Salen and Eric Zimmerman, found that, "games can inspire the loftiest form of cerebral cognition and engage the most primal physical response, often simultaneously."[17] Unique to the modern gaming experience, these simulated, real-life impasses mirror and routinely activate internal conflicts and conscious and unconscious discrepancies present in the individual and often epidemically rampant in society.

Currently, international friction and war activate choices pertaining to duty versus personal ethics, and self-preservation versus sacrifice, continually demanding redefinition of conceptual splits between self and other, moral and immoral, absolute and indefinite. Domestically, economic decline and family system strife also require confrontation with discordant drives and clashing obligations regarding security and growth, certainty and flexibility, responsibility and the capacity to re-envision.

In video games, these same internal battles are activated—the story structure is identical—but the settings, characters, and situations are typically fantastical. In video games, one is instead confronted with whether or not to abandon a team-member to zombie dismemberment so that others can escape, or to risk failing the mission for the sake of an "all-for-one" mentality. Or perhaps, one is presented with the possibility for savage and unnecessary violence, but not required to do so for game completion. Or yet again, when the going gets tough and frustrating, one can proceed forward or hit the restart button, save progress or wipe the slate clean.

At first glance, these artificial scenarios appear removed from actual experience—and almost escapist from it—yet a closer look exposes deeper themes that are wrestled with on a daily basis. Game mechanics encourage real-life struggles to be perpetuated on the screen, in a format that breeds experimentation of choice.

In serving one of myth's functions[18] of upholding and validating or challenging a culture's value system—a shared set of social mores—video games acquire a status of collective and psychological relevance:

> Chutes and Ladders is not just a children's playtime activity, but a cultural document with a rich history, designed to express a religious doctrine of a particular time and place. The Sims is not merely a simulation of suburbia, but a representation of cultural interaction that relies on an ideological reality located beyond the scope of actual game play.[19]

Any game that establishes a formidable cultural presence automatically unites with cultural frameworks. Not all games are pillars of mythic importance, but all games, whether epic and psychoactive, or merely time-filling and puzzle-oriented, possess elements of narrative; many of which are worth paying attention to. Brian Reed illustrated how relatable story variables are discreetly inherent, even in the most simplistic games:

> A game without a story can still have a story. You're playing *Tetris*. All is going well…until it isn't. You accidentally drop a piece in the wrong place. You stumble, trying to recover from that mistake, and make another. Soon the screen is too full, and the blocks falling too fast, and you succumb. There's not a single word on the screen, not a bit of dialog to sell you, but you've got a series of emotions that hit you the same as if you'd just been told a story about failing to overcome odds. (October 19, 2012)

These relevant narrative threads mirror societal and universally germane realities. Viewing games as cultural language and symbol suggests how their use of storytelling devices demonstrates the prevailing drive for meaning and mythmaking in society. Although video game production is a business, and games themselves are frequently confined by industry agenda, they, as a responsive communication medium, serve higher masters and deeper motives. As opposed to perceiving narrative design as a gaming function (as a business model might claim), Stephen Dinehart believes that "Game design is a narrative function" (November 8, 2012). In this way, video game design and play are tools that support the mythologizing exigencies of the public. In his *Forbes* article, "Why Playing Video Games Makes You a Better Dad," author and video game advocate, Jordan

Shapiro, asserts, "I think video games can function as interactive mythology. They can be understood as non-linear stories that help individuals derive meaning from the complicated paradoxes of everyday life."[20] The primacy of narrative formation within cultural systems is indicative of the presence of particular needs that mythologies meet, chiefly, the developmental necessity of individuation.

There is a reciprocal nature to the exchange that takes place between the gaming narrator and the player, which opens up possible pathways for transformation to occur. Storytelling devices within a game can impact a participating playing group, issuing transformation from the inside out. Narrative structure can also be implemented in such a way as to invite innovative agency of the player, with the player ultimately affecting the way the game is manipulated. This personalizing employment of mechanics can result in change from the outside in. The balance between a game's pre-fabricated story and the ability for a player to alter narrative is what makes for enjoyable and transformative play. Bissell observed that, "Even though you may be granted lunar influence over a game's narrative tides, the fact that there is any narrative at all reminds you that a presiding intelligence exists within the game along with you."[21] A video game cannot subsist without the engagement of a player, and conversely, a player's actions derive meaning within the context of a game's narrative parameters.

If video games and the participating public reflect and respond to each other, how do game designers play a role in being a type of middleman? They do so by intentionally or unintentionally channeling the collective unconscious voice and making it explicit in relevant forms that resonate with the given population. Depth psychologists and mythologists have long observed that the storytellers of a given age are the ones typically receptive to the nuances of unconscious language and possessed the skill to translate these messages and themes into approachable expression. Shamans, poets, authors, and filmmakers have all been credited with the ability to communicate the psyche's silenced needs and present them in a manner that speaks to the public in ways that are recognizable and appealing. Sigmund Freud noted that an artist holds "a sensitivity that enables him to perceive the hidden impulses in the minds of other people, and the courage to let his own unconscious speak."[22] In this tradition, video game designers also take on the responsibility of tapping into the collective unconscious. Much of the time, a game's success requires that they are able to do so.

Interview participants also recognized the importance of allowing the unconscious material to govern a project. In his approach to designing, Armando Troisi always seeks to nurture the hidden life of his work, seeing it as possessing its own motives and needs to be rendered into being. He claimed, "It's funny, because I really believe projects can and do have a mind of their own and it's my job to foster that impulse" (October 15, 2012). The desire to bridge the personal perspective with the larger human experience is echoed by game designer, Edmund McMillen, the co-creator of the hit sensation, *Super Meat Boy*. In the documentary, *Indie Game*, he admits, "My whole career has been me trying to find new ways to communicate with people."[23] The impulses to connect, reveal, and transform are inherent in the work itself, and strongly felt by the masters of the craft.

Aside from universal, overarching, mythic themes, some games are now venturing into new territory by attempting to address the unconscious issues of specific societal problems and phenomena. Brian Reed offered the game, *Papa & Yo* as a fitting example of a game that is endeavoring to do just that. In it, the player is cast as a young boy, exploring the metaphoric aspects of the relationship with his alcoholic father. The father appears as a monster who is at times friendly, and at others, terrible and deadly. While the game was profoundly moving and evocative,[24] evidencing the revelatory and even cathartic power of story when it came to players who could relate to the boy's trials, it received mixed reviews due to play mechanic limitations and restricting narrative.

Throughout history, artists of every kind communicate deeper, mythic themes and psychological realities by employing the use of archetypes. Jung[25] described archetypes as universally applicable images that relate to psychic functions within the unconscious. Jungian scholar, Marie-Louise von Franz, expanded,

> These are innate irrepresentable structures that always and everywhere on suitable occasions produce similar thoughts, mythological images, feelings, and emotions in human beings, parallel to the instincts, those impulses to action that are characteristic of the human species.[26]

James Hollis, a Jungian analyst, builds on this definition by emphasizing that through the archetypes within our narratives, we are able to garner meaning that enables us to transcend the confines of the day-to-day:

> It is our imaginal capacity (...) that constructs the requisite bridges to those infinite worlds which otherwise lie beyond our rational and emotional capacities. Without the archetypal imagination, we would have neither culture nor spirituality, and our condition would never have transcended brutish rutting in the dust en route to becoming dust itself.[27]

Archetypes make culture possible, and through their symbolic trappings, point toward psychic truths that carry transformative properties.

Game designers utilize archetypes to orient the player and to instigate a chain reaction of associations within the individual that triggers complexes and ultimately promotes engagement. This engagement occurs when a player recognizes the archetypal themes and images as akin to those in his or her own real life experiences, either consciously or unconsciously. For Troisi, "The monomyth reigns supreme" (October 15, 2012).

The monomyth is the well-known hero's journey motif, outlined by Joseph Campbell.[28] Lindsay Morgan Lockhart claims, "We end up employing similar techniques as mythical storytelling, engaging people in deep, cultural symbols/archetypes that we can convey without a lot of highly detailed explanation" (October 29, 2012). These techniques encourage symbolic recognition in the player, and support an ease of communication that moves the story along organically. Troisi refers to the online social game *Bedazzled* and its use of the gemstone/diamond image as representative of value (November 18, 2012). He laughingly states that if people lived in a world where pickles were instead a highly-prized and sought-after commodity, we would be playing *Bedazzled* with pickles in lieu of diamonds. The image itself is not important; it is the archetypal reality that lies beyond, which is the critical aspect. Shane Neville spoke of the art and consideration that goes into choosing effective archetypes: "It's quite easy to make a system work, but making something that resonates with people is something else entirely" (September 27, 2012). A video game system can perform on a basic level without archetypal symbols taken too seriously, but when pursuing mythological relevance, they are what sanction association and a sense of familiarity in the player that is fundamental for a gratifying, interactive experience.

The interactive quality of game play is the biggest determinant of the manner in which narrative is integrated into the video game structure, and the extent to which a player can dictate courses of action. Interactivity has been described as such: "it takes place within a system, it is relational, it allows for direct intervention within a representational context, and it is iterative."[29] The emergence of possibility is a direct result of the existence of choice. As systems can be constructed to be open, the video game medium enlists the player to be instrumental in the co-creation of story. It is incumbent upon the game designer to be conscientious of the dynamic ebb and flow of narrative control, to remain mindful of releasing power when necessary, and helpfully guiding when appropriate. In this light, the designer's job resembles that of a therapist's role when creating an open and exploratory setting for a client, while simultaneously holding the tension between freedom and containment:

For designers who want to change and startle gamers, they as authors must relinquish the impulse not only to declare meaning but also to suggest meaning. They have to think of themselves as shopkeepers of many possible meanings—some of which may be sick, nihilistic, and disturbing. Game designers will always have control over certain pivot points—they own the store, determine its hours, and stock its shelves— but once the gamer is inside, the designer cannot tell the gamer what meaning to pursue or purchase.[30]

Just as the therapist's duty is to facilitate, follow, and protect the self-initiated directives of the client, a game designer must stay cognizant of shaping structure that can then occasion fertile free play on behalf of the participant. In reference to transmedia storytelling, Dinehart claimed that the purpose is, "Not just to provide the answers, but to beg intrigue" (November 8, 2012). Fostering autonomous activity does not, however, mean an absence of embedded narrative. On the contrary, optimally, narrative themes should be durable, yet hover as only an allegiant presence. "Although I enjoy the freedom of games, I also appreciate the remindful crack of the narrative whip—to seek entertainment is to seek that whip."[31] Effective storytelling in video games requires maintaining the equilibrium between embedded and emergent narrative, or the intrinsic and the spontaneous narrative.

Many of the interviewees posited that producing purposeful story and hooking the attention and involvement of the player depended on finding a narrative strength and tone that fit the particular project. Reed observes that, "games get the stories they need in the shape they need them to be in. We'll lather on the plot as needed, or we'll not say a thing" (October 19, 2012). Similarly, Troisi describes the process of gauging the suitable amount of embedded narrative for a particular work to be similar to adjusting a volume dial in order to find the ideal level (November, 18, 2012). He also expounded on his preferred storytelling style of narrative minimalism. For him, this involves laying down a critical path, or narrative spine, that runs throughout the entirety of the game, but is flexible enough to be appealing to audiences with differing predilections of agency and range of experience. The primary narrative only serves to provide the bare essentials of plot to guide the player. One could solely engage with the game in this way if he or she favors to do so. Troisi also spoke of the inclusion of secondary story elements that are made available to the individual only if sought out. These supplementary details enrich the game play, but are not requisite for use. This electoral arrangement also mirrors a divide that is seen in the outside world, where people choose varying levels of engagement in their own lives.

Superficial pathways are sufficient, but there are multiple layers of meaning and depth always accessible.

Active engagement with narrative can sometimes be fostered through the inclusion of nuanced and relatable video game characters. A player commits to a video game character when he or she projects onto and identifies with archetypal symbolism. Jung described projection as a process that occurs when the unconscious material within a subject is seen as being located in and belonging to an object/other.[32] Unconscious attributes typically consist of repressed, forgotten, or underdeveloped parts of the ego, and regardless of their positive or negative nature, these aspects are perceived as residing externally to the self. However, when a projection takes place, an unconscious, emotional tug of recognition results and subsequently causes an attraction or repulsion response. With video games, these types of responses increase the players' ability to claim ownership over certain characters or resonate with particular goals or themes. Rick Davidson stated that, "The best stories allow the player to project themselves into the story, either onto a faceless avatar or through empathy onto the leading characters. Games let players 'be the story' rather than passively 'observe the story'" (November 20, 2012). Reed added, "You hear Players recount, 'I jumped off the cliff.' 'I found the secret door.' 'I was driving through the city,' and not 'Gordon Freeman pushed the cart into the reactor'" (October 19, 2012). Projection is at the root of the allure of the hero archetype or the visceral response to obstacles and triumphs. The seduction of embodying these images or facing exhilarating conundrums can account for hours of unparalleled absorption.

Projective ownership, made increasingly more urgent through agency, generates palpable player experience. Tangible game-traits are enticing, in part, because human designers not only intentionally utilize collective archetypes, but also because they, themselves, unavoidably infuse their own unconscious content into the products they create and the worlds they spin. Jonathan Blow, the game developer of *Braid*, one of the most critically-acclaimed indie games to date, stated, "let me take my deepest flaws and vulnerabilities and put them in the game."[33] Often, what constitutes a deep flaw or even a personal celebration is universally applicable, the representations of which join others through shared story experiences that are eerily resonant with collective paradigms. In a recent study, researchers, Leonard Reinecke, Ph.D. and Sabine Trepte, Ph.D., found that player perception of in-game self-efficacy significantly predicted performance and enjoyment.[34] This could imply that due to self-identification within the game system, an individual's emotions and actions are thereby susceptible to virtual events. Bissell poetically spoke to the power of projection and the expectations that can arise from internalizing identification:

So what have games given me? Experiences. Not surrogate experiences, but actual experiences, many of which are as important to me as any real memories. Once I wanted games to show me things I could not see in any other medium. Then I wanted games to tell me a story in a way no other medium can. Then I wanted games to redeem something absent in myself.[35]

It is as if the player is capable of permeating the digital membrane of code lines and programming to assimilate into the game world, and the game, too, periodically forgets its artificial boundaries and dares to come alive.

Another strategy that game developers are taking in pursuit of propagating meaningful play is to engage the interacting individual as an actor in a play. Jeffrey Yohalem[36], the lead writer on *Far Cry 3*, draws his inspiration from the traditions of method acting and the teachings of Constantin Stanislavski and Lee Strasberg. The aim of method acting is to instill, in the actor, ownership over a character by intuiting into that character's thoughts and feelings. Yohalem claimed that mere simulation in games was insufficient; the player should be consumed by his or her role: "Simulation leads only to brief moments of contradictory understanding in a sea of mundanity. That isn't art. That is life. The purpose of art is to give the viewer a distilled, purposeful experience."[37] When Stephen Dinehart was asked to speak to his favorite factors of game design, he answered, "Creating a space of possibility in which meaning can manifest; a space in which the audience becomes actor, a protagonist ready to manifest her will into being" (November, 8, 2012). When considering narrative and collective amalgam, they too are subject to the immediacy of experiential expression. "Myth is not created; it is the phenomenological dramatization of our encounter with depth."[38] Video games, as a modern storytelling medium, compose opportunities for spontaneous involvement and are themselves shaped by authenticating interactions of the moment.

Transcendent Technology

Aside from the dynamic between player and narrative explored thus far, video games impact psychological processes directly though catharsis of untapped socially-incongruent propensities, and also afford space for compensatory realities to be lived out in a symbolic fashion. It was previously discussed in this article that repressed or latent human qualities left undeveloped by the ego inevitably manifest through projection. When psychic potential is exiled to the unconscious as a by-product of cultural imbalance or pathology, this content builds frustrated energy, seeking expression. Open communication between the conscious and unconscious mind is paramount to the individuation process, and from this perspective, video games can serve the crucial function of cultivating acceptable, vicarious enactment of repressed components, and endorsing psychic reparation through offering environments that offset daily life.

Historically, as a society grows progressively larger and more domestic, it maintains its civility through morally and legally evicting human behavior that does not support the mores and values of the group. In Western society, most behavior linked to the loss of control or the expression of emotional extremes is not condoned. Forms of aggression, exhibitionism, or dishonesty may be punishable by law, but lesser violations of propriety and upstanding expectation are subliminally policed by the pre-existing cultural parameters informed by religious and political heritage. Unfortunately, it is in the more broadly sweeping and insidiously subtle regulatory processes that many tendencies, innate to normal adaptation, are deemed unacceptable and are denied an arena or digestion zone. These inclinations are then silenced and relegated to the unconscious life of the populace. This does not mean that they do not endure or hold sway over the public, but that they surface instead in undesirable disguise.

Without a space for the spectrum of human characteristics to be experienced, the repressed content falls into the unconscious and can be seen arising in disfigured ways like drug addiction, self-inflicted anger (depression), passive aggressiveness, anxiety, and an inability to communicate. It is also obvious, when listening to popular music on the radio or observing the images and themes in movies, that violence, lust, and anger maintain substance within the public sphere. The full scope of psychic reality is something that cannot be changed, as every positive aspect possesses a countering shadow. Denying the existence of or devaluing these propensities only lends to their unconscious strength, and whatever is unconscious eventually breaks through into the cultural life, whether summoned or not.

Video games can offer a location for otherwise unacceptable tendencies to be symbolically articulated. Lockhart explained their function in this context:

> Why an explosion of games in the most recent century? As we are able to automate more and more of our lives, and as these traditional skills we're wired for become unnecessary, it has bred a certain restlessness in our culture. We have a lot more free time to fill and basic instincts going unmet. Video games come in to fill the role. (October 29, 2012)

Social media scholar and professor Henry Jenkins agrees, saying, "Many current games are designed to be ethical testing grounds. They allow players to navigate an expansive and open-ended world, make their own choices and witness their consequence."[39] Jenkins believed that providing an appropriate space to explore darker themes does not propagate maladaptive behavior. Due to the configuration of the game itself, the player is able to make the distinction between virtual and literal value systems. "Two players may be fighting to death on screen and growing closer as friends off screen. Social expectations are reaffirmed through the social contract governing play, even as they are symbolically cast aside within the transgressive fantasies represented onscreen."[40]

Through games, an individual enters a liminal space of suspended reality, where underdeveloped human tendencies are intentionally engaged. By confronting and owning these properties, a catharsis is invited to take place in which the unconscious material is appeased and cultural norms are simultaneously upheld. This perspective is only a piece of the complex subject of game violence, and there are many fascinating questions surfacing around the crucial roles communities are not currently playing in creating a containing space for such material to be explored by the youth. For most of the adult population, however, although not exhaustive, this viewpoint speaks to the emergence and popularity of such narrative themes in our culture.

In addition to contextually sanctioning and purging repressed human behavior and emotion, games also afford a compensatory escape. Often, the video game environment is replete with opportunities for locating that which is lacking from modern life. Much can be absent from the contemporary, daily routine— particularly connection with others and personal perceptions of achievement, cooperation, discovery, valor, completion, victory, and optimal challenge, just to name a few. Davidson explained,

> Different genres of games satisfy different needs. It is not so much that person A belongs to genre A and so on, it's more that need A can be satisfied with genre A. If you are feeling that need to compete and prove yourself, you may fire up an FPS. If you are feeling cooperative and supportive you might play your MMO with your clan. If you are feeling preoccupied and need a moment's respite, you might play a quick casual game on your phone. (November 20, 2012)

Davidson went on to say that "philosophically, society craves possibility. Without possibility, there is only resignation and cynicism. Games often help people kickstart their imagination and see possibility in everyday life." With the desire for possibility at the seat of humanity's existential searching, video games offer easy access to uncharted territory.

Connection is a primal, human need. In regards to video games, connection can occur when two or more people sit down together to share a console experience or—more increasingly—online, thanks to the advancement of digital, interactive technology. In response to the question of how games are important, Nathan Moller replied, "Pretty much the same way any art or form of storytelling is important. It's a way for people to connect" (October 15, 2012). Lockhart gave a personal account of how connection through gaming made an impact on her childhood:

> For a shy kid living in the middle of the woods, having a vehicle to interact with so many people from all over the world in an environment that provided chances for competition, collaboration, exploration, and general shared experience was key to my development as a person. (October 29, 2012)

With the online component, especially, video games connect communities and transcend national and ethnic boundaries through a larger experience. The complexities and specifications of the individual identity fall away in the act of joining.

Connection also materializes when the public forms a relationship with the game narrative itself, and partakes of a universal story. In this way, an individual might play a single-person game and still feel connected to a grander design. Lockhart described this reality faced by the contemporary Westerner:

> We love stories, especially big, sweeping, epic, mythic stories, because they speak to the shared experience that is "us" as a species. While everyone might dream of leading a "big" life, the fact is that individually, most people's lives are quite "small" in the grand scheme of things. Even people who were well known in their day are generally forgotten, but what persists is the collective stories that we write, either through our real collective experience or through our representations of our collective experience. (October 29, 2012)

She continues, claiming, "People love challenge. We're wired for it, love to struggle, to create, to overcome." It is easy to understand how a compensatory refuge inside a game-world could provide vital relief from the current milieu of economic turmoil, cultural apathy, and generalized disenchantment. The player is lifted out of frustration and ushered immediately into a controllable situation where he or she can be found victorious.

Because life does not necessarily provide instantaneous atonement for circumstantial short-comings, people, for better or for worse, have come to accept digital accomplishments as real. In talking about central archetypal hero symbols of today, Reed stated,

> The archetype we see most (…) is the person in control, who is just on the edge of losing that control completely. From Pac-Man to Superman, from Mario to Spider-Man, we always seem interested in the person who is most likely to fail, yet somehow pulls through. I think we identify with that. We want Spider-Man to beat the bad guy and save the girl. We want Master Chief to save the galaxy. Their triumphs are there for us when our own may either be few and far between, or a very long time coming. (October 19, 2012)

While digital adventure and the accompanying sensations of optimal challenge, triumph, and power are no replacement for literal struggle and victory, some video games do fabricate representational means for nurturing those feelings during times when hope runs dry or inspiration fails.

Playing video games does more for sustaining its participants than merely providing compensatory or mimetic experiences; play, as practice and as enactment, in and of itself, is key to individual and social development. From a Winnicottian stance, all play is consequential because it is a symbolic exercise that references deeper psychological truths, and also because it is spontaneous, absorbing, and animating. Psychoanalyst, Donald Winnicott,[41] believes that play is not a pastime reserved only for children, but is rather an equally essential activity for adults, in that it cultivates authentic selfhood, or ego strength. Sociologist, Johann Huizinga, writes that with play, "there is something 'at play' which transcends the immediate needs of life and imparts meaning to the action. All play means something."[42]

Dusty Everman claims that enactment is a biologically ingrained tendency, responsible for evolutionary success (November 16, 2012). He describes what he called the Caveman Principle, involving theoretical cavemen A, B, and C, to illustrate the primacy of practice and play in human survival and advancement. Hypothetically, Caveman A sits in the cave around a fire. That is all he does. Caveman B is proactive and ventures out to kill saber-toothed tigers. Caveman C envisions killing saber-toothed tigers, and imaginally practices before encountering his foe. From an evolutionary standpoint, Everman posits, Caveman A, left to his own devices, would die from lack of practical application. Caveman B, although displaying initiative, would also have low chances of survival due to frequently placing himself in harm's way without adequate preparation. Caveman C, however, because of his implementation of imagination and fantasy to problem-solve, would be better equipped to effectively approach the dangers of prehistoric life (November 16, 2012).

Through play, the historical legacy of practice and enactment has evolved to include internal solidification of concepts and narrative, in addition to physiological advantages. Play is a safe way to encounter difficulty, both physical and psychological. Everman pointed out that our belief systems are founded on the bedrock of such repetition (November 16, 2012). People commonly run through mental scenarios, plan, and daydream. These acts are all demonstrations of adult play, which are meant to help prepare an individual to face future situations. Moral dilemmas, projections of the self, and fixations often take place within an imaginal space.

Video games construct venues for fantasy, not only to enforce cultural ethos and promote advantageous attributes, but when emergent storytelling is available, they can also stimulate new responses and thus establish seminal paradigms in the player. This level of play is made possible by games suitable for adult projection and enactment. While American children play video games, the center of the gaming market focuses increasingly on mature themes, as the original, digitized generation ages.[43] Adult play is not frivolous: "Play is oppositional, parodic and sometimes revolutionary; this rhetoric is opposed to a 'work ethic' view of play as a useless activity."[44] Video games provide a ripe context for play to be progressive. Sociologist, Gary Alan Fine, wrote that, "the external constraints that affect other social worlds (physical possibility, social acceptability, and temporal organization) do not affect fantasy so directly; anything is possible, given the belief that it should be possible."[45] The liminal zone of fantasy invites participants to challenge status quos, toy with Pandoric possibility, and ultimately invent new narrative guidelines to live by.

Although play and enactment carry the potential for strengthening or changing an individual's self-concept, the freedom to experiment with outlawed internal characteristics or to imaginally manipulate cultural mores does not destroy the valued ethics held by the player. The process of moral re-enforcement and the act of testing those values is not mutually exclusive. Troisi notes compelling evidence that supports this statement: Upon the release of *Mass Effect 2*, Bioware tracked players' decision tendencies. The gathered data was intended to determine where to invest future efforts in project development. The *Mass Effect* franchise is notorious for its presentation of moral dilemmas and choice crossroads that, once moved across, direct a player down a particular path. Troisi remarks that two types of choices were tracked: paragon and renegade. Paragon choices in the role-playing setting are described as those that occur when the player pursues the morally superior path through morally superior means. The renegade choice refers to taking the morally superior path through any means possible. Troisi claims that he was surprised to find that more than 90% of players took the paragon route, even when doing so was not rewarded (November 18, 2012).

Everman reports similar findings in reference to information gained from tracking choice trees in the game series, *The Walking Dead*. Records of choices are cataloged throughout the game and averaged against the choices of other players. At the end of the game, these statistics are presented to the player. Echoing the results of Troisi's study, Everman notes that the vast majority of players make choices that are congruent with our culture's value system. To this he proudly states, "We want the *option* to be bad, but we don't want to *be* bad. People want to be good, and *are* good, even when it is not required" (November 16, 2012). Regardless of the testing ground for tampering with cultural norms, the gaming public demonstrates that even within a medium that is accused of glorifying violence and base impulses, the player is still the ultimate narrator that dictates chosen outcome.

Shadow and Sun

All things possess both light and dark attributes, positives and negatives. The focus of this article has mainly been on the interplay between the game-playing public and the video game itself. In being mindful of balance, it is imperative to mention the shadow aspects of gaming as well. When a medium so powerfully captivates and absorbs projective fantasy, and when it fills so many vital roles, the game itself is at risk of becoming too important. Davidson had much to say on this topic:

> The evolution of interactive media, when viewed through a sociological lens, is a double-edged sword. On the one hand, the multi-platform, always-connected technology offers a rich canvas to immerse players in worlds and experiences that they have never experienced before. On the other hand, this technology and the applications which leverage its power have the real ability to shift a significant portion of societal interaction from in-person, physical, and face-to-face to disturbed, online, and potentially impersonal in nature. [...] Rant aside, games tap into fundamental psychological needs more so than passive media (such as TV or movies) because of how in-control a player feels of their gameplay destiny. Games set goals, provide feedback, allow for the feeling of achievement, they motivate, they share, they allow people to connect. (November 20, 2012)

When needs are so easily met in a virtual world, the motivation to connect in person may not be as profound. Dinehart also lamented this trend:

Sadly, digital media is fortifying the wall between the ego and reality. Interactivity itself seems like a farce in the face of a culture where people can barely seem to say "hello" and "good morning." I say this not lightly but in full commitment to the idea that while we study making HCI [Human Computer Interaction] more meaningful the very building blocks of what makes us human are crumbling. (November 8, 2012)

Today, with digital media being so accessible, many game designers are conflicted about the impact of their products. When convenience and simulated experience undercut authentic interaction, it signifies a problem.

Aside from issues with interpersonal connection, games can also become surrogates for a wide range of otherwise unmet needs. Davidson continued,

Video games are also degrading parts of society by shifting energy from productive work to leisure. For example, many young men who in years gone by would have validated their worth by learning a trade, committing to advance studies, helping run the family business and so on, are finding all they need from video games. They get the recognition, accomplishment and purpose from games which means they don't need to get these things elsewhere. (November 20, 2012)

There are many gamers who, in finding their fix, catharsis, and connection through technological avenues, become apathetic to extending themselves back into their day-to-day lives. It is in the way in which technology is wielded that determines whether the use is pathological or not. Imbalanced personalities will always seek equilibrium through some means; unfortunately, in Western culture, the modalities for compensation can become unhealthy, in themselves. It is important to recognize, however, in critical analysis, that games could not fill a need so adeptly unless there was a need to begin with. By their appeal, games starkly highlight what is being abandoned in society. Upon this insight, it is imperative to instead interpret this medium as a reflective compass and to first make peace with the shadows in our shared collective unconscious, to integrate, develop, and yes, to move as toward a north star, in the direction of individuation. Dinehart took this conversation full circle:

[A game] brings about discourse, engenders wonder, beauty and, ultimately, brings joy to the world. Playing in the systems of life is at the very core of what makes us sentient beings. Life and living in the bureaucratic present can often seem like a burden. No art frees us more from the bonds of servitude than games and the meaningful play [that] well designed video games bring about. Our culture needs play now more than ever. (November 8, 2012)

In the spirit of defining something by that which it pursues, video games demonstrate that what is at the heart of human yearning is noble, indeed. Even though the video game is still a relatively new medium, and we are only now beginning to grasp its positive and negative implications, it distinctly highlights desires for communication and connection with collective story that points toward potential applications for growth. Meaningful adaptability should be celebrated, and new ways of navigating tumultuous times supported.

Digital Horizons

Video games are a young and untried medium. With the rapid advances in technology, it is anyone's guess where it could progress from here. It is helpful, however, to speculate, and to gage the tenor of the development process in order to predict how games will continue to relate to the public. Xbox designer, Christopher Raykovich, claims that he found it exciting to be at the threshold of discovery and implementation, stating that finally, "the benefits have outweighed barriers to entry" (November 1, 2012).

Neville agreed with the locomotive temperament in the industry: "Change is constant. Business models will change. Development processes will change and the challenge will grow" (October 19, 2012). Davidson expanded on this prediction further still:

We will see advances in technology, more cross-platform development, more reliance on the cloud as well as more sophisticated vehicles for storytelling, deeper content and sexier visuals. I think we will also see more of a blur between what is the game and what is regular life. The subtle advances of gamefication, turning mundane tasks to interesting challenges, is cool. (November 20, 2012)

Shifts and improvements are undeniably underway, and with video games in particular, limitations seem to be set only by the imagination of their creators.

The future of gaming depends upon the skills and intuition of the programmers, the responsive plasticity of the medium itself, and also upon technological innovation in all spheres. David Berner expounds upon how video game refinement is going to be instrumental in scientific growth in the upcoming years:

Gaming is going to be taking on a vast new frontier, as some scientific teams are utilizing artificial intelligence and game programming to be able to advance the field of medicine. For example, there are teams that are teaching computers and peripherals to be able to not only map out the genome structure, but to also teach it how to "heal" itself. Much like computers are able to find their own virus and correct the problem, scientists are applying the same mentality to the human body. (November 12, 2012)

Long the subject of science fiction quandary, artificial intelligence would add an even more visceral layer of relatable interactivity to the gaming system. Narrative and authorial privilege could reside increasingly more within the game itself, while retaining an autonomous and emergent quality. Dinehart expressed his vision:

I see [gaming] diversifying to the point that we come to have many forms of entertainment which today we cannot imagine. We will not even call them games. We will develop new words to describe the experiences that blend the sister arts into the new art—the next art. (November 8, 2012)

Toner admitted that, even now, the ability to continually re-imagine and re-visualize the potential of games is not only what will propagate quality game experience, but, at this point, seems a necessity in keeping pace with the demands of a growing audience (October 20, 2012). The dynamic relationship between the gamer and the game results in an amalgam entity that evolves reciprocally. Just as leaps in technology elicit fascination and involvement on behalf of the public, games are sensitive to the playing population's needs and respond accordingly.

The unconscious needs of the masses will always require an artist to step forth and form bridges of communication between the known and unknown psychic realities and to perpetually initiate the excitement of promise and a belief in possibility. Neville conveyed his personal zeal in regards to contributing to his craft:

It's easy to just make 'product.' You can make a very good living churning out product. I want to make games that add something to the medium. I want to innovate, try new things and bring those things to the medium for other developers to experiment with and expand upon. (October 19, 2012)

Reed, also caught up in the enthusiasm, mused over the potential of video games:

I want to help push this art form forward and reach that next level of involvement. We can make our audience laugh, we can make them angry or happy. Can we make our audience cry? Can we make them love? That's the stuff I think is next. (October, 19, 2012)

It is in the vested interests of artists like these whose hands the future of game development rests.

There may be nothing more important than story. Narrative seeks to communicate the deepest aspects of the psyche in an attempt to integrate them into consciousness in the push toward wholeness. Mythic narrative has accompanied humankind throughout history as we seek to find meaning in pain, challenge, and accomplishment. The archetypal imagery populating story is used to point beyond itself toward transcendent truths that are otherwise only vaguely intuited.

It is in this contemporary form of storytelling, the video game, that the collective voice in culture has manifested as interactive art. Dinehart whimsies, "We stand on the brink of something wholly new for humanity; a magic unlike anything the world has known—a powerful form of art propaganda that will surely come to shape the world as we know it" (November 8, 2012). Through the interplay of projection, the release of catharsis and compensation, and the thrill of immersive fantasy and play, games prepare their audience for the future by guiding the individual and influencing cultural winds. Video games and their gamers will continue their relationship into the unknown days ahead, tending to and reflecting each other's needs and co-creating their shared story.

Notes

1 Daniel Siegel, *Pocket Guide to Interpersonal Neurobiology*
2 Carolyn H. Miller, *Digital Storytelling: A Creator's Guide to Interactive Entertainment*
3 Isaac Newton, *The Principia: Mathematical Principles of Natural Philosophy*
4 Carl G. Jung, "Conscious, Unconscious, and Individuation"
5 Jung, "Aion: Researches into the Phenomenology of the Self", 3.
6 Jung, "Conscious, Unconscious, and Individuation."
7 Ibid, 279-280.
8 Ibid, 281.
9 Murray Stein, *Jung's Map of the Soul*, 176.
10 Rollo May, *The Cry for Myth*, 15.
11 Joseph Campbell, *The Hero with a Thousand Faces*, 3.
12 Steven Kent, *The Ultimate Guide to Video Games*
13 Tom Bissell, *Extra Lives: Why Video Games Matter*, 11.
14 Ibid, 71.
15 Elizabeth Shepherd, "Heroes and the Collective Unconscious: Explorations of Mythic Relevance in Film"

16 Miller, *Digital Storytelling*, 214.

17 Katie Salen and Eric Zimmerman, *Rules of Play: Game Design Fundamentals*, x.

18 Joseph Campbell, *Pathways to Bliss: Mythology and Personal Transformation*

19 Salen and Zimmerman, *Rules of Play*, 507.

20 Jordan Shapiro, "Why Playing Video Games Makes You a Better Dad," para. 16.

21 Bissell, *Extra Lives*, 39.

22 Sigmund Freud, "Creative Writers and Day-Dreaming," in *The Freud Reader*, 387.

23 *Indie Game*: The Movie

24 Patrick Klepick, "When Fantasy and Reality Collide"

25 Carl G. Jung, "Archetypes of the Collective Unconscious"

26 Marie-Louise von Franz, *Projection and Re-Collection: Reflections of the Soul in Jungian Psychology*, 23.

27 James Hollis, 6.

28 Campbell, *Hero*.

29 Salen and Zimmerman, *Rules of Play*, 59.

30 Bissell, *Extra Lives*, 155.

31 Ibid, 40.

32 Carl G. Jung, "Concerning the Archetypes, with Special Reference to the Anima Concept,"

33 Pajot and Swirsky, *Indie Game*.

34 Leonard Reinecke and Sabine Trempte, "The Pleasures of Success: Game-Related Efficacy Experiences as a Mediator Between Player Performance and Game Enjoyment"

35 Bissell, Extra Lives, 182.

36 Jeffery Yohalem cited in Mathew Kumar, "Far Cry Wants to Turn Players into Performers."

37 Ibid.

38 Hollis, *The Archetypal Imagination*, 17.

39 Henry Jenkins, "Reality Bytes: Eight Myths About Video Games Debunked"

40 Ibid.

41 Donald Winnicott, *Playing and Reality*.

42 Johan Huizinga, *Homo Ludens: A Study of the Play Element in Culture*, 446.

43 Jenkins, "Reality Bytes".

44 Salen and Zimmerman, *Rules of Play*, 519.

45 Gary A. Fine, *Shared Fantasy: Role-Playing Games as Social Worlds*, 231.

Bibliography

Bissell, Tom. *Extra Lives: Why Video Games Matter*. New York: Vision Books, 2011.

Campbell, Joseph. *The Hero with a Thousand Faces*. Princeton, NJ: Princeton University Press, 1973.

Campbell, Joseph. *Pathways to Bliss: Mythology and Personal Transformation*. Novato, CA: New World, 2004.

Fine, Gary A. *Shared Fantasy: Role-Playing Games as Social Worlds*. Chicago: The University of Chicago Press. 1983.

Freud, Sigmund. "Creative Writers and Day-Dreaming." In The Freud Reader, edited by Peter Gay. Translated by James Strachey. (pp. 436-443). New York: W. W. Norton, [Original work published 1908] 1989.

Hollis, James. *The Archetypal Imagination*. College Station, TX: Texas A & M University Press. 2000.

Huizinga, Johan. *Homo Ludens: A Study of the Play Element in Culture*. Boston: Beacon Press. 1955.

Indie Game: The Movie. DVD. Directed by Lisanne Pajot and James Swirsky. Canada: Blinkworks, 2011.

Jenkins, Henry. "Reality Bytes: Eight Myths About Video Games Debunked." PBS, Date unknown. http://www.pbs.org/kcts/videogamerevolution/impact/myths.html

Jung, Carl Gustav. "Aion: Researches into the Phenomenology of the Self." In The Collected Works of C. G. Jung, edited by Herbert Read, Michael Fordham, Gerard Adler, and William McGuire. 2nd Edition, Vol. 9. Translated by Richard F. C. Hull. Princeton, NJ: Princeton University Press. [Original work published 1959] 1975.

Jung, Carl Gustav. "Archetypes of the Collective Unconscious." In *The Collected Works of C. G. Jung*, edited by Herbert Read, Michael Fordham, Gerard Adler, and William McGuire. 2nd Edition, Vol. 9. Translated by Richard F. C. Hull, 3-41. Princeton, NJ: Princeton University Press. [Original work published 1954] 1990a.

Jung, Carl Gustav. "Concerning the Archetypes, with Special Reference to the Anima Concept." In *The Collected Works of C. G. Jung*, edited by Herbert Read, Michael Fordham, Gerard Adler, and William McGuire. 2nd Edition, Vol. 9. Translated by Richard F. C. Hull, 54-72. Princeton, NJ: Princeton University Press. [Original work published 1954] 1990b.

Jung, Carl Gustav. "Conscious, Unconscious, and Individuation." In *The Collected Works of C. G. Jung*, edited by Herbert Read, Michael Fordham, Gerard Adler, and William McGuire. 2nd Edition, Vol. 9. Translated by Richard F. C. Hull, 275-289. Princeton, NJ: Princeton University Press. [Original work published 1939] 1990.

Kent, Steven. *The Ultimate History of Video Games*. New York: Three Rivers Press. 2001.

Klepek, Patrick. "When Fantasy and Reality Collide." Giant Bomb. September 12, 2012. http://www.giantbomb.com/news/when-fantasy-and-reality-collide/4361/

Kumar, Mathew. "Far Cry 3 Wants to Turn Players into Performers." Gamasutra, November, 15, 2012. http://www.gamasutra.com/view/news/181662/Far_Cry_3_wants_to_turn_players_into_performers.php#.ULtmjeT7KSo

May, Rollo. *The Cry for Myth*. New York: Norton and Co. 1991.

Miller, Carolyn H. *Digital Storytelling: A Creator's Guide to Interactive Entertainment*. Burlington, MA: Focal Press. 2004.

Newton, Isaac. *The Principia: Mathematical Principles of Natural Philosophy*. 1st Edition. Translated by Julia Budenz, Bernard Cohen, and Anne Whitman. Oakland, CA: University of California Press. [Original work published 1687] 1999.

Reinecke, Leonard and Sabine Trempte. "The Pleasures of Success: Game-Related Efficacy Experiences as a Mediator Between Player Performance and Game Enjoyment." *Cyberpsychology, Behavior, and Social Networking*, (14) 2011. 10.1089/cyber.2010.0358

Salen, Katie and Eric Zimmerman. *Rules of Play: Game Design Fundamentals*. *Cambridge*: The MIT Press. 2004

Shapiro, Jordan. "Why Playing Video Games Makes You a Better Dad." Forbes, 2012 http://www.forbes.com/sites/jordanshapiro/2012/11/15/why-playing-video-games-makes-you-a-better-dad/

Shepherd, Elizabeth. "Heroes and the Collective Unconscious: Explorations of Mythic Relevance in Film." Master's thesis, Pacifica Graduate Institute. 2010.

Siegel, Daniel. *Pocket Guide to Interpersonal Neurobiology*. New York: W. W. Norton & Co. 2012.

Stein, Murray. *Jung's Map of the Soul.* Peru, IL: Open Court. 1998.

von Franz, Marie-Louise. *Projection and Re-Collection: Reflections of the Soul in Jungian Psychology.* Translated by William Kennedy. La Salle, IL: Open Court. 1980.

Winnicott, Donald. *Playing and Reality.* New York: Routledge. 1989.

Elizabeth Shepherd *is a writer, therapist, and all-around creative. She received her M.A. in Counseling Psychology from Pacifica Graduate Institute, and has completed her coursework for Pacifica Graduate Institute's Ph.D. in Depth Psychotherapy program. She is currently working on her dissertation. In her ongoing research, she is passionate about exploring storytelling and collective phenomena. When Elizabeth is not writing, engaging in projects, or seeing clients, she can often be found relaxing with a glass of wine, adventuring in the nearby Pacific Northwest's mountains, shooting her longbow, or chasing after the occasional unicorn.*

Mythic Ringtones

Hello Hermes! We've Come to Talk with You Again

By
Diane P. Coffey

The melody embedded in memory moves from present to past, from music lyrics to ringtones, and a riff segueing from endings to beginnings.

> Hello darkness, my old friend
> I've come to talk with you again,
> Because a vision softly creeping,
> Left its seeds while I was sleeping,
> And the vision that was planted in my brain
> Still remains
> Within the sound of silence.[1]

Ringtones are a kind of trumpeter breaking the silence—a herald calling for attention. When I reflect on the swift changes in technology, specifically the smartphone, I hear the lyrics from the song "The Sound of Silence" as a kind of overture.

The opening lyrics, "Hello darkness, my old friend," were written in 1964 by singer-songwriter Paul Simon in his parents' bathroom with the lights turned off and the water running.[2] The bathroom tile provided an acoustic reverberation in a place where no one was listening. Over the years, the lyrics have been interpreted in a number of different ways. Some hear the dream of someone surrounded by crowds of people, perhaps a cheering audience, paying homage to something great. Others may hear the words of a song lamenting the lack of communication between people. Through the lyrics I hear a mythic presence reflected in the brief history of the smartphone.

The smartphone has strong archetypal images with a pantheon of mythical underpinnings. The mobile phone moves swiftly like Hermes wearing iconic symbols of round hat and winged shoes. The polymorphic Hermes is denoted as the interpreter, the messenger, the herald, and the best communicator. The god of wealth holds the purse strings of communication and exchange. Known as a night traveler, Hermes crosses privacy boundaries secretly collecting data and mapping routes. The metal associated with Hermes is mercury. The alchemists called it quicksilver because of its liveliness, its malleability and its capacity to transform itself. Mercurial qualities can be frustrating, but ultimately, symbolize an agent of metamorphosis.

There is great enthusiasm whenever an inventor has a flash of success with a new idea or re-imagining of an existing one. During the mid-2000s ringtones became an aural fashion accessory for personalizing mobile phones making known the presence of Hermes and the technical creativity of the first lyre.

There he found a turtle:
And it brought him
Lots of fun;
Hermes was the first
To manufacture songs
From the turtle he encountered
Outside the door,
As it was eating
the splendid grass
Outside the door of their home.[3]

A smartphone is generally understood to be a mobile telephone using wireless cellular technology with advanced functionality. Turned on and tuned in users of the smartphone move from basic phone conversations to real time applications, streaming entertainment and finessing new releases in technology. We meet the contemporary smartphone at the intersection primed for guiding us through the principles of liaison, communication, movement, and adaptation.

The brief history of the smartphone bears Hermes' shape shifting imprint influencing buying decisions, manipulating profits, and stealing data. The concept for this essay was conceived between Apple visionary Steve Jobs' death in October 2011 and prior to the Apple iPhone 5 launch in the fall of 2012. The essay re-writes took place in early spring 2013 around the time the Samsung Galaxy S4 was announced and updated again in the fall of 2014 as the mercurial smartphone morphed in size with the release of the Apple iPhone 6. Hermes, master of crafts and skills, rules all new arrivals connecting one generation to the next.

iHermes: Archetypal Branding

On February 25, 2007 Apple Computer introduced the iPhone in an advertisement that hundreds of millions of viewers watched during the 79th Academy Awards on ABC network television. A black and white history of telephony eclipsed into full color and the sound of silence disappears with each caller saying "Hello" in a series of sound bites. The audience sees images beginning with Lucille Ball, of the 1950 famed *I Love Lucy* show, answering a rotary telephone. The thirty second commercial continues through a succession of thirty-one film and television clips featuring iconic characters from the dinosaur cartoon era of the Flintstones to the Incredible Super Heroes all using telephones. Actor Robert Redford connects with the nearly extinct public pay phone. Sara Jessica Parker cradles a cordless phone in the intimacy of her *Sex in the City* on-stage bedroom and French actress Audrey Tautou's "Bonjour" greeting bespeaks of a global network.[4]

Earlier in 2007, prior to the Academy Awards, Apple's charismatic CEO Steve Jobs, announced to MacWorld Conference attendees: "Today Apple is going to *reinvent the phone!*"[5] Steve Jobs was a magnetic pitchman selling ideas with flair and charisma. German sociologist Max Weber defined charisma as "a certain quality of an individual personality, by virtue of which he is set apart from ordinary people and treated as endowed with supernatural, superhuman, or at least specifically exceptional powers or qualities."[6]

Apple's vision for the future of the phone was delivered with a kind of messianic zeal to change the world. Editor and Publisher of *Cult of Mac,* Leander

Kahney described Steve Jobs as the communicator who crafts and delivers the story behind the Apple brand. "Jobs has turned his keynote speeches at MacWorld into massive media events. They are marketing theater, stages for the world's press."[7] Quick on his feet and with the magic power of persuasion, Jobs knew what to say and what not to say.

In New York City, a statue of Hermes stands atop the enormous gilded clock on the facade of Grand Central Terminal where the Apple Store launched the iPhone 5 in September 2012. The statue of Hermes holds a caduceus in his left hand, a symbol of the herdsmen and given by Apollo:

> I'm going to give you a marvelous wand for fortune and wealth,
> made of gold and triple-leafed, and it will keep you safe when
> you are carrying out all the decrees of favorable words and
> actions which I say I know from the voice of Zeus.[8]

The magic wand represents, by extension, the multitudes of trades and negotiations. JP Morgan's chief economist, Michael Feroli, estimated fourth quarter 2012 iPhone sales could realize the miraculous growth surge needed to boost a sluggish U.S. economy.[9] While the iPhone was the best selling smartphone during the 2012 holidays the American economy remained unchanged.

In the Fall of 2014, Apple released two sizes of the iPhone 6. Sales exceeded the previous initial launch revenues with combined sales for the "iPhone 6 and 6 Plus totaling ten million dollars in the opening weekend."[10] The redesigned sapphire crystal 4.7" diagonal screen offers a faster and more efficient chip compared to the iPhone 5S. The transparency of the crystal symbolizes the immaterial of the messenger. Crystal also symbolizes an intermediate level between the visible and the invisible. The color sapphire blue represents the color of dreams symbolizing the road to infinity and the shift from real to the imaginary.

The iPhone 6 Plus with a 5.5 inch screen has garnered the name "phablet," a term used to describe an intermediate screen size between the typical smartphone and tablet computer. The iPhone 6 heralds the arrival of Apply Pay a service and digital wallet application that stores payment card data and initiates payment for goods. With a quick tap of the phone the presence of Hermes, the merchant, drives the smartphone into the circulation of wealth and the network of alliances.

Crossing Boundaries

The smartphone personifies the "geniusphone," an advertising term used to elevate the capacity for rich conversations in real time, the intelligence of touch screen applications, music with authentic beats, and picture perfect images. The smartphone has an archetypal resonance with Hermes' the silver-tongued clever merchant. The youthful Hermes was not content to live a dull existence sequestered in a dark cave with his mother Maia:

We're not going to stick around here, as you want, the only two among all the immortal gods without any gifts, without even prayers! It's much better to spend every day talking with the gods, rich, bountiful, loaded with cornfields, than to just sit around home here in this creepy cave. As for honors, I'm going to get in on the same ones that are sacred to Apollo. And if my father won't stand for it, I'll still try, I'm capable certainly, to be thief number one.[11]

Strategic incentives drive consumer demand from limited supply to pricing structures that create exclusivity in an elegant seduction that persuades consumers to purchase, upgrade, and download digital technology.

With an almost religious devotion, bloggers and the media christened the iPhone the "Jesus Phone." The online PC Magazine Encyclopedia defines the Apple iPhone nickname as having religious overtones.[12] As a medial tool, the smartphone enables communication between people, access to data on the Internet, and connections to online communities. Subjectively, it stands for the innumerable ways in which messages are received, interpreted, and adapted. From a depth psychological perspective this clever external device is a transitional virtual object with hidden meanings.

The term *hermetic* means recondite—hidden from sight or concealed. In this respect, Hermes is what Jung calls "*deus absconditus*, which means hidden god."[13] He is the great trespasser and a wind god with the ability to cross boundaries. The name *Hermes* is derived from the term *herm,* the name for a pile of stones making a boundary. Whatever the hidden meaning a myth can hide historical fact, economic gains and losses, a psychological complex, political struggles and workforce displacement.

American consumers eulogize Hermes, god of merchants and thieves, through increased sales, economic recovery, and worldly success. Shopping mall customers browse the retail environment seeing products first hand then the unfaithful consumer turns to the smartphone to seek a better price. Hermes the con artist seduces merchants with false in-store shoppers who leave the retailer to seek the advice of their social network for feedback on pending purchases. The term *showrooming* denotes the act of consumers using brick and mortar retail stores to touch and see merchandise prior to making online purchases. As god of commerce, Hermes presides over the fecundity of money.

The Herald and the Art of Communicating

Some mythic stories credit the Three Fates, the Greek goddesses of destiny, with inventing the five vowels of the alphabet and "Hermes who reduced the sounds to characters, using wedge shapes because cranes fly in wedge formation, and carried the system from Greece to Egypt."[14] The smartphone culture has adapted the alphabet substituting alpha characters for entire words such as the letter "r" for the word "are" or "urs" to mean "yours." Medial acronyms express feelings like "LOL" meaning to laugh out loud. Emoticons, colon-hyphen-parenthesis, are configured and interpreted by the computer operating system in the image of a smiling face ☺ and other image based emoticons. Tweets are limited to 140 characters that may include the hash tag symbol "#" and the ampersand symbol "@." Hash tags categorize keywords in tweets and help to facilitate Twitter searches. The "@" symbol is used to signify where a particular post is addressed to. From the early days of Twitter, the "@" symbol has grown to be used in many different ways and may develop expanded purposes as users become more clever with its use.

These changes in language might resemble code that approximates the shrinking vocabulary of "Newspeak" as described in George Orwell's novel *1984*. Orwell reveals the aim of language control in the passage:

Don't you see that the whole aim of Newspeak is to narrow the range of thought? In the end we shall make thought crime literally impossible because there will be no words in which to express it.[15]

Steve Jobs might have argued that the changes in language are not an attempt to eliminate words; rather any email, text, or tweet can be edited to be simple and provocative. Abbreviations and symbols are tools for the short message. I am inclined to believe the fickle nature by which humans adapt and modify technology is bound to change with each new generation.

The art of crafting catchy communiqués is revealed in the cunning use of vocabulary and images discovered through metaphors. A text message might be compared to a kind of Haiku writing with individuals creating an interactive style of poetry. Unlike the traditional art of Haiku there is no obvious link to nature, or specific number of syllables, nor formal decorum for linking. Some might say the allure of charm gets lost–there's no back and forth dialogue, and no deep diving reflection.

The art of text messaging is ambiguous. Text messages generate their own demand and are viewed by some to be better than a phone call.[16] In text messaging and e-mail you can present yourself as you wish to be "seen," you can process messages as quickly as you want, and hide as much as what is displayed. There is no commitment and there's a sense of control over the conversation. A text message can be answered anytime, anyplace, and it's your choice to respond or ignore the message. Screen communication serves a dual-purpose for quick responses and as a place to reflect without reacting.

Some people share a lot of information through social media postings and quick message responses. I see this as a kind of chameleon persona, a thin veneer of who they really are. It's the "them" that they choose to make visible and perhaps reveals multiplicity rather than a single identity.

Mercurial

Hermes has the psychological capacity to establish relationships. The persuasive herald shares many signs of friendship and mingles with "Likes" on Facebook, adds users to Google Plus, draws followers on Twitter, and organizes a group hyper-network to fuel action similar to flash mobs. *Flash mob* is a term used by the media to describe a "fad in which large crowds carry out a public performance and post the results on YouTube."[17] Crowds respond like Hermes, adapting quickly to situations in the face of twin pressures of internal drives and external stimuli.

> And in the naked light I saw
> Ten thousand people, maybe more.
> People talking without speaking,
> People hearing without listening,
> People writing songs that voices never share
> And no one dared
> Disturb the sound of silence.[18]

The lyrics of "The Sound of Silence" denote smartphone users all over the world communicating "without speaking" by using text messages, sharing photos, and by clicking thumbs up to "like" products. In India 53.2% of the population have mobile phones while the 2011 census data on household amenities reports only 46.9% of the population have a toilet.[19] Mobile connectivity in this developing country has a greater demand than plumbing in individual homes and personal comfort.

Our brains are adapting at a speed like never before. High daily exposure to technology stimulates brain cell alteration and neurotransmitter release, gradually strengthening new neural pathways in our brains while weakening old ones. The smartphone, "in the naked light," comes to life with pings, colored lights, and ringtones. Various psychological phenomena such as cognitive pleasure, regression, narcissism and addiction may be associated with the smartphone. The neurochemical response to every ping and ring tone seems to be one elicited by what neuroscientist Jaak Pannksepp calls the "seeking" drive, a deep motivation of the human psyche.[20] The addiction to a process rather than a substance follows the same neural pathways in the brain that reinforce dependence on substances.

Feelings of euphoria are linked to brain chemical changes that control behaviors ranging from a seductive psychological draw to a full-blown addiction. The qualities, desires, and fantasies that people project onto the smartphone and its virtual world arise from some basic human needs and longings.

> Fools, said I, you do not know
> Silence like a cancer grows.
> Hear the words that I might teach you.
> Take my arms that I might reach you.
> But my words like silence raindrops fell,
> And echoed
> In the wells of silence.[21]

With a kind of Pavlovian conditioning people "hear without listening" with somatic responses. We sense a vibration or see a smartphone illuminate and the brain responds with a surge of dopamine. Dopamine is responsible for the euphoria that addicts chase. Gary Small, Director of the Memory and Aging Research Center at Semel Institute for Neuroscience and Human Behavior, describes the neurochemical response, saying, "Dopamine transmits messages to the brain's pleasure centers, causing addicts to want to repeat those actions over and over again even if the addict no longer experiences the original pleasure and is aware of negative consequences."[22]

In 2010 the term *nomophobia* was coined from a UK study to mean the kind of anxieties associated with the loss of a cell phone, when access is not available due to expired battery life, depletion of credit, or when there is no network coverage. As users of these clever external devices, we are given the contents of the mythical Pandora's Box and the sufferings of human life. What cleverness is needed to locate an inner drive to create a movement that is neither mechanical nor an adaptation reducible to computation? To heal technology's addictiveness one may need to call for a creative escort to read between the lines, ask new questions and craft meaning.

There are some who believe that the connectivity culture provides an individual zone. Technology writer Kevin Kelly, first editor of *Wired*, says that he is replenished in its cool shade:

> At times I've entered the web just to get lost. In that lovely surrender, the web swallows my certitude and delivers the unknown. Despite the purposeful design of its human creators, the web is a wilderness. Its boundaries are unknown, unknowable, it mysteries uncountable. The bramble of intertwined ideas, links, documents, and images create an otherness as thick as a jungle the web smells like life.[23]

Perhaps the smartphone is to be perceived as a liberating device, a machine of soul that finds inner quiet and freedom from distractions. The transition from unconscious to the conscious mirrors Hermes in myth as a heroic mercurial sojourn into the land of inner and outer meanings, paradoxical truths, and multiple interpretations

Selfie Portraits

In March 2013, Samsung Electronics announced the Galaxy S4, a new generation of smartphone with several quirky software features. The "air gesture" feature, like air movement from a fluttering wing, allows the user to scroll, through photos or Web pages without touching the phone. When you look away from the phone, the "smart pause" feature puts a video on hold. The dual camera feature allows the user to take a photograph with the front and rear-facing cameras simultaneously. For example, at a basketball game, a user can shoot a photograph of the game with the rear camera and the user's reaction to it with the front camera; the two shots appear in one photograph.[24]

The smartphone digital camera feature serves as a sort of mirror and creates a photo image with twin like reflections. Self-portraits known as *selfies* are photographs typically taken by a cell phone camera held at arm's length or in a mirror. In "The Myth of Narcissus and Echo" Narcissus stares not once, but twice, so the image of himself is echoed visually through him:

> And he gazes in dismay at his own self; he cannot turn away
> his eyes; he does not stir; he is as still as any statue carved
> of Parian marble. Stretched out along the ground, he stares
> again, again at the twin stars that are his eyes.[25]

There is no separating Narcissus' duplicate imagining from the symmetrical virtual space where there is no distinction between good and bad, real and unreal as compared to the real world, which is asymmetrical, and where such differences do exist and have significant consequences.

He now is struck with wonder by what's wonderful in him. Unwittingly, he wants himself; he is the seeker and the sought, the longed-for and the one who longs; he is the arsonist—and is the scorched.[26]

The Narcissus myth suggests a self-fixation that paralyzes. The impulse to become fixated on a single image within a small pond is only a shadow of what is possible. The virtual world can be a place to play and to recognize other qualities that double with possibilities of new knowledge.

Anthropologist Victor Turner writes that we are most free to explore identity in places outside of our normal life routines, places that are in some way "betwixt and between."[27] Turner calls them *luminal*, from the Latin word for "threshold." A sixty-year-old woman describes how her smartphone is a place of hope: "It's like having a little Times Square in my pocketbook. All lights. All the people I could meet."[28] The plethora of computer games and applications available on smartphones enable us to be transported from the mundane daily commute into places and time zones far away. We search Web sites that lead into adventures of the unknown and unknowable. Smartphones with GPS capabilities guide us out of the forest to a safe return home.

The term *puer* is Latin for young man. Hermes, the *puer,* thrives on fantasy and creativity and moves with mercurial insight. Today's teens and twenty-somethings are at the start of a new millennium and are history's first "always connected" generation.[29] The Pew Research Center report, "Millennials: A Portrait of Generation Next," identifies the millennial generation as more likely than older adults to say technology makes life easier and brings family and friends closer together.[30] Steeped in digital technology and social media Hermes type individuals move with comfort and ease between the worlds of Facebook, Twitter, Skype, Email, Instant Messaging, and Internet search engines.

"Perhaps the puer spirit may not be meant to manage but to imagine. In the hands of the puer are shapes and gestures, the puer touch, but not the reins of will."[31] The Greek word *metis* means a quality that combines wisdom and cunning. Metis engendered with manual finger dexterity scrolls through smartphone icons with a flick of a fingertip like the flutter of a wing. Phalanges brush with the lightness of air to cross application thresholds. It's at the crossroads, George Elder writes,where things split open, promising other directions to take. Crossroads open to the past and the future...opens the space of Hermes where directions were given, where a new orientation becomes possible.[32]

The process of Hermes' shape shifting antics and mercurial qualities offers alternatives, breaks from the status quo, and guides us on a journey into the unknown.

Master Thief

The truth about stealing, leaking, stalking, or spying is not about thieves snatching devices, but the ease with which companies can gain access to the personal information stored on a smartphone. Unauthorized permission may provide access to device locations, read contact lists and telephone logs. The boundary between what is mine, such as privacy, and what data is sold for marketing research, stolen by computer hackers, or gleaned secretly by a government is a line Hermes crosses. James Hillman notes the helmet of Hermes "makes the wearer invisible."[33] Through a turned on smartphone an individual's current location can be identified and a detailed profile of recent whereabouts disclosed.

In *The Works and Days,* Hesiod tells the legend of how Pandora was designed by Zeus as punishment for the human race to which Prometheus had given fire. Zeus ordered Hermes to contrive within Pandora lies, crafty words, and a deceitful nature.

> But into her heart Hermes, the guide, the slayer of Argos
> puts lies, and wheedling words of falsehood, and a treacherous
> nature, made her as Zeus of the deep thunder wished, and he, the
> gods' herald, put a voice inside her, and gave her the name of woman,
> Pandora, because all the gods who have their homes on Olympos
> had each a gift, to be a sorrow to men who eat bread.[34]

Whistleblower Edward Snowden's recounting of the government's giant location tracking database was revealed in 2013 by the *Washington Post.*[*] The National Security Agency (NSA) is reportedly collecting about five billion cell phone records per day under a program that monitors and analyses highly personal data about precise locations of individuals. The NSA monitors the results using a sophisticated mathematical technique that maps overlapping patterns of cell phone movements. Specific cell phone locator tools such as one code-named "co-traveler" enable the NSA to search for possible associates of intelligence targets:

---

[*] See the *Washington Post* article, "Edward Snowden comes forward as source of NSA leaks." June 9, 2013.

Co-traveler and related tools require the methodical collection and storage of location data on what amounts to a planetary scale. The government is tracking people from afar into confidential business meetings or personal visits to medical facilities, hotel rooms, private homes and other traditionally protected spaces.[35]

Notorious for lying and breaking boundaries, Hermes, with the speed of winged shoes, joins forces with the NSA to create kaleidoscopic footprints of people's private lives.

Conclusion

Hermes, the mercurial god, changes location, changes form, alters the truth, keeps a conversation moving, and manipulates market prices. Shimmering with seduction, Hermes' quicksilver nature can change in a nanosecond. In alchemical theory, the presence of a second element, "the fixed," is needed for change to be actualized. The principle of change is insufficient until joined to its opposite. Hermes' flighty opposite is found in Hestia's fixedness. In Greek mythology the hearth-goddess Hestia is said to be the inventor of domestic architecture. She symbolizes family unity, by extension, and as goddess of the public hearth she embodies social contact.

Features of the smartphone are designed to warm users at the electronic hearth with feeling tones. Emoticons express emotions in images depicting happy faces, hearts, and photo images. The hearth connotes a kind of nostalgic homecoming to the origins of one's being. I am drawn back to a nostalgic moment remembering my family connection through rituals of routine phone calls. The telephone has been our connection to the other; the missing, not visible, lost sound, or that of the other voice. Nostalgia calls forth memories of family connections, fantasy conversations, and messages forgotten and remembered.

In 2013 the Library of Congress selected "The Sounds of Silence" for long-term preservation. Upon the announcement, singer Art Garfunkel told the Associated Press "When you look at the little mesh wire microphone… and you address people on the other side of the mic, you hope that your performance will be special, and you hope that it will have lasting power."[36]

And the people bowed and prayed
To the neon God they made.
And the sign flashed out its warning,
In the words that it was forming.
And the signs said, the words of the prophets

Are written on the subway walls
And tenement halls.
And whispered in the sounds of silence.[37]

Life changes with each new smartphone connection. It's a transformative experience that's magnetic, seductive, captivating and imbued with superhuman charisma. The archetypal and symbolic resonances of the smartphone is a modern myth that leads the way into 24/7 connectivity with GPS mapping and a narcissist camera that captures selfies and echoes self love. Life experiences are saved in Internet archives and unchecked facts mutate and spread in Tweet messages of 140 characters. Our fluid identities shift with the ebb and flow of changing social networks.

The smartphone culture symbolizes archetypal change. We hear the voice of the dreamer in everyday interactions through the paradox of the title of the song. Enchanted partners and collaborators read between the lines and are drawn to connections in a network of contacts. There is no need to reject or disparage technology. The desire to get in touch with another human being has not decreased. It requires the same cultivation of mutual caring and understanding and the same painstaking exploration of shared and unshared meanings.

Notes

1 Simon, 1964
2 Simon, 2004
3 Boer, 1987, 19
4 Academy Awards iPhone Commercial
5 Gallo, 2010, 175
6 Weber, 1964
7 Gallo, 2010, 137
8 Boer, 1987, 55
9 Plumer, 2012
10 Paul, 2014
11 Boer, 1987, 29-30
12 Jesus Phone 2014
13 Jung, 1979, par 209
14 Graves, 1960
15 Orwell, 1950, 45
16 Turkle, 2011, footnote Chapter 14.1. French psychoanalyst Jacques Lacan talks about the analytic encounter. The offer to listen creates a demand to be heard. "In short, I have succeeded in doing what in the field of ordinary commerce people would dearly like to be able to do with such ease: with supply, I have created demand." See Lacan, 1977, 254.

17 Wasik, 2012

18 Simon, 1964

19 "India Census: Half of Homes Have Phones But No Toilets," 2012

20 Turkle ,2011, footnote Chapter 11.14. Washington State University neuroscientist Jaak Panksepp describes a compelled behavior he calls the "seeking drive." When humans (indeed, all mammals) receive stimulation to the lateral hypothalamus (this happens every time we hear the ping of a new email or hit return to start a Google search), we are caught in a loop "where each stimulation evoke[s] a reinvigorated search strategy." See Pannksepp, 1998, 151. The implication is that search provokes search; seeking provokes seeking. Panksepp says that when we get thrilled about the world of ideas, about making intellectual connections, about divining meaning, it is the seeking circuits that are firing.

21 Simon, 1964

22 Small & Vorgan 2008, 49

23 Turkle, 2011. Retrieved from www.kk.org/thetechnium/'archives/2009/06/techno-philia.php. 275

24 Chen & Wingfield 2013

25 Ovid, 1993, 94

26 Ibid.

27 Turner, 1969

28 Turkle, 2011, 3

29 "Millennials: A Report of Generation Next: Confident. Connected. Open to Change," 2010

30 Ibid, 6

31 Hillman, 2005, 220

32 Elder, 1987,166

33 Hillman, 1979, 29

34 Hesiod, 1991, 75-85

35 Gellman & Soltani 2013

36 Mastropolo, 2014

37 Simon, 1964

Bibliography

Academy Awards iPhone Commercial. (n.d.). Retrieved from YouTube: www.youtube.com/watch?v=TBoG1qbzeog

Boer, C. (1987). *The Homeric Hymns*. Dallas: Spring Publications.

Chen, B. X., & Wingfield, N. (2013, 03 14). *Samsung Introduces New Galaxy Phone*. Retrieved from the NY Times: http://www.nytimes.com/2013/03/15/technology/samsung-introduces-new-galaxy-phone.html?_r=0

Elder, G. (1987). Crossroads. In *Encyclopedia of Religion* (M. Eliade, Trans., Vol. 4). New York, Macmillian.

Gallo, C. (2010). *The Presentation Secrets of Steve Jobs: How to be Insanely Great in Front of an Audience*. San Francisco: McGraw Hill.

Gellman, B., & Soltani, A. (2013, 12 4). *NSA Tracking*. Retrieved from Washington Post: http://www.washingtonpost.com/world/national-security/nsa-tracking-cellphone-locations-worldwide-snowden-documents-show/2013/12/04/5492873a-5cf2-11e3-bc56-c6ca94801fac_story.html

Graves, R. (1960). *The Greek Myths: Combined Edition*. New York: Penguin.

Hesiod. (1991). *The Works and Days*. Ann Arbor: University of Michigan Press.

Hillman, J. (1979). *The Dream and the Underworld*. New York: Harper Perennial.

Hillman, J. (2005). *Senex & Puer*. Putnam: Spring Publications.

India Census: Half of Homes Have Phones But No Toilets. (2012, 03). Retrieved from BBC News: http://www.bbc.com/news/world-asia-india-17362837

Jesus Phone. (2014). Retrieved from PC Mag: http://www.pcmag.com/encyclopedia/term/59933/jesus-phone

Jung, C. G. (1979). *The Collected Works* (Vol. 9 Part 2). (H. Read, M. Fordham, G. Adler, W. McGuire, Eds., & R. F. Hull, Trans.) Princeton, NJ: Princeton University Press.

Lacan, J. (1977). The Direction of the Treatment and Principles of Its Power. In *Ecrits* (A. Seridan, Trans.). New York: W. W. Norton.

Mastropolo, F. (2014, 03 10). *50 Years Ago: Simon and Garfunkel Record "The Sounds of Silence"*. Retrieved from Ultimate Classic Rock: http://ultimateclassicrock.com/simon-garfunkel-sounds-of-silence/

Millennials: A Report of Generation Next: Confident. Connecte. Open to Change. (2010, 02 1). Retrieved from Pew Research Center: http://www.pewresearch.org/millennialspg

Orwell, G. (1950). *1984*. New York: Signet Classic.

Ovid. (1993). *The Metamorphoses of Ovid*. (A. Mandelbaum, Trans.) New York: Harcourt.

Pannksepp, J. (1998). *Affective Neuroscience: The Foundations of Human and Animal Emotions*. Oxford, England: Oxford University Press.

Paul, I. (2014, 09 22). *Record Broken*. Retrieved from MacWorld: http://www.macworld.com/article/2686209/record-broken-iphone-6-iphone-6-plus-sales-top-10-million-in-opening-weekend.html

Plumer, B. (2012, 9 20). *How Apple's iPhone Could Single-Handedly Rescue the US Economy*. Retrieved from Washington Post: http://www.washingtonpost.com/blogs/wonkblog/wp/2012/09/10/how-apples-iphone-could-singlehandedly-rescue-the-u-s-economy/

Simon, P. (Composer). (1964). The Sound of Silence. [P. Simon, & A. Garfunkel, Performers] Columbia Records.

Simon, S. (2004, 05 12). *Weekend Edition Saturday*. Retrieved from National Public Radio: http://www.npr.org/templates/story/story.php?storyId=1951161

Small, G., & Vorgan, G. (2008). *iBrain: Surviving Technological Alteration of the Modern Mind*. New York: Collins Living.

Turkle, S. (2011). *Alone together: Why We Expect More from Technology and Less from Each Other*. New York: Basic Books.

Turner, V. (1969). *The Ritual Process: Structure and Anti-Structure*. New York: Aldine De Gruyter.

Wasik, B. (2012, 01). Crowd. *Wired*, 80.

Weber, M. (1964). *Theory of Social and Economic Organization*. (A. Henderson, & T. Parsons, Trans.) New York: Free Press.

Diane P. Coffey, Ph.D., *has a long history convening and collaborating with nonprofit organizations serving the imperfections of being human. Her international humanitarian work has traversed rural areas of China and crisscrossed through Central and South American countries. She holds a certificate in Chinese Art and Culture from the International Living Tao Institute in Fujian Province, China and a Ph.D. in Mythological Studies and Depth Psychology from Pacifica Graduate Institute. She is also a certified canine behavioral therapist. Current art and writing projects include a book reflecting the art of forgiveness, and an illustrated series of picture books about healing abuse. Her 2010 essay "Abu Ghraib Enhanced Interrogation: The Iconography of Evil" appeared in the anthology* Challenging Evil: Time, Society and Changing Concepts of the Meaning of Evil. *She writes on archetypal patterns and the dynamics of canine companion relationships at www.dianepcoffey.com. She resides in Philadelphia, PA, with her loving husband and routinely returns to her multigenerational family homestead in Santa Barbara, CA.*

Elevator Football

Dennis Patrick Slattery

Nothing cryptic about
The news
Unless you want to
Correct what every story
Forgot
Like their hope that
You forgot the 14 times
 yesterday
You watched a camera
From a high in the corner
Record a football player
With arms as thick as a shark's torso and
The strength of
Superman punch the lights out of
His fiancé
And in case you missed it
While reaching for a gin and tonic
To wash down your Doritos or
A handful of peanuts without salt
Let's show you again—
The grainy gray-black
Rage of a thing gone berserk
In the confused confined space
Of an elevator at a ritzy hotel
Striking out at a woman
Wearing no NFL-approved helmet
On her fragile head
Drop to the floor like someone
Who forgot she was carrying a

Football to the TD line on
The far side of the elevator,
There by the doors not yet
Ready to open
While a newscaster's voice
Drones on
Aware you really are not hearing
His reading from a prompter
Again
And the violent images revived
And play once more instantly in case you
Had gone to the bathroom
So it obliges you
Pleads for you to see this
Impromptu pick-up football play
Not yet in the coach's stable of
300 others for just this game
Then the NFL player showing
Either compassion or disgust
Drags the motionless body
Across the TD line
There, where the elevator
Leaves a gash in the floor
Victorious
But only 6 points?
Will he try for 2 more or simply
Kick her through the goal posts
And settle for the safety of one?
In the stands of my living room
We have all ceased to eat
And drink.

Dennis Patrick Slattery, PhD. is the author, co-author, editor or co-editor of 24 volumes, including 6 volumes of poetry and over 200 articles. Learn more about Dennis' work at www.dennispslattery.com

Reincarnative Gaming

The Hard Death and
The Intransient Self

By

John Brendan Loghry

Jñāna yoga, one of the spiritual practices of Hinduism, encourages a stance of detachment from the circumstances of daily life. This detachment is achieved through discrimination between the transient and essential aspects of the self—between that which will pass away and that which is believed to survive the body's death. The latter, the more eternal aspect of oneself, is one's Atman, while the former could be seen as the role one plays in a particular place and time. Huston Smith wrote that, according to jñāna yoga, the task of the individual is, "to drive a wedge between her skin-encapsulated ego and her Atman," and that, in order to do this, she will often, "think of the former in the third person," and, "reinforce the assertion by visualizing herself from a distance."[1]

We could think of this as avatar-practice, akin to the practice of mindfulness. It is a practice that facilitates what we could call *Atman*-consciousness—the holding separate of one's essence from the circumstances of life. One who achieves such consciousness would be able to distance herself at least temporarily from her life, to tack back and forth between engagement in, and detachment from the world, seeing circumstances both from within, as a participant, and from above, as an observer. A person with this ability would almost necessarily be less likely to get swept up in a difficult narrative and tossed about like the grass of the field.

This dispassionate stance is, in a sense, the state of Vairāgya advocated in jñāna yoga, though it is not necessarily a total renunciation of bodily pleasures or pains—certainly this would be a part of such detachment, but it would be more appropriate to see this as a renunciation of the chains of narrative, which elicit rote (or determined) reactions rather than the measured and free actions of which we are capable. As we achieved such a state, we would become freer to enter narratives without being mired in them, to become at least partially enlightened. This state of the mind—of not being inextricably tied to our given role in a story but also not rejecting that story altogether—would potentially preclude bad action and foster a more peaceful stance toward others.

The presence of past lives—of histories within us that both were and were not our own—would almost necessarily bring about the same effect as the avatar-practice of the jñāna yogi and would potentially be more effective in doing so. Coupled with transmigration of memory—the transfer of memories from a former life to each of subsequent incarnation—reincarnation would have a profound impact on the structure of the psyche, which would be formed by a series of discrete (separate) histories. And with each of these histories would come a unique perspective, almost the ghost of a past life. An individual with such a multi-layered psyche would possess an innate tendency toward reflection and would be predisposed to a certain level of detachment from the circumstances of life. But no such transmigration of memory appears to have occurred. The unavoidable fact is that this kind of detachment does not appear to be naturally occurring in our species, even in those that believe in reincarnation—hence the need for the jñāna yogi's practice.

There is a technology, however, that could offer a way of simulating just such a state. Video games already facilitate a kind of avatar-practice through the explicit visualization of an avatar in its own world during gameplay. But this practice, at least in its current form, does not appear to induce the kind of multi-layered psyche-state I have described and may in fact serve to reinforce a kind of surface-consciousness in the gamer.

The French postmodern philosopher, Jean Baudrillard, wrote of Disneyland as a virtual reality so garishly virtual that it keeps us from recognizing that the rest of our lives—our "real" lives—have become virtual as well.[2] The video game could be seen as a variation on this red herring, this planted virtuality, which

Baudrillard described as, "the imaginary concealing that reality no more exists outside than inside the limits of its artificial perimeter."[3] The video game could, then, solidify our attachment to the circumstances of our lives outside the game, keeping us from considering how transitory those "real-life" circumstances may be. What could be a technology of depth would appear to have remained a technology of surface.

A video game with certain features, however, could create a state of detachment by simulating the presence of past lives. In fact this simulation of reincarnation could be as effective within the psyche of the gamer as true past lives and transmigration of memory would have been, were they to have occurred. Such a game (or cluster of games) could lay down virtual past lives, virtual (closed) histories within the psyche of the player, creating a multi-layered (and thus deeper or broader) psyche, the kind of psyche that would be more prone to act out of a kind of *Atman*-consciousness.

Before I describe such a game, it will be helpful to identify the ways in which current games have fallen short of this vision. There is one element in particular that has kept video games in the realm of surface technologies, and it is one that is so ubiquitous that it is taken for granted. That element, which has been with us since the earliest beginnings of cartridge-based gaming, is the easy death.

The Easy Death

The easy death is death without any significant consequence. It is the death that can be remedied by pushing the reset button or by simply waiting for the game to return automatically to its beginning.

It is of course the mitigated significance of actions within the game-world that gives video games their liminal quality. One can destroy a virtual enemy and face no consequences in the real world—no threat of incarceration, no angry relatives of the deceased knocking on one's door at night. But that strength is also a liability. The relativity of virtual death keeps current games from functioning as platforms that would facilitate *Atman*-consciousness.

As to the easy death of the other—either of the avatar of another gamer, who can simply reset and reenter the game, or of a character endemic to the game environment (a non-playable character, or NPC)—many have suggested that the repeated, virtual killing of such others can foster sociopathic qualities, a kind of detachment that predisposes people not toward reflection but toward violence. There were early games that at least attempted to make such actions— for instance, the unnecessary killing of NPC's—a liability. In *Return to Zork*, killing an innocent bystander would essentially render the game un-winnable, although players quickly found a way around this—by tossing their accumulated possessions to the ground before the Guardian came to remove them, players were able to preserve their ability to move forward in the game despite their bad action. But for the most part, the virtual violence against virtual others has gone on unabated. What is of primary concern to the current argument, however, is not the easy-death of the other, however cumulatively consequential that may be, but the easy death of the self, of one's own avatar.

The easy death of the self is one that both comes easily—with death occurring relatively often—and is easily overcome by reset. Both aspects of the easy death have become ubiquitous, so that the gamer's expectation when coming to any new game is that when one's avatar dies, the game-world will return to a pristine state of naiveté, in which no mushroom has been pounced upon and no zombie slain, while the avatar is returned to its origination point. The avatar then proceeds from the same origination point as before and navigates the same terrain and obstacles as before, only now it is controlled by a gamer with foreknowledge, someone who can anticipate the obstacles ahead. The easy death becomes the advantageous death. The gamer develops a god's-eye-view of the game-world through a series of trial runs that do not count—up until the point at which he can save his progress and solidify a new (advanced) origination point or until he finally beats the game.

The return of the game-world to its pristine state—the offer of unlimited resets—is of course meant to serve the gamer. But the easy death carries an unconscious trap—it withholds efficacy or potency from the gamer. One has no lasting effect on the game-world at all, except, on occasion, to open up new, previously withheld portions of the world for further exploration. No matter his level of mastery, the gamer's participation in the game-world is restricted to the immediate experience, and the game can always reset itself to its pristine state, as if all the gamer's actions had been negated—as if it were all simply a dream or as if he had never existed.

And so for the gamer, there is this task always waiting. Even when he has mastered a game, he could always come back to it, always start over from the same origination point in this game-world in which he is both a god (with his god's-eye-view) and a Sisyphean prisoner, thrust again and again into the same points in time, unable to achieve any action that has any lasting consequence. He is de-legitimized in the face of the game-world, isolated from it by his limited efficacy. The gamer remains solitary, detached, and ultimately inconsequential.

More recent, open-ended games—the massively multi-player online role-playing games (MMORPGs)—have made progress in terms of overcoming this limitation. In *World of Warcraft* (*WoW*), although a dead avatar can be resurrected, it is not an easy process—it involves a period of weakness (resurrection sickness) and the degradation of the arsenal of weapons that have been amassed through gameplay. And the world itself does not reset with the gamer, who is but one of a number of players in a shared virtual space. Thus death in *WoW*, although it can be overcome, is not as easy as in traditional games, either in frequency or effect. What keeps it from fostering the kind of *Atman*-consciousness I describe is the fact that it is still not a true death, because the avatar is able to return to the world. It is not death at all, in fact, but rather a penalty period for less-than-laudable gameplay. And it is this that keeps even this not-quite-as-easy-death from enlarging the gamer's psyche through the laying down of discrete histories.

What kind of game would shift a gamer's identification away from the more transient features of life toward the more stable elements of him- or herself—in essence facilitating a detachment from the circumstances of everyday life? My answer is a game that would, in fact, lay down discrete histories within the gamer by following the conceptual scheme of reincarnation—what I have called reincarnative gaming (RG).

Reincarnative Gaming

Reincarnative gaming (RG) would build upon the model of play established in currently available MMORPG's, although it would differ from these in two significant ways. The first would be the finality of death.

Achievement of *Atman*-consciousness through game-play requires the hard death (or true death) of the avatar. It is through hard death—the inability to re-enter a game-world as a deceased avatar—that previous game-play becomes, not a trial run but a history, a previous life that is accessible now only in memory. When such isolation from the circumstances and events of the past-life is achieved, one is automatically thrust into a state of detachment and reflection. The gamer becomes the avatar's *Atman*—that which both preceded and survived the now-dead avatar. The loss of access to these avatars, the act of dying, caps off their histories. Building up a number of such past (virtual) lives—or even a single past life—would simulate the state of having been reincarnated with transmigration of memory and would facilitate a shift toward *Atman*-consciousness in the gamer.

In order to mimic reincarnation, the RG platform would need to operate a number of ages (time periods) or locations simultaneously, with each age or location isolated from each of the others—each operating as its own, coherent world. This separation, which is already part of MMORPG's such as *WoW*, would ensure that there would be only two options for moving from one age or location to another. The first would be to create a cohort of avatars in different ages or locations within the game and to play one at a time, as many currently do in *Second Life* or *WoW*, choosing which of their many avatars to play at any given time. The second would be the hard death and the decision to reenter the game.

Of course if reincarnation is the conceptual scheme of RG, reentry is a given. But with the degree of personalization that is available to players in current MMORPG's—the degree to which players can choose the characteristics of their avatars—what would keep the gamer from recreating the lost avatar, of uncapping a capped history, of cheating the hard death as players of *Zork* cheated the figure meant to bring consequences to their actions? The answer is fate.

An element of fate would keep the hard death hard. There would have to be at least a degree of randomness to the identity or attributes of each new avatar. Each avatar will need to remain distinct in an individual's mind if it is to act as an internal locus of a past history, and for this to be achieved, the avatars could not be subject to the degree of personalization available in many current games. Those that believe in reincarnation do not have any illusions of having had the ability to choose their own characteristics or circumstances when they were thrust back into the physical plane. Those reentering the RG platform would likewise be subject to qualities applied randomly, beyond their control. This would not only apply to the features of the avatar but to the starting point at which one entered the game-world. The probability would need to be that the gamer reentering a given world would begin not only as a different avatar but from one of a great many potential starting points to be randomly selected by the game. Through such acts of fate, each specific avatar would be inextricably tied to a specific history. Although it would be the desire of many gamers to retrieve the lost avatar, to rescue it from the hard death, it is in the act of death that the avatar would gain a measure of immortality within the psyche of the gamer—for with each death would come the encapsulation of a virtual lifetime as a complete, distinct layer within the psyche. For an RG platform to succeed, such recovery of past lives would have to be made virtually impossible.

Whether it would be possible to be attacked and killed when not playing— as territorial claims can be attacked in one's absence in the augmented reality, GPS-based game, *Ingress*—or whether one would have to consent to attack, as is the case in many portions of the several *WoW* worlds, would be left to the game-designer. Whatever the means, the death of the avatar would have to be final. In order to facilitate the laying down of a multi-layered history, the only intransient aspect of gameplay, the only aspect of the avatar that would survive from one game-world to the next or one incarnation to the next, would have to be the gamer himself.

One might think that to mimic reincarnation, RG would have to offer a series of successive ages—that one would have to move linearly from an older time period to a newer one. But what matters is not that the gamer progresses sequentially (as if he is moving through a world's history). Attempts to establish such a lineage of avatars would be difficult, anyway, due to the already-established tendency of gamers to create and maintain multiple avatars within current MMORPG's. So it would not matter whether subsequent lives were lived in subsequent or previous ages. It would not even matter whether each of the RG game-worlds were created by a single game developer or whether each game a gamer played had been released by a different developer. What matter are the two elements that ensure the encapsulation of distinct histories, the two elements lacking in currently available gaming platforms—the element of fate and the eventual capping off of an avatar's personal history, such that a specific avatar could accumulate a specific history.

Beyond this the games do not need to be of any particular character. A game such as *Second Life* could function as an RG platform, as long as there was the possibility (perhaps the probability) of a hard death. It also would not matter whether death was abrupt, with the gamer immediately exiled from the game-world, or whether the game eased the avatar into death, as a kind of lingering spirit, able temporarily to continue inhabiting its world as a presence that could only sometimes be seen by others and having a sharply diminishing ability to have any physical effect on the world itself. As long as this ended with the true death of the avatar, it would still have the intended effect.

Virtual past-lives built up in this way would function within the psyche no differently than actual past lives, because the unconscious portions of the psyche have difficulty distinguishing between fantasy and reality. In addition to these discrete histories, the avatars themselves would be internalized and would continue to exist as doubles of the (no-longer accessible) avatars, as distinct personages within the psyche—almost as ghosts that continue to inhabit the mind of the gamer. Although it is counterintuitive, it is actually the hard death that leads to the preservation of the avatar as a living presence within the psyche, whereas the easy death prevents it from ever becoming more than a shallow icon on a screen. And it is the element of fate that offers this internal figure a living personality—this avatar that is unique, that cannot be recreated.

It has not taken long to describe the structure of RG—or the relatively few changes that would have to be made to current games for such a gaming platform to come into being. The idea behind this argument is simple, namely that having lived through a variety of perspectives that now exist as discrete histories within the psyche would almost necessarily produce a broader perspective in the individual, who would then be the Atman of the various past lives—that it would induce the ability to detach from circumstance long enough to avoid the kind of reactionary behavior commonly seen in our species. Even in such an artificially induced state of Atman-consciousness, one would be much more prone to find the ability to tack back and forth between detachment and engagement—an engaged Vairāgya. No longer would the individual be bound to the earth, as it were, where circumstances may be overwhelming or where passions may flow as freely as blood on a field of virtual battle. Rather the gamer would become someone with an instinct for both presence and distance, someone who could see his circumstances from above even as he engages with them on the ground, as does the jñāna yogi as she does her avatar-practice.

Conclusion

One might think that the potential for loss of one's digital life—the closing forever of an avatar's being—would cause increased feelings of attachment to that life and thus would increase one's tendency to focus on it to the exclusion of other things or to become angry over its loss. This is indeed likely, especially the first time a gamer's avatar faces the hard death. But with the accumulation of past lives will come the ability to see beyond the immediate loss, to gain some inner distance from it.

It is likely that the traditional structure of video games—the easy death of the disposable avatar, the constant threat of a forced return to the origination point (the hard or soft reset)—has caused the intense reactions often seen during and following traditional gameplay. In the kind of game I describe, not only would death not come easily (the player's death-anxiety for his avatar would thus be diminished—more a possibility in the future than a near certainty in the very short-term), but the player's actions would never be completely negated. For in death, the avatar's history would be sealed. It would become a fact of the gamer's history, laid down in his psyche like a story in a religious text. In a hard death, such an avatar gains some measure of immortality within the gamer himself.

This effect is in stark contrast to that which takes place in more traditional gaming, where an avatar's life is as disposable as a paper cup. As I wrote above, although the return to the apparent naiveté of the origination point becomes in some ways an advantage to the player, it is also a curse, as the eternal task given to Sisyphus was a curse. The gamer gains a temporary state of excitement during such gameplay but also finds his body flushed with stress-hormones, burning himself out as he chases after diversion. And in the end, all his efforts have been eternally nullified—his play negated.

Reincarnative gaming would allow not only for entertainment—a slower burn, a more intentional, more paced form of gameplay, as is found in many current MMORPG's—but also for a kind of enlightenment. With its elements of fate, which allow avatars to remain as distinct personages within one's memory, and with the finality of death, which forms an avatar's history into a coherent and discrete (capped) narrative, reincarnative gaming would potentially simulate the state of having lived—and remembered—past lives. In the absence of actual past lives (at least ones we can recall) and of a naturally occurring form of *Atman*-consciousness, such a simulation and its very real effects in the gamer's psyche would likely be quite worthwhile.

Notes

1 Huston Smith, *The World's Religions* (New York: HarperCollins, 1991), 31.
2 Jean Baudrillard, *Simulacra and Simulation*, trans. Sheila Faria Glaser (Ann Arbor, MI: University of Michigan Press, 1994), 12-13.
3 Baudrillard, *Simulation*, 14.

Bibliography

Baudrillard, Jean. *Simulacra and Simulation*. Translated by Sheila Faria Glaser. Ann Arbor, MI: University of Michigan Press, 1994.
Smith, Huston. *The World's Religions*. New York: HarperCollins, 1991.

John B. Loghry, *M.A., M.A., Ph.D., is a social worker, writer, and artist in Oklahoma.*

The Great Internet Daydream Machine

By
Jason Sugg

The Internet is perhaps the most inviting medium ever created for that curious phenomenon known as the daydream. We do not usually think of it this way, but to be online is to be steeped in metaphor, and to be steeped in metaphor is to be in a dreamlike state. The Internet sucks us into metaphorical consciousness because the basic acts of "being online" are themselves metaphors, although they have become so fundamental to our thinking that they have become difficult to ferret out. Instead, these metaphoric actions operate unseen, effectively obscuring the contours of a way of being that has become one of the mainstays of contemporary culture.

In the early-to-mid-1990s, I was a painfully shy computer science student at MIT. It was an odd, liminal time; the Internet and the World Wide Web had not yet exploded into public consciousness, but already the Internet was a labyrinthine museum of wonders, filled with hidden corners, secret passages, cultural artifacts, and heated discussions that ranged from benign humor to paranoid conspiracy theory. For me it became a kind of refuge, a garden of virtual delights that could stand in for all that I was missing in my physical life, dominated at that point by a blur of classes and problem sets, with the bulk of my time spent in drab classrooms, lackluster lecture halls, or the warren of monk cells that filled my dorm.

One night, while staring out the window in an attempt to avoid dealing with some particular problem set, I was startled by the sound of gunfire coming from a room down the hall. A "rat-a-tat-tat" exploded into the excited and surprised cries of a group. Standing outside the doorway peeking in, I witnessed a cadre gathered around a computer, watching something that took a moment for me to understand. The glowing screen featured a *first-person* perspective of a character in a video game, as if the character actually *was* the individual playing the game. This was unheard-of at the time; the PC had always lacked the necessary computing power for such a thing. Before, the player's perspective had always been from above, looking down on the action from a god-like point of view. That framing had always mandated an emotional distance into the games, making them into abstract puzzles more than visceral experiences.

But here in the darkened dorm room in front of my very eyes was something completely different—the kind of thing that only appeared in futuristic projections. This particular point-of-view character held in his visible and beefy arms a very large gun. I watched in fascination as he roamed through a post-apocalyptic landscape, when suddenly a demon appeared. Bullets flew, made contact. Blood and guts sprayed across the screen. It was gory and visceral. More than just a game, it was an experience, and its riveting carnage was greeted with howls of satisfaction from my dorm mates. I watched, queasy, uncertain what to make of this gore, both fascinated and repulsed, as demon after demon was blown to bits. id Software's *Doom* had arrived.

At this point there are so many layers of abstraction at work in the operation of the Internet that it is hard to even pin down exactly what the Internet is physically. At the level of most peoples' experience a "user" "visits" a "site." The "page" one views often contains "menus," "banners," "site maps." When "shopping" online, one "puts" "items" in one's "cart" before "checking out." The original, physical sense of these actions has been subverted, leaving instead a purely as-if sense. Manipulating this physical equipment, it is as-if one were taking these physical actions.

But that metaphor rests upon another one a layer down, a metaphor referred to as the HyperText Transfer Protocol (HTTP). At that layer a "client" "sends" a "request" to a "server" and "receives" a "response." That metaphor rests upon yet another, the Transmission Control Protocol (TCP); in this metaphor a "client" establishes a "connection" to a "port" on a "server" over which it "transmits" a "stream" of "data." In the TCP metaphor, "messages" are always guaranteed to be "delivered" in full or an appropriate "error" "returned," "data" is never "lost." The TCP metaphor, in turn, rests on an Internet Protocol metaphor, and so forth. The further down the chain one gets, the closer to actual hardware doing physical stuff, the more difficult it is to actually connect the *metaphor* in which a human user of the system operates to its *physical embodiment*. At bottom is little more than a host of tiny machines capable of detecting electromagnetic fluctuations (and even the concept of electromagnetic fluctuations is a metaphor!). Everything above that is based on an assignment of meanings to those fluctuations and, while, arbitrary, is widely agreed-upon. Metaphor stacked upon metaphor. Modernity encapsulated.

No wonder then, that the Internet is so conducive to the fantastical. The very act of engagement with the online world entangles one in metaphor. To "surf" the "Web," to "chat," to "game" are all activities that are only possible via analogy, via seeing the physical world through a particular metaphorical lens that channels one into a different mode of thinking, a mode that analytical psychologist Carl Jung referred to as "dreaming or fantasy-thinking."[1]

Jung actually defined two different modes of thinking. The first, which he termed "directed thinking," is what is usually meant when one talks about thinking. Rational and logical, it is, according to Jung:

> reality-thinking, a thinking that is adapted to reality, by means of which we imitate the successiveness of objectively real things, so that the images inside our mind follow one another in the same strictly causal sequence as the events taking place outside it... It has in addition the peculiarity of causing fatigue, and is for that reason brought into play for short periods only.[2]

Jung also noted that this type of thinking was intimately tied up with language: "Any very intensive train of thought works itself out more or less in verbal form,"[3] with the consequence that "so long as we think directedly, we think *for* others and speak *to* others."[4] In other words, directed thinking is, at its core, a mode of social adaptation.

But for Jung, fantasy-thinking affects its occupant quite differently: "This sort of thinking does not tire us...it leads away from reality into fantasies of the past or future. At this point thinking in verbal form ceases, image piles on image, feeling on feeling."[5] This is the kind of thinking that happens in the dreams of both night and day. Indeed, Jung asserted that "between day-dreaming and night-dreaming there is not much difference,"[6] and the empirical research of recent years has backed him on this, leading to the conclusion that "waking and dreaming mentation are continuous."[7]

Jung's description of fantasy-thinking describes the experience of being online remarkably well. Who has not lost track of time on the Internet, unexpectedly wiling away hours surfing from website to website? How many hours have we collectively wasted on Facebook? Time can disappear online; indeed years and years of experimentation and design evolution have gone into making the online world just the kind of environment that can lead one into fantasy. User experience designers refer to this sort of design as "immersive"—one becomes enveloped in it and forgets that one is interacting with a metaphor at all.

This was the experience of *Doom* as well. The god-like point of view of previous games made it much easier to remember one was not really in the game, that in reality one was merely engaged with a puzzle. But *Doom's* first-person perspective and responsiveness made it difficult not to get pulled into the world of the game. It was so popular precisely because, more than any game in history up to that point, it was so easy to slip into the daydreams of its designers, to follow the corridors of their fantasies until those fantasies were one's own. As an experience it wormed its way into my psyche, so much so that I often found my nighttime dreams as well as my daydreams set in its world, following its particular metaphors of movement and mayhem.

While essentially similar, there are important differences between the dreams of night and day. Night dreaming is almost always unconscious—setting aside the unusual phenomenon of lucid dreaming—while daydreaming always contains an increased possibility of consciousness stepping in. It is substantially easier to watch yourself daydream, to become conscious of the activity as it is happening, than it is to become consciously aware of the activity of night dreaming. Imaginal psychologist Mary Watkins used the presence or absence of this type of awareness to distinguish daydreams from what she terms waking dreams:

In daydreaming, the ego's attention becomes attached to the imaginal contents in the same way it does to our daily concerns…One could say that daydreams are a form of sleeping wakefulness, as opposed to the state of wakefulness even while sleeping that characterizes a waking dream.[8]

In other words, in the daydream, "awareness becomes absorbed and attached to the emotion, thought, or action, we become it…That identity, created by the fusion of awareness with the emotion, causes us to lose recognition of the experience."[9]

For the time being let us view the daydream as a potential waking dream, fantasy content that one might become aware of under the right circumstances. In this light, the daydream seems as important to consider psychologically as the night dream. Indeed, the increasing conclusion of empirical research in this area has been that "when waking conditions are altered to reduce both external sensory input and the conscious demand for cognitive process (relaxed wakefulness), the resultant free-floating thought is quite similar to, and may even surpass, dreaming mentation in its imagistic-hallucinatory quality."[10]

The daydream, it might be said, is a kind of fifth column infiltration by the dream's nightworld into the fortress of rationality modernity has erected around our daytime activities. That kind of breakthrough happens only under certain favorable conditions; a tunnel of sorts must be opened between dream and waking consciousnesses to allow the oneiric contents to emerge. The Internet is so captivating to so many precisely because it provides such a welcoming environment for these kinds of infiltrations. The remove from physicality; the legions of others who, because of their implicit anonymity but distinctive content, provide ideal hooks for projections; and the increasing access from anywhere all work together to make it a kind of incubator for daydream fantasies.

This effect is so prevalent that almost all non-enterprise Internet activities, in one way or another, involve states of reverie. Social networking, online shopping, gaming, pornography—all of these activities involve daydream fantasy, in whole or in part. In my personal experience, even searching on the Internet is often driven by daydream, as something forgotten comes to the front of my mind and I turn to the virtual world to deepen into that fantasy. The Internet is a giant daydream machine, and almost every Internet business makes its money by abetting the indulgence of fantasies, whether those fantasies be of sex, of life with some new acquisition, of human connection, or of what it would be like to live in a whole different world.

I held out for a week or so, but in the end everybody was simply having too much fun without me. I already felt isolated in that rigorous academic world, and now the people I knew the best, the handful of people I did have connections with, were all absorbed in this phenomenon from which I had excluded myself. Telling myself I just wanted to have the experience of playing so I could share in my friends' conversations, I finally downloaded and installed *Doom*.

There is a particular kind of mind-eye-hand coordination required by video games that I have always found elusive. But though I would never master this game with the same level of dexterity as others I knew, it turned out to be surprisingly easy to control relative to my past experiences with other games. Soon enough I, too, was blasting my way through its demon-filled moon base. Just when my interest would flag, the game would present some intriguing new possibility—a rocket launcher I could use instead of a machine gun, or a secret room happened upon by accident. The game's designers clearly had a subtle understanding of how to sustain interest in the virtual world they had created.

It didn't take long before I was as sucked into this world as my friends had been. Far from just being a way to have something to talk about with friends, I had come to really enjoy the virtual violence and gore. My inner schoolhouse nun was scandalized; my inner ten year-old was delighted. This game was a hell of a lot more fun than problem sets, and it soon began to dominate my time. The fantasy world of the game had enveloped me, and I had no idea why.

In retrospect it seems unsurprising that a bunch of brainy yet awkward computer science and engineering students would become absorbed in outlets for aggression. We sat in classes or in front of computers all day long. Few of us had any clue how to approach women. Our bodies were young, in their prime, and no doubt revolting against the diligent and disciplined strictures into which we had locked them. In these often shockingly violent games, all that pent-up energy found an outlet—not a physical one, obviously, but a fantastical one. Such is my supposition after the fact, at least. At the time, all I knew was that I had mysteriously and compellingly been pulled into the hyper-violent world of this game.

Jung's one-time mentor, Sigmund Freud, classified daydreaming as a continuation of the childhood tendency towards spontaneous play. "The growing child, when he stops playing, gives up nothing but the link with real objects; instead *of playing*, he now *phantasies*. He builds castles in the air and creates what are called *daydream [sic]*."[11] For Freud such play was essential to the child; his daughter Anna, a prominent psychologist in her own right, identified the child's play as the precursor to the adult's.[12] Sigmund himself declared, "A child's play is determined by wishes: in point of fact by a single wish—one that helps in his upbringing—the wish to be big and grown up."[13] For the child, Freud noted, the activity of play was intensely pleasurable, "the child's best-loved and most intense occupation."[14]

But for the adult, Freud observed, "A happy person never phantasies, only an unsatisfied one. The motive forces of phantasies are unsatisfied wishes, and every single phantasy is the fulfillment of a wish, a correction of unsatisfying reality."[15] Jung was kinder to the adult's fantasies, staking out a position that declared fantasies essential to bridging the gap between the modern rational mind and the instinctual bases upon which it rests—"Through fantasy-thinking, directed [rational] thinking is brought into contact with the oldest layers of the human mind, long buried beneath the threshold of consciousness."[16]

So from Freud we are given to understand these fantasies, much like dreams, as wish fulfillments. From Jung we are given to understand them as the arising of archaic contents that the modern mind has been trained to ignore. These two points of view are not at all incompatible—it should be assumed that our wishes might follow archetypal forms. The popularity of *Doom* among my cadre of friends could thus be understood dually, from the Freudian perspective as the satisfaction in virtual form of an unconscious drive towards aggression, and from a Jungian perspective as the acting out of the unsatisfied and age-old instinct towards war.

Further, both Freud and Jung identify this proclivity for fantasy as the root of the human tendency to produce myth. Freud proclaimed, "It is extremely probable that myths…are distorted vestiges of the wishful phantasies of whole nations, the *secular dreams* of youthful humanity."[17] Jung asserted, "The conclusion that the myth-makers thought in much the same way as we still think in dreams is almost self-evident."[18] Though we were not its creators, we were active participants in the mythos that defined *Doom's* world.

It is common these days in depth psychological circles to hear the plaintive question, "What are the new myths?" But the answer to that question is obvious to anybody who has ventured online. The new myths populate YouTube; they define the worlds of the hugely popular MMORPGs (Massively Multiplayer Online Role-Playing Games) such as Everquest or World of Warcraft; they fill the host of political chain emails suggesting that President Barack Obama was secretly born in Kenya or that he is going to herd all white people into cattle cars and ship them off to concentration camps. The history of the cinema provides a handy companion here as a medium it was initially dismissed as a fad by the bearers of culture's flame. But as it became clearer that film was here to stay, the dismissal was replaced by pietistic complaints about its prurient subject matter.[19] All the while, though, film was busy developing a language to express what had gone unexpressed in mass culture up to that point. The whispers of folk tales around campfires, the virulent rumors that spread through the ranks of those at the bottom of society, the fascinations of those who lacked access to the culture's advancements—all of these became the subject matter of the cinema, and all of them were giving expression to the repressed preoccupations of large segments of society.

Something similar happens on the Internet. *Doom* gave visceral expression to an aggression that lies at the heart of modern life, an expression much richer than previous attempts had been. The videos on YouTube often speak to some irony of modern life. The wizards and warriors worlds of MMORPGs speak to a longing to live in a more enlivened world. Those lunatic chain emails speak to an unspoken fear of the other or to a desperate sense of insecurity in the face of modernity. The Internet is a stew of phantastical metaphors, and as we interact online, gravitate collectively towards this and away from that, those metaphors become shared. And a shared metaphor is a myth. If we want to find the new myths, then we need merely to look online, for they stare us in the face there.

Why is it so difficult for us to acknowledge these myths? Is it because they do not speak to transcendence, to bliss, to rapture, but instead to dirtiness, to all those dark corners of our souls that we don't like to acknowledge? If so, then we must answer the question of why these prurient things hold such a clear mass interest for us. As with all depth psychology, to get a really satisfactory answer to that question we are forced to move beyond moralizing and into curiosity.

At the time, *Doom* was a revolution, providing an immersive first-person experience, an unprecedented precision in the rendering of its world, and, perhaps most presciently, a networked mode that allowed multiple players on a network to play against one another. This networked mode, a kind of precursor to today's MMORPGs, added a new dimension when we grew tired of the canned nature of the game as packaged. Suddenly we could act out violence upon each other in a completely harmless way. Not only did it make the game world more interesting—and frustrating—to be playing against other human intelligences, but it also provided a relatively harmless conduit for a certain natural but otherwise unacknowledged competitiveness among us. In this activity a set of unspoken rules developed concerning what could be done to whom under which circumstances. Out of *Doom*'s mythos emerged a set of rituals; those rituals served both to express our aggression and contain it appropriately.

Group life was important in this process. There were those who chose not to participate in our games, for whatever reason, and it did not take long before we felt they were different, lacking the cementing experience we shared. Those of us who played shared a mystery; we were fellow initiates. Nor was that fellowship limited to our immediate vicinity. *Doom* was an Internet-wide hit, and we therefore had a fraternity with all of its wide-flung fans, whether we had any direct contact with them or not. We belonged.

Much has been made of the Internet's ability to build communities around identities that often remained hidden in the pre-Internet era. It seems clear that the relatively anonymous nature of Internet interaction is one factor in this phenomenon, as that easy anonymity has erased the threat of social opprobrium that once threatened these identities. With that hazard removed it has become possible for people aligned around common identities to find each other in a way that was much more difficult before, or even to find these commonalities with the people that they already knew.

This phenomenon has appeared around a broad range of organizing centers, from the trivially silly—for example, the Ice Chewers Bulletin Board at www. icechewing.com—to the life-saving—for example, emptyclosets.com, an online community providing support and advice for those coming out of the closet. There are communities for racial identities, for all sorts of fetishes or peccadilloes. Some of these are criminal, such as communities catering to pedophiles, but most are more about helping people define their particular identities. The physical world seems filled with increasing pressures to conformity; but in the online world one's quirks are defining and cultivated.

In their seminal introduction to group psychotherapy authors Irving Yalom and Molyn Leszcz defined Universality as one of group therapy's 13 key therapeutic factors. By that they meant the realization that "no human deed or thought… lies fully outside the experience of other people,"[20] a realization can provide a "'welcome to the human race' experience."[21] This was certainly my experience in the world of *Doom*. In retrospect it seems highly unlikely that *Doom* fostered my aggression; rather it appealed so much because it channeled an otherwise repressed energy that was already there. In large measure that aggression had remained repressed precisely because it was socially unacceptable, and therefore was forced to remain a private matter—if necessary even private from myself out of fear of what might happen should it be tapped.

But seeing others engaging with their aggression in this relatively harmless way simultaneously said that others have this experience, and that it would not be the end of the world to tap into it. I want to be clear; before this I did not know I had this aggression, even though in retrospect it seems obvious. The communal engagement with aggression was revelatory, because through it I found my own aggression. I suspect the same is true of any virtual phenomenon. It holds power because it taps into long-dormant and hidden urges—Freud's unfulfilled wishes, Jung's archetypal energies. Online that power is amplified as the Internet provides a community of others similarly engaged. The games speak to what we fail to acknowledge in ourselves, the violence and aggression that rule our inner lives in this day and age. Perhaps that is a good thing—better that violence should find expression virtually than be acted out in the world.

On the Internet individual stories weave together, engagement with experience breeding others' engagement with their own similar experiences. Once this was the province of the storyteller around the campfire, giving symbolic expression to the otherwise inexpressible. But now it happens on the Internet, stories tumbling over stories, building on each other, cannibalizing and interbreeding until bizarre trends like the LOLcats—funny pictures of cats with captions of what the cat might be saying (www.lolcats.com)—are generated and become widely acknowledged at the same time we struggle to explain their comic hold.

This social aspect of all Internet is critical, perhaps its greatest feature. It is mightily difficult—and dangerous—to engage with these forces in isolation. They need a social container to hold them, to give them a form acceptable to the group. My experience was that a group together playing with these games was both a form of permission and a check on my worst impulses. In the context of the group one could be led and, in turn, lead towards unacknowledged impulses—aggression and sexuality that could find no outlet in the larger society was acknowledged and engaged in a group. Somehow that made things less scary, even though we rarely, if ever, talked about it in explicit terms.

This is the Internet as culture generator, as spawner of collective stories that carry weight for the entire society. This, I believe, suggests the appropriate way to regard the Internet, as the greatest temple ever built to what Henri Corbin called the *mundus imaginalis*,[22] the world of fantasy. We go to the Internet to participate in the *mundus imaginalis*, not alone, in an introverted and isolated way, but in a public, extraverted, shared manner. The Internet allows our personal fantasies to weave together with those of others, my fantasy life and your fantasy life interpenetrating and informing each other within the various containers out there, the different game worlds, the subcultures and forums, Facebook and Google+. A new fabric emerges, a fabric that in previous eras would have gone by the name of culture.

For that is really what we have witnessed on the Internet. As it has accelerated commerce and interactions, and enhanced our abilities to track larger and larger amounts of information—we should be reminded of the "external brain pack" from the cartoon Dilbert, as well as a study from earlier this year suggesting that humans use the Internet as a form of memory[23]—it has also had the effect of accelerating the process known as culture. In past generations culture evolved through an interplay of a society's elements—economic, technological, religious, artistic, and so forth. It happened at the pace of cash exchange, the pace of letter delivery over long distances, the pace of stories told around a campfire. It happened in the rhythm of the seasons, on timescales of months, years, decades, and centuries. Now, as the last few political races have revealed, it happens at the pace of electrons, on timescales of hours and sometimes minutes, on the rhythm of a seemingly ever-shortening attention span.

Years later I had a dream that hearkened back to *Doom*. I descended into an underground chamber and machine-gunned a group of people. It startled me, but not my therapist, who I suspect was already well aware of my unacknowledged aggression. In retrospect, given my enthusiasm for those games, my naiveté seems almost willful. Somehow I had touched upon those aggressive instincts in my game play without really defusing them. Clearly, just getting in touch with one's unspoken urges is not enough. Something else must happen in order to bring those contents into real relationship with the rest of being. Daydreaming alone is not enough.

The question for us as a civilization—I refer here to the global civilization of which the Internet is part and parcel—is the extent to which this culture process draws us away from the world. At what point does the temple to the *mundus imaginalis* become a prison? At what point does the fascination of the virtual, the narcotic of the fantastic, displace the tangible world? These are perhaps concerns of the old for the way things used to be. I can certainly grow nostalgic for rotary phones and simpler times, but fantasy can be captivating. In a world going to shit all around, maybe we are too sucked in by this enchanting fantastical world, with the result that our day-to-day life becomes all-the-more drab.

Mary Watkins distinguished daydreams from "aware participation in the imaginal."[24] She noted that in daydreaming "there is no awareness during it or memory afterward of what was going on."[25] This implies that one might move from daydream to more conscious engagement by bringing awareness. How might we bring more awareness to our activities on the Internet? It is, after all, a realm seemingly designed to make it as easy as possible to operate without conscious awareness. What seems to be demanded is what James Hillman referred to as "seeing through," by which he meant "a process of deliteralizing and a search for the imaginal in the heart of things by means of ideas."[26] Through that process we can achieve what both Hillman and Jung described as the "depersonalization" of the anima's effects, which is the way out of an anima-possession.[27]

But perhaps we are not there yet. Perhaps it is too soon, the virtual world too young a phenomenon to be amenable to the kind of self-awareness that would be necessary. Perhaps for the generations growing up without ever knowing a pre-Internet world the charms of the virtual will be less enticing. Perhaps as the virtual merges with the physical the body will once again become part of the equation, bringing with it an awareness grounded in corporeality. Perhaps we will revisit our deteriorating physical environments, and use the self-knowledge gleaned in our virtual interactions to design structures that can intrigue us in the same way the online world can.

But in the meantime, game on.

Notes

1   Carl G. Jung, "Symbols of Transformation: An Analysis to the Prelude of a Case of Schizophrenia" (1911), Vol. 5, 2nd ed., *The Collected Works of C. G. Jung*, 1967, 18.

2   Ibid., 11-12.

3   Ibid., 11.

4   Ibid., 12.

5   Ibid., 17.

6   Ibid., 18.

7   Ross Levin and Hugh Young, "The Relation of Waking Fantasy to Dreaming," *Imagination, Cognition, and Personality*, 21(3, 2002): 202.

8   Mary Watkins, *Waking Dreams*, 1984, 18.

9   Ibid., 19.

10   Levin and Young, "Waking Fantasy", 202.

11   Sigmund Freud, "Creative Writers and Day-Dreaming" (1908), in *The Standard Edition of the Complete Psychological Works of Sigmund Freud*, vol. 9 (London, England: Hogarth, 1959), 145.

12   Anna Freud, "The Concept of Developmental Lines," *Psychoanalytic Study Of The Child*, 18 (1963): 245-265.

13   Freud, "Creative Writers," 146.

14   Ibid., 143.

15   Ibid., 146.

16   Jung, *Symbols*, 29.

17   Freud, "Creative Writers," 152.

18   Jung, *Symbols*, 24.

19   Michael Chanan, *The Dream that Kicks: The Prehistory and Early Years of Cinema in Britain* (London, England: Routledge, 1996), 158-159.

20   Irvin D. Yalom and Molyn Leszcz, *The Theory and Practice of Group Psychotherapy* (5th ed.) (New York, NY: Basic Books, 2005), 6.

21   Ibid.

22   Henry Corbin, "*Mundus Imaginalis* or the Imaginary and the Imaginal," in *Spring* 1972, 1-19.

23   Rob Waugh, "Are Our Brains Being Boggled by Google? Study says Humans Now Use the Internet as our Main 'Memory'—Instead of our Heads," *Mail Online*,

January 25, 2012. http://www.dailymail.co.uk/sciencetech/article-2091127/
Google-boggling-brains-Study-says-humans-use-internet-main-memory.html

24   Watkins, *Waking Dreams*, 18.

25   Ibid.

26   James Hillman, *Re-visioning Psychology* (New York, NY: HarperCollins, 1976), 136.

27   James Hillman, Anima: An Anatomy of a Personified, Notion (Putnam, CT: Spring, 1985), 117-121.

Bibliography

Chanan, Michael. *The Dream that Kicks: The Prehistory and Early Years of Cinema in Britain* (London, England: Routledge, 1996).

Corbin, Henry. "*Mundus Imaginalis* or the Imaginary and the Imaginal," *Spring* 1972.

Freud, Anna. "The Concept of Developmental Lines," *Psychoanalytic Study Of The Child*, 18 (1963).

Freud, Sigmund. "Creative Writers and Day-Dreaming" (1908), in *The Standard Edition of the Complete Psychological Works of Sigmund Freud*, vol. 9 (London, England: Hogarth, 1959).

Hillman, James. *Anima: An Anatomy of a Personified Notion* (Putnam, CT: Spring, 1985).

Hillman, James. *Re-visioning Psychology* (New York, NY: HarperCollins, 1976).

Jung, Carl Gustav. "Symbols of Transformation: An Analysis to the Prelude of a Case of Schizophrenia" (1911), Vol. 5, 2nd ed., *The Collected Works of C. G. Jung*, edited by H. Read et al, translated by R. F. C. Hull. (Princeton, NJ: Princeton University Press, 1967).

Levin, Ross and Young, Hugh. "The Relation of Waking Fantasy to Dreaming," *Imagination, Cognition, and Personality, 21*(3, 2002).

Watkins, Mary. *Waking Dreams* (3rd ed.) (Dallas, TX: Spring, 1984).

Waugh, Rob. "Are Our Brains Being Boggled by Google? Study says Humans Now Use the Internet as our Main 'Memory'—Instead of our Heads," *Mail Online*, January 25, 2012. http://www.dailymail.co.uk/sciencetech/article-2091127/Google-boggling-brains-Study-says-humans-use-internet-main-memory.html

Yalom, Irvin D. and Leszcz, Molyn. *The Theory and Practice of Group Psychotherapy* (5th ed.) (New York, NY: Basic Books, 2005).

Jason Sugg, MA, LPC *is an Austin-area counselor and a Ph.D. candidate in Pacifica Graduate Institute's Depth Psychotherapy program. He has a strong interest in the cultural and political applications of depth psychological theory. He also holds B.S. and M.Eng. degrees in Computer Science from the Massachusetts Institute of Technology. He lives in south Austin, TX, with his wife and two children.*

Finding the Connections

Depth Psychology and Social Media

By

Donna May

We are like islands in the sea; separate on the surface but connected in the deep.

—William James

No man is an island, entire of itself; every
man is a piece of the continent.

—John Donne

Recently, I was talking with a woman, whom I will call "Sara." She was interested in interviewing me about my work with dreams for one of her upcoming podcasts. It was a soul-filled conversation, including discussions on imagination, dreams, art, writing, and the collective unconscious. I felt a deep rapport and connection. Separated by continents and a major ocean, this dialogue with Sara would never have taken place a few years ago; I wouldn't have even known about her existence. What made this "meeting" possible was the Internet and social media.

I have heard it said that the Internet is a metaphor for the collective unconscious. Personally, I have come to believe that this is true, that social media is impacting the very nature of Psyche herself. Experiences like the one with Sara have brought me to an understanding about how these sites can be powerful ways to link like-minded individuals, as well as to educate and direct focus towards important matters. There is a common ground below the surface of things, asking that we dive deep and see more than what we are conscious of. Social media is part of this deepening and joining process.

I came to this belief haltingly. As a true "techie immigrant," I was deeply suspicious and phobic about all things related to computers, especially the Internet and social media. Like many of my professional peers, I regarded these kinds of social platforms as suspect forms of communication, offering very little depth to the possibility of connections and interactions. After all, early exposure to Twitter and Facebook, for many of us, was all about what one was baking for dinner, or where they happened to be at the moment. More, being restricted to 140 characters to type a message or idea on Twitter seemed limiting almost to the point of uselessness.

I also had concerns that these new forms of online posting and discussion could be quite dangerous. Reports of government and corporate gathering of information, the toppling of politicians and others over an ill-thought-out "tweet," not to mention the reports of defamation, bullying, and sites with evil intent, are just a few of the shadow areas of social media that have been documented. For years I stayed clear of all things social media, including Facebook, Twitter, Pinterest, and LinkedIn. While the connective capacity of Facebook and LinkedIn was intriguing; the "short form" updates and info available via Twitter unique; and the images on any topic one might desire accessible on Twitter, the fear of the unknown kept me from imagining beyond that which I could consciously see.

This began to change for me in about 2008. I had "retired" from my position as a system administrator within a county behavioral health system. I did this to devote myself more fully to Psyche's call to/for me: to bring depth psychology concepts and tools to as many people as I could—both in and out of the therapeutic container. I had witnessed the transformative power of the imaginal and I wanted to devote myself more fully to this work. Because I live in such a rural area, I was forced to broaden who and how I worked and associated with people. One way to do this was via the Internet and online communities.

This has been an organic process of learning and growth. Here are some of the key benefits and values I have experienced through my use of social media:

Personal and Professional Connections

Prior to using social media, I yearned for the days of graduate school, often traveling thousands of miles to attend a conference or workshop just to be with others interested in depth psychology. Now, because of the Internet and social media, I feel connected and sustained with the work I do, even with people who live on other continents. Via Internet and video conferencing, I am able to consult and converse with people in New York, England, Canada, New Zealand, Australia, and elsewhere. I easily learn of new research, publications and workshops; I am also involved in various online depth psychology forums, and because of my increasing presence in social media, was even invited to serve on the board for Depth Psychology Alliance, a large dynamic online community dedicated to bringing together those who are interested in delving into soul.

Not only can I find others, but they can find me. Soon after signing up on Twitter, an author and professor specializing in metaphor and education privately messaged me via the platform. She was up in my area, writing another book, and wanted to meet. We have become friends and I would never have met her if I hadn't been posting on Twitter. I have also been able to connect with old friends and alumni, find new friends and colleagues. Facebook, Twitter and other sites helps one find tribes within tribes, something not possible in pre-Internet days.

Community Networks

Social media, fueled by the power of the World Wide Web, is helping to bring together like-minded people in my community, as well as reach many who have never heard about depth psychology, but who are very much interested in active imagination, dreams, art, writing, music and other tools of individuation. They will attend a workshop and/or come for individual consultations and say how relieved they are to know that I am in their area. It is not uncommon for someone to nervously share a dream then state that they had been afraid to share it with someone for fear of being labeled mentally ill: "I thought they would think I was crazy." I also have been contracted to consult, facilitate and do supervision specifically utilizing these concepts and tools–many of these agencies and directors staying connected with me via various social media sites.

Opportunities for Learning and Sharing

Social media is a way for an ever-growing number of people to learn from, and stay in touch with, me. Facebook, Twitter, LinkedIn, and Pinterest, for example, are great ways to share forward many of the things I know and learn about. I am also able to inform people about my availability for consultations and upcoming classes, groups, and workshops.

Many of the individuals I am connected to on social forums have little or no past understanding or information about depth psychology. I trust the process of Psyche and I have observed many times how the introduction and offering of the tools to go within, giving permission to people to follow their images and dreams, can be valuable and empowering—not just for the individual, but for their relationship, family, community and for Earth Herself.

The Internet is an important way to get these tools and ideas out into the world in the 21st century. The Internet, including social media, can be a means to focus and gather light, to make conscious, to gather new imagistic threads and connections together to create and weave a new story, a new myth, which gives context to the dark, the traumatic, the awful, without one being swallowed up in the apocalyptic story unconsciously being played out in the world today.

However, I am neither naïve nor Pollyanna-ish; the fears about social media are often justified. Can the limited character count that Twitter demands and the high speed at which information comes and goes end up trivializing things? Yes, it can. Does Facebook have a shadow, a dark side, with the capacity to create dangerous connections or unhealthy situations in a person's life? Definitely. Do social media platforms serve, for some, as a way to become more of an island, disconnected and less engaged with one's family and community? Absolutely, this can and does happen.

But, in the face of all this, we cannot deny there are other isles of consciousness and possibility we simply fail to glimpse out there beyond our current intellectual and psychological horizons. Several hundred years ago, Earth's inhabitants would look out onto the ocean and believe that the world was flat, that there was nothing beyond what they could see. The fear of dropping off the "edge" kept many from venturing out onto the waters that lay gleaming before them. It took individuals like Ferdinand Magellan who had the capacity to envision and look beyond the visible horizon to trust and set sail towards lands not seen.

There is also the other side of things: Social media can be a lifeboat that reduces one's feelings of isolation, and a means of finding connections with others doing this work—others who have heard and answered Psyche's call but live where they feel stranded and alone.

Social media serves as a breath of fresh air when we find like-minded others, when we need validation or confirmation for those images, dreams and knowings that emerge. The very nature of both Facebook and Pinterest, for example, is to have us noticing, recognizing, and interacting with images, topics, and individuals. How we do this begins to change the very essence of how we perceive our imaginal and conscious minds.

More than ever, Psyche is calling out to each of us to create, to be, to share and to engage. We are living in times of great collapse and change. We need each other, those of us who are dreaming and creating and sharing the new images and stories into being. New dreams are emerging and it is worth the journey via social media to find, create and sustain these connections that may not be visible to the naked eye. Venturing forward with a compass, knowing one's True North, can help us find and stay on course, to help and be helped, to know we are not alone, nor crazy, and that we all have important things to say and contribute.

I began this essay with the story of my conversation with Sara. Continents apart, I felt an instantaneous link with her, immersed in a beautiful and soulful container made possible by the miracle of connecting through social media. Venturing out, engaging in and with social media, can help each of us discover many "Saras" along the way. Indeed, none of us is an island, but inextricably linked by something deep, emerging, and important.

Donna May, M.A., L.M.F.T. *is a therapist, consultant, educator and author of the upcoming book* Psyche's Call: Putting the Soul Back into Psychology. *She is an adjunct faculty member at College of the Siskiyous, where she has taught courses in dreams, life story writing and human services. Donna graduated from Pacifica Graduate Institute, where she studied counseling psychology with a specialization in depth psychology. She has conducted classes, groups and workshops on writing and story for over twenty years. She also has extensive training in dreams, and dreams, writing, art, and active imagination are key elements in the work that she does with others.*

Donna lives is beautiful Etna, CA with her husband Bruce and their three dogs and three cats, where she loves to read, write, walk and explore the wild nature all around. Donna can be reached via her website: www.psychescall.com.

Through the Looking Glass

Reflections and Adventures in Social Media

By

Eva Rider

Alice had got so much into the way of expecting nothing but out-of-the-way things to happen, that it seemed quite dull and stupid for life to go on in the common way.

—Lewis Carroll, *Alice's Adventures in Wonderland and Through the Looking-Glass*

How can you squander even one more day not taking advantage of the greatest shifts of our generation? How dare you settle for less when the world has made it so easy for you to be remarkable?

—Seth Godin

Traveling through the hi-ways and byways of the Internet, we inevitably stumble on a full spectrum of perspectives, attitudes, and beliefs. Through our aloneness, whether it be in the guise of wrenching loneliness or its cure, solitude, we ultimately bump into one another. We are souls traveling side by side.

Technology developed the highway; we are the ones who are creating the threads that weave us together into a global tapestry. We are not alone as we feared; rather, we are mirrored. It seems that new bridges are being formed between the realms of spirit and matter. We are spinning and extending Soul through the airwaves, the galaxies, and back into matter. Our bodies and hearts and minds and souls are linking us and catapulting us into higher frequencies. We are as though quickening, evolving, and the Internet may be our manifest vehicle. Surely this is a Renaissance unprecedented in our history.

Our reflections on ourselves and on the universe are mirrored back to us in a palette of colors we could never have imagined even a decade ago. We are hurtling through multitudes of realities. Like Alice, we have fallen down the rabbit hole and entered the parallel world on the other side of the looking glass. What we encounter makes no sense. Perception bends and changes direction. It can go inward, outward, up or down. All things are possible. We are on a wild and magical ride carrying us we know not where and our only allies are trust and surrender.

Consciousness allows for an awareness that we are still standing in darkness and merely peering into the light, blinded by its glare. It is the yearning towards love and for reunification to a source we no longer remember that draws us forward. It is our saving grace as humans that we long for a way home. We may find it in each other, in our world and in the galaxy. Everything is reflected back to us; all that is, that was, and that will ever be exists in the imagination to the ends of nowhere and back again.

"If the world has absolutely no sense, who's stopping us from inventing one?" wondered Alice in Lewis Carroll's 1865 classic Alice's Adventures in Wonderland. Alice's adventures, both in Wonderland and through the looking glass, have renewed depth of meaning, almost as though Carroll had a glimpse into our current reality. We are reminded that without imagination, we are lost; with imagination the universe can be recreated. Imagination is that which points humanity towards creating the future out of the torn fabric of yesterday's mistakes.

Swiss psychologist C. G. Jung insisted that loneliness "does not come from having no people about one, but from being unable to communicate the things that seem important to oneself, or from holding certain views which others find inadmissible."[1] Loneliness and isolation inevitably permeate our communication in a world engulfed in consumerism, propaganda, and violence. In the midst of this unprecedented expansion in technology, we are forced to reinvent the shape and design of communication. Perhaps, this global linking in consciousness is the answer to the grief and devastation that engulfs both us and the planet, even as it seems to widen in scope, endangering life on earth. In the bubble of the worldwide web, we can see the edges of microcosm and macrocosm blur and shift as we bump and bounce off each other like atoms in space. Cosmos and matter are merging through thought in space and time.

New Beginnings

Although we live in an era of historically unprecedented change and cataclysm, although our very existence on this planet is endangered, and although we may already have passed the point where a way back is possible, there is still the "transcendent third" that Jung[2] invoked, describing the apex of the triangle, where the magnetic tension of the opposing poles splinters the system of security that has become outworn and transports into an entirely new reality. This is our destiny and the place it will deposit us can only be our rightful home. T. S. Eliot's profound and prophetic words resound more clearly than ever: "We will return to the place where we started and know the place for the first time."[3]

The biblical story of the Tower of Babel is appropriate to our current crisis. Once upon a time humans spoke one language; the implication is that it was a language of the heart and soul and this is that which we yearn to reclaim. Humanity's course as conscientious stewards of the earth was interrupted when the God Yahweh (whose traits have much in common with the Greek god, Saturn) shattered the Tower of Babel and unleashed a force of division that erupted in "babble," a nonsense language, incomprehensible and bereft of meaning and incapable of being understood. This resulted in a scattering of humanity across the earth. This division in language without the inclusion of metaphorical, symbolic understanding leaves us lost and wandering in a banal universe, bereft of soul.

It is the result of this symbolic dismemberment that has been responsible for encasing human beings in cages of loneliness and isolation. We have forgotten that we once shared a resonance that transcended speech. Without the skill to understand each other, humanity cannot attain unity and return to the original blueprint of our destiny as gods and stewards of consciousness. If we are the offspring of gods, does not our legacy lead us to become as gods ourselves?

In this myth of the Tower of Babel lives the echoes of the original exile from the Garden of Eden. This separation seems to have been essential in our subsequent wanderings across the earth, and is evident in that self-reflection is needed to integrate shadow; that which is "other." This is the only path open to us if we are to attain wholeness or individuation, in C. G. Jung's terms. In fact, the Internet is both friend and impediment to loneliness, depending on how we choose to use it.

At this pivotal juncture in time, we are encountering a tear in the fabric of our known reality. We are at a turning point of consciousness on our little planet. We have an opportunity to link back towards a unification of mind through our diversity. The Internet is a tool that is of our own making, and we can use it to whatever ends we choose, to evolve or to devolve. Logos as Mind and relatedness as Eros, dancing together, can weave new patterns of existence. The resulting design is as yet unrevealed, but it is clear that we have been called to "re-member" the original universal language we once shared.

A new language is being formed that may encompass feeling as well as thought; image as well as sound. The metaphorical and the literal must live side by side. We are seemingly being catapulted into a new frequency that transcends our three dimensional reality. We are linked to one another; intricately interdependent with all living beings and plants. This planet has graciously provided us with a *temenos* (sacred container) which nourishes us, providing sustenance, tools, and beauty for our well-being—perhaps to encourage our evolutionary journey and potential awakening to our role as creators and sustainers of life, or else to be destroyed.

Our destiny allows for choice. Will we choose the path of creativity or destruction? This is the end of the long childhood of humanity. We must grow up. Language is a tool, and social media its messenger, allowing us to remember that we were once born from the same source and we shall return. It is our destiny.

There are many theories referring to the origins of human language. In creation myths, as in Genesis, the implication is that language has existed as long as humans have walked the earth. In his article entitled "The Origin of Language," historical linguist, Edward Vajda describes one such evolutionary theory, suggesting that "as soon as humans developed the biological, or neurological, capacity for creative language, the cultural development of some specific system of forms with meanings would have been an inevitable next step."[5] This may have happened millions of years ago. What we know now is that language and society co-exist and one is intricately connected and sustained by the other. Humans are essentially social beings. We are ultimately dependent on each other for survival and our ability to make to understand one another renders this possible.

However, communication in the form of the spoken and written word, does not necessarily translate into understanding. Jung spoke of the language of the dream as being ancient and pre-verbal.[6] He suggested that we possessed images and symbols long before we had language. The dream speaks a language of the "unconscious" and is thus outside of the realms of logic and the linear format of language. It prefers to dance and play in realms of image and symbol and metaphor. Poetry and dreams are the language of soul. We inhabit these realms as technology and planetary crisis collide, and we seek one another. Without this reflection and the embracing of the Other, we are doomed to destruction.

The Rabbit Hole

The Internet and social media are perhaps the mediators that usher in this new emerging transformation, wherever it may lead us. They point us to a road that leads us into rabbit holes, through dark underworld passages and up again through sunlit meadows. But, if an inherent telepathic linking of mind through image and symbol provided a primal form of communication before language and speech developed, then the current difficulty in comprehending one another may be further complicated by the Internet communication. Nowhere is the result of the destruction of the proverbial Tower of Babel more evident than on the highways of the Internet. The Internet is still, even well into the twenty-first century, limited to those who have access to it and can use it, thus leaving out vast segments of society. This also creates a further divide.

A great deal of what is available to us on social media is noise and distraction. It takes a finely tuned sensibility to tap into what is hidden beneath the screech and clang of consumerism, sensationalism, and propaganda. However, on the positive side, the Internet may be another rung on the ladder that leads to an evolutionary leap in human global consciousness. These are the building blocks of human imagination and the tools of social media at its best.

As philosopher, visionary and, in my view, *psychopomp* (in Greek mythology, a guide of souls to the place of the dead), Terence McKenna noted, "The Internet is the global brain, the cyberspacially connected, telepathic, collective domain that we've all been hungering for."[7] Social media extends through myriads of channels, each constituting its own world, including Twitter, Facebook, Linked-In, Scoop-it, Pinterest, and Instagram, among others, and new channels seem to appear on a daily basis. Facebook, which arguably played a significant role in ushering in this revolution in social media, has been the most widely used with over 1.3 billion users in 2015—although this is also changing. It has been called "disingenuous" by some, even as its calculating and manipulative side progressively shows through in its increasing efforts at commercialization. In a 2014 *Mic* magazine article, psychologist Robert Simmermon, a psychologist who deals with mass media issues, is quoted as saying that Facebook is "psychological theater." Simmermon writes, "In a way, it's similar to reality TV, that it's not really reality and we know it. The pictures can be reality, certainly, but they're very carefully edited and chosen before they're put up," continuing, "In every facet of life, we choose to present ourselves in certain ways. But on Facebook, 'the world's most disingenuous social network,' we have increased control over our curated identities, actively deciding to post certain photos over others."[8]

Yet, in many ways, social media sites such as Facebook have created a new plane of interaction and friendship. The world of social media, its mazes and passageways has been a journey of continuous incredulity for me, I embarked on it with no idea where I was headed as did we all. We, like Alice, stumbled into a parallel universe where nonsense seemingly is possessed of its own wisdom. We are all traversing wonderland. As an experiment, while incubating this writing, I began to post images and quotes from Lewis Carroll's *Alice in Wonderland* and *Through the Looking Glass*. The affirming nods from my own Facebook depth community, confirmed to me that we have crossed the bridge into a metaphoric language. What was once nonsense has become social wisdom.

Where social media will lead remains unknown. Whether we initially entered this strange land to connect with friends and family, to make professional connections or simply to explore the worldwide web, finding like-minded souls on the highways of the net has been an unsought but welcome bonus. Our Internet exploration may have taken us to unfamiliar but resonant territory, or we may have found ourselves completely lost, arriving like Alice, through the looking glass, in strange realities. One daily meets oneself on the path, one is led astray by white rabbits and bustled along by Mad Hatters, occasionally makes the acquaintance of wise caterpillars, strange unicorns, bumbling and pretentious royalty, while continually finding ourselves stuck, unstuck, inflated, deflated, confused while wandering down strange passageways, rooms, path and encountering differing viewpoints unexpectedly at every turn.

So, in many ways, we are left wondering: Where are we? *Who* are we? Where did we come from? Where are we going? Perhaps, in times of unprecedented change, it is an appropriate response to adversity to surrender to being lost. At the least, it is place from which to begin the journey. Sometimes, as Alice demonstrates, anyplace is a good beginning if one trusts one's curiosity and one's instincts. The virtual world of the Internet may invite both skeptics and hopeless addicts to its charms and bedevilments, but one thing is certain: It is here to stay, presumably, at least, until it evolves into a form more organic and ethereal. It is paving the way to a potential linking into global consciousness.

As yet, the possibilities of the Internet are untraveled and the global linking leading outward although still is in its infancy, inevitable. Luddites—and even those who have ultimately adopted technology—may still protest the many problems it has unleashed—not the least of which is the invasion of our privacy.

It is not mere paranoia to feel we are being observed. If we are looking, then we can be certain that we are also being looked upon, watched, judged, and looked into as well.

On the other end of the spectrum, the Internet allows for the creation of communities that could never otherwise have been formed. It connects old friends and introduces new ones. The outcome of using social media may be unknown and perhaps it is more related to journey than arrival. The words of the award-winning sci-fi novelist, Ursula K. Le Guin are apt: "It is good to have an end to journey toward; but it is the journey that matters, in the end."[9]

Social Shadows and Slants

Social media cannot replace living intimacy but it is certainly imitating it. It is not a destination, but a steppingstone into untraveled realities. I often feel nostalgic for the Seventies, an era that now seems so simple in retrospect. Time seemed to move more slowly, even luxuriously. Telephones had solid weight and substance. They were attached to a wall socket. When they rang, we answered them in person, or if we called someone there was no answer, we simply called back later. There were no answering machines, no computers; instead there were books, television, radio, phonographs, and tape recorders. Social interaction meant you spoke on the phone and arranged to see each other in person, seeming to engender a more authentic connection to the Other. We made eye contact, read body language, tuned into facial expressions of others. I think this fostered emotional intelligence and compassion. Virtual reality existed in dreams, daydreams and visions. That was all. We must redefine a sense of boundaries. What is privacy? Where are boundaries? What image are we presenting? Is it true? Who is looking at us? We are perpetually "on stage," often caught up in an effort to be seen—or perhaps, to hide? On Facebook, some people share intimate troubles, the big events of our lives, and details of trips, meals and time with friends. The introverts tend to hide and peek out more warily.

As all things in our time, social media delivers a collision of the pernicious and the beneficial. The mythical apple offered to Eve in the Garden of Eden has been offered once again, and we, once again, have eaten of the fruit of knowledge. Curiosity ever encompasses the paradoxical curse and saving grace of humanity. Social media offers each of us a blank page from which to begin again. We can communicate a fabrication of ourselves or an image of what we hope to become. The possibilities range from a sales opportunity to a soul's opportunity. Depending on our intention, either and both are possible, and woe to the one who cannot discriminate between the two!

In the larger view, we find ourselves on an entirely different wavelength, a new frequency, traveling along at lightning speed, along this technological highway in our own human-made Milky Way. We bump into each other. Whether friend or foe, new connections emerge that transcend time and space that otherwise would not have been possible. Friends, colleagues, soul connections that were perhaps always there move through new realities as we access each other via direct synchronicity; via love of language, symbol, image, poetry, idea, music, and mutual thirst for knowledge. We link together through what are called "threads" in this global web of humanity, and we begin to feel the hum of many voices, many directions on the highways.

John Wyndham's science fiction novel, *The Chrysalids*, is about a post-nuclear Holocaust society split in two—a rigid fundamentalist community, and those "others" who are deemed "mutants" because they have a physical deformity from what was once the "norm." The mutants are the disenfranchised, and they are exiled to "The Fringes" of society.[10] In this story, we are introduced to two children who communicate in "thought shapes." They are warned to keep this "gift" hidden from view for, if discovered, they are in danger of being exiled to The Fringes. Their strange gift is perceived as curse through the lens of the old worldview, yet it is this new ability to communicate in "thought shapes" that holds the key to a new story about an evolutionary shift.

Terence McKenna imagined that the Internet would perhaps link the human race together telepathically, creating such an evolutionary shift.[11] Computers chips become smaller and may eventually evolve into tools that have been integrated by body so that psyche will no longer rely on them. We will learn to connect in new ways. We are evolving. We, as humans, continue our journey between stardust and earth matter.

Depth psychologists, philosophers, theologians, poets, artists, dreamers, and spiritual seekers may now meet and dance together on their own frequency and create new worlds. We who have traveled through the universe on parallel journeys never imagining we would meet are suddenly traversing the skies and airwaves intersecting, sprinkling stardust and laughter and tears. We do not shy away from a search for meaning, hope and solutions in this world gone mad, in the throes of a revolutionary atmosphere unprecedented in recorded Western History. We share news, jokes, poetry, and events. This is the bright spark.

The dark is equally as black. We hear of Internet stalking and facile access to pornography, including that produced through trafficking and the manipulation and abuse of innocents. We are daily exposed to stories that overwhelm us by amplifying the horrors of war and climate change and its impact on us all, and which provide very few solutions. The dark underbelly of the world wide web is as surely at our fingertips as much as its gifts. We are wise to travel with caution, to heed signs and warnings from instinct, intuitions, signs and synchronicities along the way. We choose where we tread as we may in all of life, especially if we are aware and conscious of life's unfolding mystery.

In a video interview captured for the documentary film, *A Matter of Heart*, Jung said that "the world hangs by a thin thread: the psyche of man" and that the hope of the world lies in this.[12] If we can connect in mind and heart, perhaps it will lead us back to our deep embodiment and ensoulment in nature toward a Utopia that some of us have always dreamed may be possible.

The shadow lurks behind social media in more insidious ways than in life because it peers into our living rooms with judgments and yearnings and whatever disowned material rises to the top. We are caught between the yearning to be seen and the fear of being exposed. The witness in us reels crazily between judgment and the yearning for relatedness—between Saturn and Eros. Being reflected accurately is a rare thing: such is the trickster aspect of projection. Yet it is the nature of the soul of humanity to long for relatedness and for wholeness. It is our source and beginning and to it, we will return in one form or another.

As social media develops and emerges into a new phase of its existence, the vision of Terence McKenna of the Internet as a potential vehicle for linking the human mind together telepathically, begins to seem more real. Perhaps we are indeed creating a ship that carries us together to the same star, and with conscious cooperation, our star may continue to flourish and thrive on Earth. Where the trajectory of the Internet and its social implications will lead us we have yet to discover for certain. We, as humanity, are its sole architects. We are a grand experiment. If we remember our source, the path on which we travel may once again become visible beneath our feet and we may return to our birthright and sit side by side with the gods.

French Philosopher and Jesuit Priest, Pierre Teilhard de Chardin's words illuminate the inborn hope of humanity for this possibility future: "Someday, after mastering the winds, the waves, the tides and gravity, we shall harness for God the energies of love, and then, for a second time in the history of the world, man will have discovered fire."[13]

Notes

1   C. G. Jung, *Memories, Dreams, Reflections*, 1989, 356.

2   Jung, "The Structure and Dynamics of the Psyche", CW 8, 1969.

3   T. S. Eliot, *Little Gidding V*, 1971, 47.

4   Jung, 1989, 356.

5   Edward Vadja, The Origin of Language , n.d., para. 6.

6   Jung, 1989.

7   Terence McKenna, Interviewed in Podcast 351 – "What Is Truth?", 2013.

8   Robert Simmermon quoted in "There's a Reason Engagement Photos Irritate Us" by Ellie Krupnick, *Mic* Magazine, 2014.

9   Ursula K. Le Guin, *The Left Hand of Darkness*, 1969.

10   John Wyndham, *The Chrysalids*, 1959

11   McKenna, 2013

12   Jung, in a video interview captured in *A Matter of Heart*, 1986

13   Pierre Teilhard de Chardin, *Writings in Time of War*, n.d., 143-4

Bibliography

Chardin, Pierre Teilhard de, *Writings in Time of War*. New York, NY: Harper & Row, n.d.

Eliot, T. S. Little Gidding V, *Four Quartets*. Orlando, FL: Harcourt, 1971.

Jung, Carl Gustav, "The Structure and Dynamics of the Psyche". Edited by R. F. C. Hull. The collected works of C. G. Jung, Volume 8. Princeton, NJ: Princeton University Press, 1969.

Jung, Carl Gustav. *Memories, Dreams, Reflections*. Translated by R. Winston & C. Winston, Edited by Aniela Jaffe Ed. New York, NY: Random House, 1989.

Krupnick, E. (2014). "There's a Reason Engagement Photos Irritate Us—And It's Not Because We're Bitter". *Mic magazine*: http://mic.com/articles/103596/the-trouble-with-all-those-engagement-photos-on-facebook Retrieved from http://mic.com/articles/103596/the-trouble-with-all-those-engagement-photos-on-facebook

Le Guin, Ursula K. *The Left Hand of Darkness*. New York, NY: Walker & Co., 1969.

McKenna, Terrence. Podcast 351: "What Is Truth?", 2013: http://www.matrixmasters.net/salon/2013/05/podcast-351-what-is-truth

Vajda, Edward. *The Origin of Language*, n.d: http://pandora.cii.wwu.edu/vajda/ling201/test1materials/origin_of_language.htm

Whitney, Michael. *Matter of Heart*. Written by Michael Whitney Produced by Kino International Corporation, 1986.

Wyndham, John. *The Chrysalids*. New York, NY: New York Review Books, 1955.

Eva Rider MA, LMFT, *is a Jungian depth psychotherapist, workshop leader and lecturer. She holds a BA in History from McGill University and an M.A. in Psychology from John F. Kennedy University, where she taught as adjunct instructor. Eva is a graduate of the Marion Woodman BodySoul Rhythms™ Leadership Training, a certified hypnotherapist, and dreamwork teacher, exploring personal and archetypal dream processes using fairy tale, myth, music, art, poetry and movement. Eva's passion is a journey of unveiling the feminine through correspondences between Jungian theory, alchemy and Psyche/Soma as revealed through the glyph of the Hermetic Tree of Life. She can be reached at www.reclaimingsoul.com*

Madness and the Map

By
Drew Foley

Digital Space

As I type the words for this sentence, I am presented with familiar characters on the screen as my fingers move across the QWERTY keyboard on my MacBook Pro. The arrangement of the letters on the keyboard is nearly unchanged from my first experience with the vintage Royal manual typewriter, a relic of my father's college days. My fingers move in patterns not unlike those I learned on the IBM Selectric, circa 1978. The distinct hum of the Selectric has yielded to the whisper of my 2011 MacBook Pro.

The ink-stamped letters of the IBM typewriter are now replaced with pixels illuminated on the 15" screen of the laptop computer. The familiar contours of the Times New Roman 12 point font are the analog of the internal digital structures in the computer's physical memory. With a press of the *power* button, the electronic signals that inhabit the computer's volatile memory are cleared and the map between the digital code and analog image is broken.

As anyone who examines the binary representation of a computer data file can attest, the grammar of digital information spaces is a foreign terrain for humans. While human language is comprised of symbols used to construct analog representations of phenomena, the bits stored in digital space appear undifferentiated. It is only that grammar of the machine that interprets a string of zeros and ones as a digital photograph, moving image, sound file, software application, or book chapter. Without this mapping of digital to analog, the computer representation appears as gibberish.

Without a map, it is madness.

Entry

Entry into new spaces requires a map. The creation of new maps presupposes entry into new spaces. Therein lies the dilemma. This dilemma is an ancient one.

To map new spaces, the unmapped space must be entered. This experience of entering into an unknown and unmapped space is at once a foreign experience and a familiar one. Long before the disorientation of entry into new forms of digital space, the notion of *being lost* referred to crossing new frontiers of physical space.

Physical Space

This work has its origin in classical questions of navigation:
Where am I?
Where is the nearest point of reference?
What path do I follow to travel from my current location to my destination?

Navigation is the set of skills and knowledge that we apply to answer questions of location, orientation and direction.[1] Questions of navigation are woven in the oldest stories of heroes crossing the threshold between the domain of humans and the realm of the gods.[2] Questions of navigation likewise arise in our everyday experience of traveling from home to school, to work, or to meet friends in a gathering place.

This form of everyday navigation from one known referent to another is termed *way finding*.[3] Way finding is informed by nature, such as Micronesian sailors using patterns of birds, wind, and tides to navigate the complex chain of islands. Way finding is also based in instrumentation, such as the crew of a naval carrier steering the ship safely into port. It is when we are confronted with the unknown that navigation shifts from the practice of way finding to something more akin to wandering.[4]

To consider the connection between way finding and wandering, imagine yourself as a contemporary Alice in Wonderland, passing through the rabbit hole or looking glass to an unfamiliar terrain. With no map of this new place, you wander in search of familiar referent. As you explore the surroundings, you begin the process of creating and extending a map that connects internal experience with the external environment. Mapmaking is prescriptive as well as descriptive. In the imagination of the mapmaker, our understanding of the world is shaped. The mapmaker becomes part of the map.[5] Not only is Alice in Wonderland; Wonderland resides in Alice.

Similarly, each of us holds within us a map of all that we have experienced. Collectively, these maps form a shared understanding of the world that addresses questions of boundaries, relationships and paths.[6] *Boundaries* articulate the border between the known and the unknown, the safe and the forbidden. *Relationships* establish the context for the connections among the domains that we inhabit. *Paths* delineate the ways that we traverse among the boundaries and relationships that comprise the known world. To reach the boundary of the known is to stare into the abyss of the unknown. To cross the threshold into the unknown is to break from the relationships that provide grounding for our lives. To explore the unknown is to create, rather than to follow, a path.

This is the kind of exploration that poet Antonio Machado describes when he writes, "Wanderer, there is no path; You lay down a path in walking."[7] This is the kind of exploration beyond the edge of the known world that resigned the Greek hero Ulysses to one of the lowest circles of Dante's Hell as punishment. This is the kind of exploration referenced by author Robert Pirsig when he states, "To go outside the mythos is to become insane."[8]

This is the kind of exploration that is a kind of madness.

Origin

Exploration is based in concepts of origin, direction, and destination. Similarly, personal stories are woven from elements of source, narrative and goal. Such stories represent guides that make sense of experience. To lose this sense is to fall into confusion.

To follow a story, it is helpful to understand its origin. Yet, it may be through the act of departing the known and entering into the unknown that this origin is understood. Like Alice astray in Wonderland, home is most clearly conceived in its absence.

Myth is a Map

This story has its origin in the opening remarks at the 2012 *Study of Myth Symposium* at Pacifica Graduate University. Robert Walter, Executive Director for the Joseph Campbell Foundation served as host for the event. In his introduction, Walter said, "Myth is a map."[9]

Long after I left the auditorium that evening, Walter's words echoed in my thoughts.

Myth is a map.

Through years of research, I sought but never found such a lucid description. Walter's words unlocked a portal that provided a glimpse into the special significance of myth. I felt as if I had gained admission to a treasure room, hidden in plain sight. Ancient tales that serve as origin still have power to orient explorers in the digital age.

Those who research and write about myth face the question of relevance. Describing the practical value of myth can prove elusive. As ancient architects ceased building statues of Venus and temples to Apollo, it is tempting to conceive of myth as the distant stories and alien beliefs of another people and another time.

Yet, we architects and inhabitants of the digital age are no more bereft of myth than we are missing maps. In the 21st century we think of the world as mapped.[10] We live in a time in which the outermost reaches of space are mapped by telescope and the innermost fragments of our genetic material are decoded by electron microscope. With mathematical models, we may even map events of the distant past or imagined future.

Where the term *myth* suggests an act of the imagination and the term *map* implies a product of reason, both myth and map draw upon the imagined and the reasoned. As such, they are not in opposition, but rather operate in tandem as part of a grammar that is both familiar and invisible. Together, they act as origin and orientation that form the foundation of how we perceive the world.

Mapmaking incorporates not only the cartographic aspect of the physical world, but also the symbolic forms that express the language and logic of the surrounding world. Where cartography articulates quantitative measures of distance and time, symbolic maps speak to qualitative dimensions. In short, a cartographic map yields the distance to the airport. A symbolic map depicts the purpose of the airport. Contemporary maps incorporate *both* cartographic and symbolic information.[11]

Myth is a Path

Maps are more than cartography and myth is more than story.

The term *mythopoesis* refers to the way that shared stories give rise to new myths.[12] Just as we refer to mapmaking, so mythopoesis refers to mythmaking.

One misunderstanding of myth is to describe it as a means by which primitive societies seek to explain mysterious phenomena. Another misconception is to view myth strictly as the province of the imagined.

While its expression is symbolic rather than analytic, myth arises from the same underlying inquiry as mapmaking. It is rooted in our direct apperception of the physical world. The myths we make serve to "give meaning, re-orient, and re-inscribe that reality"[13]

Myths, like maps, serve as navigational guides. Individuals, organizations, groups and even entire societies choose guiding stories. The Sanskrit term *marga* refers to the path or process that is articulated by a guiding story.[14] Unlike the cartographic idea of path as a route to be traveled, this form of path is a process to be enacted. Guiding stories serve as the mythic equivalent of way finding. Such myths, like cartographic maps, function in terms of boundaries, relationships, and path.

Take, for example, the guiding stories at play in post-9/11 America. More now than ever, stories of terrorist threats heighten our awareness of boundaries as security portals. Leisure travelers, students, and families are required to pass through microwave scanning machinery. Electronic messages are collected and dissected in unmarked buildings reminiscent of a Kafka novel. Automated drone weapons are sent on missions to strike at targets on a digital grid. Enemies are detained indefinitely based upon suspected affiliations with enemy groups. This paradoxical path leads free people to freely surrender their freedoms in order to preserve the very freedom they surrender.

Such stories are more than descriptive. They ascribe meaning and orient our reality as individuals and as a society. Those who reject the guiding story still inhabit the *storied context* even as they reject the dominant interpretation.[15] Even those who disagree with the wisdom of creating a surveillance society must still argue within the context of the very surveillance society they decry.

This variation in ways of perceiving the same guiding story creates a *strange map*.[16] The map is strange not because of the terrain, but rather because of the tension between the competing realties that are conceived. This tension may be resolved through an overarching narrative that supports both of the competing conceptions. This kind of synthesis serves as a *canopy* that weaves together disparate ways of understanding the world, connecting religion and science, individualism and collectivism, free will and determinism, personal freedom and national security. The term *canopy* itself is taken from the natural world. It describes the canvas of intertwined leaves and branches that supports the ecosystem of the South American rain forest. In the human ecosystem of ideas and the imagination, the canopy refers to the fabric of the grand narrative. It is the story from which all stories arise. It is the myth that gives rise to myth.

It is the mythic space.[17]

It is problematic to ask the question of *where* mythic space is located as it is inhabits a storied space that is co-existent with physical place. Such alternate spaces date back to the oldest stories from both Eastern and Western traditions. The aboriginal people of the Australian continent speak of song-lines, or magic lines of power, that traverse the land. These lines form a path to be walked as the land is sung into existence.[18] The songs arise from the same source as story. It is the source that awakens the mythic space into our awareness. The mythic space does not fade, only our perception of it.

Mythic space is found in the sacred and in the sublime. It is a threshold just out of view, a portal hidden in plain sight. It may be entered through dreams or enacted through ritual. It may also be accessed in everyday experience.

The Magic Hour

My earliest association with mythic space has its origin in my experience of the *magic hour* between midnight and two AM. As a child I lay awake, listening to the sound the world made while its inhabitants slept. I equate this sound to the indigenous idea of the song lines that cross the land.[19]

As a young adult, I spent several years working the late shift as a night computer operator at a financial institution. The sound I heard at midnight was the hum of the machines, running the background processes queued to start during periods of low activity. As the bank customers rested, their accounts were being updated, logged, and backed up to reels of magnetic tape.

Later, I came to discover online message boards, Internet chat rooms, and entire virtual worlds, still active in the quiet hours of the night. The machines and their users seek connection to other machines and other users. Digital protocols stream data across communication lines, linking the hum of my computer to others.

Presented with a log-in screen, I enter my credentials and access code to join other digital wanderers. In his space, time assumes a qualitative rather than quantitative dimension. Secrets are hidden and discovered. Battles are waged. Love is found and lost, and found again. The magic hour may last mere minutes or it may end only when the threshold of sunrise has been crossed. I log out and my screen returns to a blinking cursor or a row of neatly arranged icons. Awareness returns to the physical space of the room that I inhabit and to a sense of time as chronological, rather than ceremonial.

The magic hour is but one lived example of entering into the mythic space. This is the space where new myths arise. It is a space not of way finding, but of wandering.

Digital Kangaroos

I first ventured into the immersive possibilities of computer programming in 1980. On the Commodore VIC-20 personal computer, I created an arcade style game called 'Roos on Fire. The 8-bit game, programmed in the BASIC computer language, featured a kangaroo attempting to escape a burning building. The graphics for the program resided in the computer's 64 kilobytes (64,786 bytes) of computer memory. I sold approximately 100 copies of the game through a computer hobby magazine.

One day, I received an unexpected phone call from one of my initial customers, who had spent many hours playing 'Roos on Fire. He reported the first bug (glitch) in the game. When the kangaroo was in the lower right corner of the screen and the joystick was pushed to the right for several seconds, the kangaroo's head would disappear. The headless kangaroo would then continue its journey through the burning building.

What happened to the kangaroo's head is a cautionary tale for the digital age. The kangaroo's graphic image was stored in the computer memory location adjacent to the memory space for the bottom right of the screen display. The joystick algorithm that overwrote the graphics memory for the kangaroo's head was the mistake of a novice programmer. From this experience, I gained insight into a fundamental difference between analog and digital grammar. Digital logic is based in the binary logic of zero and one. Whereas analog grammar offers distinctions of degree along a continuum, digital grammar works in terms of on and off.[20]

The digital storage of information in computer memory is an abstraction. Yet the binary code has an effect that is manifest in the perceptual space of the analog world. When a one is turned to zero, the kangaroo loses its head.

The Digital Age

The typewriter provides a familiar example of this analog/digital distinction. With a manual typewriter, the force with which my fingers strike the keys influences the resulting image on the paper. A tentative touch on the keys may result in a faint image on the paper. With the digital keyboard, once the threshold for the key's sensitivity is reached, the letter is recorded in the computer's memory and a pattern of pixels is illuminated on the screen.

In 1980 when I wrote the BASIC program for 'Roos on Fire, the digital logic of the machine was new to me. In the intervening years, many areas of daily life have entered this digital paradigm. I awake in the morning to the greeting of a digital alarm clock, listen to digital music as I get ready for the day, use digital tools in my commute to work or school, and communicate with friends and family through digital devices. In the evening, I relax with digital entertainment systems and end the day reading a digital text. The phrase *the digital age* to refer to this ascent of digital information systems.[21]

Just as we can say that we inhabit the digital age, so it can be said that the digital age inhabits us. Cosmologist Edward Harrison posits that each age is characterized by a dominant paradigm that shapes the way the universe is understood.[22] Such paradigms represent not only a collective map, but also a model for mapmaking itself. It is during times of transition that even the very rules of mapmaking are in flux.

Emblematic of this flux, we find ourselves in a universe that is betwixt and between the analog and the digital.[23] To hold a phone conversation, the analog sound waves of my voice are translated into a digital signal that is transmitted over a communication network. On the other end of the conversation, this digital signal is reproduced as analog sound waves that reconstitute my words.

In other cases, both the digital and analog representations are simultaneously present. Imagine the digital icon on my MacBook Pro that resembles an analog clock. The pixelated clock is an analog expression of a digital representation of an analog object. This co-existence of the analog and digital are found in everyday activities from brewing coffee to parking a car.

Passages

While we may think of this passage between the analog and digital as a matter of presentation, the shift in grammar is more fundamental. When information is changed from analog form to digital, organization is gained and meaning is lost.[24] The word *meaning* here can be misleading. It is not used in the sense of purpose, but rather speaks of nuance, subtlety and context.

For example, if you convert your photo albums from analog to digital, you gain the ability to search for images, to associate related content, and to track information (metadata) such as the number of times an image has been viewed or shared. Yet, the continuous colors, lighting and shading of the analog photographs are encoded in discrete pixels that do not age with time. The Internet itself, as a map of the world's information, represents a gain in organization and a loss of meaning.

At the time of this writing, my online query for the term *play* returns 1,240,000,000 results in 30 seconds. The search engine displays a list of prioritized results. Yet the algorithm fails to make a semantic distinction between whether I am searching for information about game *play* or a theatrical *play* or even about *play* in the sense of looseness in a mechanism (such as a steering wheel).

Conversely, when digital information is translated to analog form, meaning is gained and organization is lost. Physical book titles organized at the local library present an alphabetical array of author names. Yet, the search for a specific text is serialized rather than immediate.

A digital image printed on a 3-D printer becomes a physical object that can no longer be edited, tracked, and faithfully replicated. Even if two analog reproductions are made from the same source recording, over time each of the copies will change in different ways. Fidelity to the original fades in each of the analog copies.

The digital form itself is a kind of copy or simulation. As such, digital objects are a kind of map of an analog form. Imagine the digital terrain as an infinite plain of undifferentiated space. This digital space has no intrinsic form. It can be shaped and mapped according to our imagination.[25]

The very idea of mapping takes on a different sense when applied to digital spaces. In mapping from the analog world to digital space, we not only reflect but also actively create the space. In the passage from analog to digital, meaning is exchanged for organization. We enter into a contemporary form of madness.

This passage is the madness of the digital age.

Portals

Cultural scholar Lewis Hyde uses the term *webs of signification* to describe the grammar around terms that are paired, such as heaven and earth, life and death, good and evil.[26] It is in comparison that these terms are defined. The pairing of analog and digital follows such a web of signification. What is absent in the prior discussion of the passage from analog to digital is the ancient idea of the in-between. Such liminal space is present in new forms in the digital age. In crossing the threshold between the analog space of the physical world and the virtual space of the digital realm, our messages pass through a portal. This portal is one of many gateways that serve to link the Web of digital space.

Sacred stories and myths speak of undifferentiated space given form by divine energy. They tell of boundaries and of boundary crossing. Such tales do not simply reflect the world, but also *make the world.*[27] Hermes is the messenger god in the Greek pantheon. He is able to cross boundaries freely between the world of men, the Underworld, and Olympus, the realm of the gods. But Hermes is much more than boundary crosser. He is the creator and disruptor of boundaries. Hermes' name is taken from the root word *herm*, referring to a stone marker or border. Such boundaries represent a kind of physical map, denoting the end of one territory and the beginning of another. They map the road of the traveler and serve as points of reference for the way finder.

It is fitting that the god of markers is also the god of the unmarked. He is the god who erects boundaries, but does not abide by them. Akin to the Native American trickster figure of Coyote, he is the breaker of rules. He is the god of the road that leads home to the familiar and he is the god of the road that leads to the unknown wilderness. He is the god of the point of origin, the destination, and the liminal space that lies in-between. Not only is Hermes present in the digital age, he is present in the most intricate and vast set of gateways ever created. The Internet itself is not simply a digital network, but rather a network of networks, each connected through a gateway that directs messages.

While we tend to separate our activities into spheres of online and offline, such distinction is increasingly blurred. When I am engaged in an online classroom discussion using a video chat tool, there are multiple answers to the singular navigational question of *where am I*? I am at once physically present, seated in an office chair in front of my laptop. I am also present in the set of digital bits that stream my image and voice across the Internet. Similarly, I can be found displayed on the screens of my colleagues in physical locations around the world.

I am offline.

I am online.

I am in the in-between.

I exist in the in-between not only in those activities that I may envision as digitally mediated, but also in more routine activities in the physical world. When driving to work or school, I glance at the digital display on the dashboard of my car. The display reflects navigational information received via global positioning satellite (GPS), a system that pinpoints my cartographic position based upon readings from orbiting stations.[28] As I continue on my route, the digital display is updated based upon the movement along my route. On the display, my own position is fixed in the center and it is the world around me that moves. This form of first person perspective is similar to that in many online gaming environments in which the player's position on the display is fixed and the map shifts based upon player movement. In this GPS display, I am always the center of the map. All locations are defined in relation to me. Gas stations, restaurants, schools and hospitals appear on my map as I pass them (or rather as they pass me). This notion of self as cardinal point is evident in the ethos of the age.

The ancient term for the idea of self as center of the universe is *solipsism*. In the digital age in which I am the center of my social network broadcasting each detail of my daily routine to an audience of millions, the ancient madness of solipsism returns in a new guise. A map without myth is madness.

Hermes is present in the vast digital Internet that we have constructed. He is present in the protocols and the messages. He is present in the gateways and the waypoints. He is present on the information highway that we have created.

In unfamiliar terrain, maps alone do not suffice. We need a guide to find our way home. Left to our own cleverness, the road is fraught with hazards. Without a guide for the road, we may enter the mythic space with no way home. We may become lost in the undifferentiated labyrinth of the digital age. Like a lucid dreamer who is caught between waking and sleep, we may become lost between the offline and online realms.

The Wilderness

The story of a winter day in Newark, New Jersey in 1999 serves to remind me of how easily we may become lost in the in-between, in the wilderness between the known and the unknown. A cross-country flight had taken me from sunny Los Angeles to overcast Newark to speak to a group of financial auditors, offering reassurance about the impending Y2K threshold. The fear at the time was that at the stroke of midnight on December 31, 1999, digital information systems would fail to transition into the new millennium.

Like the headless kangaroo from 1980, computer systems built to store dates in a limited memory space are based upon a map with a finite boundary. In this case, the boundary confusion threatened chaos ranging from errors in financial calculations to airplanes dropping from the skies. Experts advised right-minded citizens to stockpile supplies in preparation for the worst.

In response to such Cassandra prophecies, I was asked to travel to various financial centers around the United States. My quest was to offer assurance that the new millennium would dawn with civilization intact. Yet, it was I who was in need of a guide. A rental car shuttle transported me to the Avis outpost at the Newark airport. From the Avis lot, I could see the Marriott hotel where I had a one-night reservation for my limited engagement. With rental car map in hand, I set out on the short trip to the hotel.

Though I was born in New Jersey, I have spent my adult life on the West Coast. Traffic signs at the Newark airport proved confusing as I found myself exiting the connector road. One sign pointed towards New York and I took the opposite turn. I unexpectedly found myself on a thoroughfare heading into the heart of Newark. While it was clear that I was in Newark, I had no point of reference by which to navigate. My first response was to attempt to mentally traverse my circumstance to determine where the path had led me astray. My next response was to admit that I was lost and to take the next exit that presented itself.

The exit took me through a gritty section of Newark. Dusk had given way to evening. The dimly lit streets offered no inviting service stations. With no helpful guide, I relied upon my experience from California in which each freeway off ramp is paired with a corresponding on ramp that enables the traveler to reverse course. I returned to the thoroughfare in hopes of heading back in the direction of the Newark Airport. Instead, the on ramp took me in the opposite direction, further from my intended destination. When signposts made no mention of the airport, I concluded that I had become lost in the wilderness of Newark.

I exited the thoroughfare once more and found my way to a grocery market in the suburbs. On a journey of less than a mile, I had traveled more than twenty miles off course. A kind grocery clerk provided me with directions to return to the airport exit and eventually to the hotel. No hotel room ever felt as welcoming as my junior suite at the Newark Airport Marriot.

Home

We need only look to the tale of the Greek hero, Odysseus, to understand the challenges of finding our way home.[29] Cursed by the gods, Odysseus wanders for nearly twenty years. Whether twenty miles or twenty years off course, the traveler is lost in a wilderness at once alarming and inviting. The hazards of Newark are tame in comparison to the intoxicating wine of the witch Circe and the lure of the lotus-eaters. Only the dedication of his crew and the guidance of the god Hermes bring Odysseus safely home to Ithica.[30]

Stories of the quest for home are found in some of our most familiar tales. Lost in Oz, Dorothy travels the yellow brick road to seek the wizard's help in finding her way home.[31] Wandering in Wonderland, what is required for Alice to return home is to wake from the strange dream that grips her.[32]

Whether we are adrift at sea like Odysseus, in the dark in Newark like the author or misplaced in a mythical place like Dorothy and Alice, the experience of being lost is part of the human story. It is woven into our myths, our maps, and our consciousness. It is likewise present in the virtual fabric of the digital information expressways that we have erected.

Hermes is the messenger god. He is also the guide figure in stories such as *The Odyssey*. In an age in which we may find ourselves overwhelmed with messages, we are more in need than ever of a guide.

Madness

The wilderness is not always a kind of madness, but madness is a kind of wilderness. Wilderness is found not only in the terrain that is outside, but also the terrain within. Like many, I encountered the wilderness within during the wandering years between age 18 and 22. At the threshold of young adulthood, I found myself in the suburban wilderness of Salem, Oregon, attending Willamette University. Away from home for the first extended time period, I encountered madness in various forms ranging from homesickness to deprivation of sleep, food and companionship.

Salem, Oregon was also the location of the state psychiatric hospital. Wandering around Salem in those years, I encountered psychiatric patients who were judged to be functional enough to be released from the facility during the daytime hours. These outpatients sometimes spoke to an invisible audience in a strange language, almost lyrical in its verse. At a yogurt shop, I sat at a table adjacent to a young man who intoned, "By this time next year I'll be locked in the winter of cold madness."

I recorded these words and others in the journal that I diligently maintained. This was not a blog or digital record, but an old spiral-bound notebook that I carried in my backpack. I recorded my own thoughts fervently, as if I was trying to find my way home through the written word.

The idea of psychiatric (or mental) illness is a phenomenon distinct from madness. The usage of *madness* in this exploration is not as a diagnostic or a clinical term. It is not even a vernacular term for abnormal thinking or affect. Rather, madness is the unmapped place to which we may travel or inhabit.

To dwell in madness is to be present in the same physical world as those around you, but to understand the world through a different map. When 15th century scholar Nicholas of Cusa reasoned the universe to be infinite, his ideas were labeled as a particular form of madness termed *heresy*.[33] Less than a century later, Copernicus provided support for his ideas, thus re-drawing the accepted map of the universe. The infinite universe was madness no more.

This is not to suggest that madness always presages genius. Yet, the madman and the prophet are two faces of the same archetype. The boundaries of the map are redrawn in every age. Just as new terrain is claimed, old terrain is lost. Harrison describes the magic universe of our ancestors in which all objects in the world were imbued with spirit.[34] In the 21st century, it would be considered a sign of madness to give thanks to the spirit of my MacBook Pro for this work.

The emerging digital age is no different. New virtual terrain is gained as we extend our shared imagination into cyberspace. Old terrain, such as newspapers and printed texts may be left behind. There are examples of times in history when entire societies have dwelled in madness. Harrison cites the witch-universe of medieval Europe as a kind of collective madness termed a *mad universe*.[35] Future societies may judge our own descent into nuclear escalation or climate destruction as forms of a mad universe. Madness is neither rare nor is it obvious even when we are faced with it. Madness may masquerade in corporate attire or the prestige of a general's uniform. Madness may speak with the cold calculus of scientific reason.

Madness resides in a map without myth.

Each of us inhabits a personal myth. As I traveled the streets of Salem, Oregon, what I wrote in my journal was a kind of personal myth. This form of self-myth serves to guide individuals along an unfamiliar path. Collectively, it is our shared stories—our myths—that serve as guide. In the digital age, it is these myths that will determine the universe that we inhabit and the universe that dwells within us.

Boundaries

When I was in high school at the end of the 1970's, I played *Dungeons and Dragons*, a popular role-playing game at the time. By the standards of current Massive Multi-Player Online Role-Playing Games such as *World of Warcraft*, my experience of *Dungeons and Dragons* may seem quaint. The game was played with dice and maps drawn on paper marked with hexagonal grids.

On this hexagonal grid, the maps drafted by the role-playing guide (given the unfortunate title of Dungeonmaster) indicated the parameters of the adventure. Locations of towns and dungeons, treasure and monsters were indicated. Play proceeded according to turns in which actions were taken or battles enacted.

Inevitably, one of the players, perhaps driven by simple curiosity or even boredom would direct his character to travel towards the edge of the map. At first, the Dungeonmaster would gently try to dissuade the player from testing the boundaries of the carefully scribed territory. When the player persisted, the persuasion became more heavy-handed. The adventuring party might be beset upon by bandits or kidnapped and taken back to town.

I draw two simple lessons from this early experience. To travel beyond the edge of the map is forbidden. Just as surely, to travel beyond the edge of the map is enticing. In each age, it is important and necessary for brave and foolhardy souls to test the boundaries of the map. Those who have done so in the past have created much of the world that we now inhabit. We are in their debt.

To borrow from Wilden's earlier description of the distinction between the analog in the digital, the relationship between maps and myth can be summarized simply.[36] Maps serve to create *organization*. Myths serve to create *meaning*.

As we map the digital world, transforming the undifferentiated space of cyberspace, we create organization. We organize our finances, our relationships, our time, and our travel. We may digitize all of our books and store them for instant access. We may even eventually encode our DNA or our own memories and store them in digital form. This organization of all the information in our internal and external worlds must be paired with meaning.

As we extend our maps into these new digital spaces, so our myths must likewise extend into these new virtual spaces. While some may be tempted to relegate myth as an ancient artifact that has been supplanted by human progress, it is important to consider the connection between myth and virtual worlds. From the earliest stories of Gilgamesh and his travel to the distant paradise of Dilmun, myths speak of travel to virtual worlds.[37]

As we travel to new digital worlds, our myths travel with us. It is these myths that permit us to venture into madness without becoming mad. It is these myths that permit us to return safely home.

Notes

1   Edwin Hutchins, *Cognition in the Wild*, 1995.
2   Drew T. Foley, *Navigating Mythic Space in the Digital Age*, Fielding Graduate University, 2012.
3   Hutchins, 1995.
4   Foley, 2012.
5   Ibid.
6   A. R. Newmann, Language is not a Vague Province: Mapping and Twentieth-century American Poetry, (Doctoral dissertation), 2006.
7   Antonio Machado, There is No Road: Proverbs by Antonio Machado, 2013.
8   Robert M. Pirsig, Zen and the Art of Motorcycle Maintenance: An Inquiry into Values, 1979.
9   Robert Walter, Opening Remarks at The Study of Myth Symposium, Pacifica Graduate University, 2012.
10 Margaret Wertheim, The Pearly Gates of Cyberspace: A History of Space from Dante to the Internet, 1999.
11 Stephan Günzel, "Eastern Europe 2008: Maps and Geopolitics in Video Games," in Space Time Play: Computer Games Architecture and Urbanism: The Next Level, 2007.
12 Maria Bittarello, The Recreation of Ancient Classical Religions on the World Wide Web: Neopaganism as Contemporary Mythopoeisis, Doctoral dissertation, 2004

13   ____. "Another Time, Another Space: Virtual Worlds, Myths and Imagination." Journal of Virtual Worlds Research, 2008, 13–14.

14   Will McWhinney, Paths of Change: Strategic Choices for Organizations and Society, 1997.

15   Ibid.

16   Ibid.

17   Foley, 2012.

18   Margaret Wertheim, The Pearly Gates of Cyberspace: A History of Space from Dante to the Internet, 1999.

19   Ibid.

20   Anthony Wilden, System and Structure: Essays in Communication and Exchange, 1972.

21   Foley, 2012.

22   Edward Harrison, Masks of the Universe: Changing Ideas on the Nature of the Cosmos, 2003.

23   Foley, 2012.

24   Wilden, 1972.

25   Bittarello, 2007.

26   Hyde, Lewis. Trickster Makes this World: Mischief, Myth and Art, 1998.

27   Ibid.

28   Foley, 2012.

29   Ibid.

30   Homer. The Odyssey, 2009.

31   Frank Baum and W. W. Denslow, The Wonderful Wizard of Oz, 1991.

32   Lewis Carroll, Alice's Adventures in Wonderland and Journey Through the Looking Glass, 2010.

33   Wertheim, 1999.

34   Harrison, 2003.

35   Ibid.

36   Wilden, 1972.

37   Bittarello, 2008.

Bibliography

Baum, L. Frank., & Denslow, W. W. The Wonderful Wizard of Oz. New York, NY: HarperTrophy, 1991.

Bittarello, Maria. B. The Recreation of Ancient Classical Religions on the World Wide Web: Neopaganism as Contemporary Mythopoeisis. (Doctoral dissertation), University of Stirling, Scotland, UK, 2007.

Bittarello, Maria. B. "Another Time, Another Space: Virtual Worlds, Myths and Imagination." Journal of Virtual Worlds Research, 1(1), 1–17, 2008.

Carroll, Lewis. Alice's Adventures in Wonderland and Journey Through the Looking Glass. New York, NY: Penguin Classics, 2010.

Foley, Drew. T. Navigating Mythic Space in the Digital Age. (PhD), Fielding Graduate University, Santa Barbara, CA, 2012.

Gunzel, Stephan. "Eastern Europe 2008: Maps and Geopolitics in Video Games." In Space Time Play: Computer Games Architecture and Urbanism: The Next Level, edited by F. V. Borries, S. P. Walz & M. Bottger, Boston, MA: Birkhauser, 2007.

Harrison, Edward. *Masks of the Universe: Changing Ideas on the Nature of the Cosmos* (2nd ed.). Cambridge, UK: Cambridge University Press, 2003.

Homer. *The Odyssey* (E. V. Rieu, Trans. 4th ed.). London, UK: Penguin Classics, 2009.

Hutchins, Edwin. *Cognition in the Wild*. Cambridge, MA: The MIT Press, 1995.

Hyde, Lewis. *Trickster Makes this World: Mischief, Myth and Art*. New York, NY: North Point Press, 1998.

Machado, Antonio. *There is No Road: Proverbs by Antonio Machado* (D. Maloney & M. Berg, Trans.). Buffalo, NY: White Pine Press, 2013.

McWhinney, Will. *Paths of Change: Strategic Choices for Organizations and Society*. Thousand Oaks, CA: SAGE Publications, 1997.

Newmann, A. R. *Language is not a Vague Province: Mapping and Twentieth-century American Poetry*. (Doctoral dissertation), The University of Texas at Austin, 2006. http://www.lib.utexas.edu/etd/d/2006/newmannd56298/newmannd56298.pdf Available from University of Texas (3244922)

Pirsig, Robert M. *Zen and the Art of Motorcycle Maintenance: An Inquiry into Values*. New York, NY: Harpercollins, 1979.

Wertheim, Margaret. *The Pearly Gates of Cyberspace: A History of Space from Dante to the Internet*. New York, NY: W. W. Norton, 1999.

Wilden, Anthony. *System and Structure: Essays in Communication and Exchange*. London, UK: Tavistock, 1972.

Drew Thomas Foley *is an educator, researcher and entrepreneur. His interest in depth psychology and the digital age traces back to his undergraduate studies in Psychology at Willamette University in Salem, Oregon. For the last 25 years, he has lived and worked in Southern California where he earned a Masters of Business Administration from Pepperdine University and a Masters of Arts in Human Development from Fielding Graduate University. In 2012, Drew earned his PhD in Human and Organizational Systems from Fielding Graduate University. His dissertation,* Navigating Mythic Space in the Digital Age, *focuses on the how digital technology shapes the ways that we live, work and learn. He continues his research as a Fellow for the Institute of Social Innovation and teaches course in organizational development and technology management.*

Century of the Selfie

Culture and Context in the Era of Electronic Waste

By
Bonnie Bright

We can no longer imagine a world without *selfies*, or hearken back to a day when the word was unknown, even if Merriam-Webster waited until 2014 to add the term to their dictionary. Not only have selfie images invaded the Internet, saturating online space via the growth of social media sites like Facebook and Instagram, it is now near-impossible to go to a spectacle or celebration, visit a historic site, take a walk on the beach at sunset, or attend a gathering with family or friends without witnessing the frenzied snapping away with a smart phone held at arm's length. More, "selfie sticks" have become an extension of our living limbs, providing a greater perspective than even nature apparently had the foresight to offer us.

Most of us are guilty of caving to the urge to capture the moment for ourselves, placing our own images front and center as we become the star of the show, but what is behind this phenomenon? What unconscious patterns are driving us to turn the camera on ourselves in a way we neither evolutionarily nor historically ever have before? Perhaps in a world that feels increasingly accelerated, we are literally seizing moments so we won't forget them, or trying to prove something to our peers by sharing these moments we believe we've managed to capture—or are we merely trying to prove something to ourselves? What does it mean to us, both individually and collectively, that we have developed technology that enables us to apprehend our images in these tiny devices and proliferate them in an instant anywhere in the world?

From a depth psychological perspective, it stands to reason that there are archetypal complexes evidenced by the compulsive trend for the selfie that lie at the heart of our modern existence, but first let us look at the facts leading to the rise of selfie phenomenon. Technology and the proliferation of smartphones has played an undeniable role. Cameras on smartphones first became commercially available in the United States in 2002.[1] By the time the front-facing camera was introduced in 2010, the capacity for users to turn the camera on themselves with very little effort gave the selfie its meteoric rise. Smartphones have become a virtual *de rigueur* for modern consumers.

Of course, the proliferation of these mobile devices, while creating a multitude of conveniences, also feeds our growing appetite for technological gadgets and contributes to a growing problem on our planet: electronic waste. This selfie-centered trend has us not only consuming smartphones with their built-in cameras a dizzying pace—but we also just as quickly discarding them as new models become available. This kind of access to technology that not only accelerates our lives but also is increasingly available at an accelerated pace has virtually sped up time, shrinking our weekends and evenings, and condensing family time, down time, and pasttimes. Not only are we more accessible wherever we go, and always "on," we are often expected to respond to messages that bombard us minute-by-minute, anytime, anywhere. We have lost the luxury of time to reflect and be still; to contemplate, cogitate, and ponder, all states linked profoundly to imagination and creative thought. It is profoundly obvious that along with all the perceived advantages of modernity, there are disadvantages as well.

The Great Acceleration

Beginning in the 1950's, after the Second World War, multiple facets of human culture seemed to speed up creating a vast shift in the human-environment relationship, a phenomenon that has been referred to as "The Great Acceleration."[2] Human population tripled in a few short decades, expediting the growth of the global economy and amplifying material consumption exponentially. Since 1950, communication and transportation options have improved dramatically, illustrated by increases in foreign direct investment, international tourism, the advent and growth of the Internet, and the sheer quantities of motor vehicles, telephones, and computers. Many of these new technologies have evolved in direct correlation with our insatiable demand for fossil fuels, even if only to transport raw materials and finished products to meet the public demand.

While many of the advances and mechanical and technological miracles achieved over the last half-century or so have resulted in significant net gains for human well-being and economic development, decades of unchecked or unmitigated man-made ecocide including pollution, contamination, toxic waste, oil spills, urban development, construction of dams, deforestation, mining, fracking, nuclear contamination, and mounting electronic waste is taking a tremendous toll.[3] "Our quest for wonderworld is making wasteworld,"[4] theologian Thomas Berry declared.

C. G. Jung, one of the pioneers of depth psychology and the study of the unconscious, insisted on the importance of reflection so that we can respond to information from the psyche in the form of symbols and dreams.[5] Jung died in 1961 at the age of 85, but even decades ago he raised concerns about what he interpreted as a decline in our ability to reflect, noting how we get caught up in the momentum that drives us forward:

> We have plunged down a cataract of progress which sweeps us on into the future with even wilder violence the farther it takes us from our roots. Once the past has been breached, it is usually annihilated, and there is no stopping the forward motion. But it is precisely the loss of connection with the past, our uprootedness, which has given rise to the "discontents" of civilization and to such a flurry and haste that we live more in the future and its chimerical promises of a golden age than in the present, with which our whole evolutionary background has not yet caught up.[6]

Technology, a significant aspect of industrialized consumer culture, is a prevalent source of distraction and an indicator by which we measure "progress"—yet another way we fool ourselves into believing our lives have meaning. Technology has profoundly amplified the speed and efficiency at which we do things, but at the same time has served to expedite the pace of our lives, leaving little time for reflection and reconnection with soul on any level. Long before the mass technological advances of the last several decades, Jung observed:

> Reforms by advances, that is, by new methods or gadgets, are of course impressive at first, but in the long run they are dubious and in any case paid for dearly. They by no means increase the contentment or

happiness of people on the whole. Mostly, they are deceptive sweeten-
ings of existence, like speedier communications which unpleasantly
accelerate the tempo of life and leave us with less time than ever before.
Omni festinatio ex parte diaboli est—all haste is of the devil, as the old
masters used to say.[7]

The "Century of the Self" and the Rise of Consumerism

The documentary *Century of the Self*,[8] which first aired on BBC in 2002, outlines the rise of consumer culture in America. This film credits Sigmund Freud's
nephew Edward Bernays with the use of Freud's theory—that humans are driven
by primitive, irrational forces—to manipulate the unconscious desires and drives
of the masses and create demand for products and services they don't really need
but rather want or desire. Ads from the 1940s reveal that, until that shift, product
marketing focused primarily on emphasizing features and functions rather than
emotional responses from customers.

By innovatively linking products with the way people feel, Bernays managed to manipulate people into desiring certain items. This process proved to be
effective time and again. By the time World War II was over and factories were
mass-producing consumer goods, the tactic of creating desire was cemented.
Before long, the era of the "consumerism" was in full swing. People no longer
bought things only when they "needed" them; rather, advertisers played on the
unconscious wishes and desires humans harbor under the surface.[9]

As our individual values changed about buying a pair of shoes or a car—
simply because it made us feel good and not because we needed to replace the
previous product that had simply worn out—companies pulled out all the stops,
bent on topping the previous year's sales with ever increasing targets and goals.
The supply chain, being systemic, responded in kind. Demand for finished products resulted in demand for raw materials. More trees were cut down for wood
or rubber or palm oil. More mines provided more copper, gold, and silver and
contributed to steel used for buildings, bridges, and cars. Businesses paid taxes;
taxes fed urban projects and funded infrastructure, leading to more opportunities
for businesses to open their doors and join in the free-for-all. Before long, our
entire western economy depended on cumulative unlimited growth, increasing
the demand for more new products that require ever more natural resources,
fossil fuels, and rare metals and minerals and leading to ever greater deposits
of refuse, non-recycled materials, and other consumer waste. If the economy

stuttered, or disaster struck, citizens were encouraged to spend more money to get things circulating again.[10]

The lure of immediate gratification captivated a culture that once valued thrift. As consumer spending rose, so did consumer debt, rising a shocking 52% from 27.4 billion dollars to 41.7 billion in just four years of the post war boom, from 1952 to 1956.[11] David Suzuki points out ways in which manufacturers have worked to keep us consuming, writing,

> When products are made to last, businesses eventually run out of cus-
> tomers. Planned obsolescence is one solution. Constantly redefining
> potential markets is yet another strategy, expanding to the third world,
> for example, and targeting elders, yuppies, children, or specific ethnic
> groups.[12]

By the early part of the 21st century, shopping malls and box stores were commonplace, and the allure of buying via the Internet was just gaining steam. Smartphones, tablets, PCs, and other electronic devices are now a common contributor to our consumer lifestyle and obsolescence as we desire the newest model each time it is released fast becoming a growing problem. As the selfie phenomenon grows in conjunction with our increasing consumption of smart phones and tablets, we might arguably refer to this century as the century of the "selfie."

Electronic Waste

The Industrial Revolution launched in the late 1700s with the leap from manual manufacturing to machines really began to take root at the beginning of the nineteenth century. Railroads, machine shops, lumberyards, meat packing plants, and iron and steel foundries increasingly served to provide the necessities people required. By mid-19th-century, improvements to manufacturing and production processes enabled consumption to go beyond what was merely instrumental, and people rapidly began to buy up radio and television sets, household appliances, automobiles, ready-to-wear clothing, and prepared food. After the Great Depression of the 1930s, the economic boom sparked by manufacturing to support World War II was a welcome era in the United States. When the war ended, manufacturers and leaders in the economic community debated ways to keep the economy going and determined that consumption was the solution. Retail analyst Victor Lebow asserted:

> Our enormously productive economy . . . demands that we make con-
> sumption our way of life, that we convert the buying and use of goods
> into rituals, that we seek our spiritual satisfaction, our ego satisfaction,

in consumption. . . . We need things consumed, burned up, worn out, replaced, and discarded at an ever increasing rate.[13]

In what has been termed by some a "throwaway" culture, e-waste and trash in general are a growing problem. A recent meme has been making its way around social media: When you throw something "out," where is "out"? We all live on the same planet, and the stark realization that the plastic bag full of trash or the discarded household goods, clothing, or broken appliances all end up in a vast landfill where they will exist for hundreds or even thousands of years to come has yet to make its way concretely into the western cultural mindset.

In 2008, National Geographic featured an article on e-waste in Accra, Ghana, stating that, while humans have always been adept at "creating trash," archaeologists of the future will note a shift that began at the end of the twentieth century when a new and particularly hazardous form of trash appeared: electronic waste.[14]

Electronic waste, or e-waste, is a growing problem. Never before have so many solid, material objects, some still are potentially serviceable, been discarded by everyday people. Mountains of computers, computer accessories, monitors, keyboards, printers, televisions, fax machines, DVD players, VCRs, stereos, cables, game consoles, microwaves, and other electronic devices—including cell phones— are tossed "out" on a daily basis as parts wear out or newer technology makes them obsolete.

The United States currently generates about 66 pounds of e-waste per person on average.[15]A United Nations report found that in 2010, the U.S. produced nearly 260 million units of used computers, monitors, TVs and cellphones. Of those, over 170 million were gathered for recycling, and almost 14.5 million were shipped outside the country. By 2012, the total weight of discarded electrical or electronic products came to about 54 million tons, an average of approximately 43 pounds for each of the seven billion people on the planet. Forecasters predict that amount will rise by 33 percent by 2017, to about 72 million tons, an amount weighing nearly 11 times as much as the Great Pyramid of Giza.[16]

An estimated 70% of computers and monitors and 80% of TVs end up in local landfills where they eventually leach arsenic, mercury, cadmium and other noxious chemicals. Most of the rest get shipped to non-industrialized nations where they are picked over and dissembled by people looking to earn a living by reselling valuable components like copper, silver, gold, and platinum. The menace emerges in the sheer number of highly toxic materials built into most devices. Computer monitors and older models of televisions contain huge amounts of lead. Other toxic materials and known carcinogens in common electronic devices include arsenic, mercury, zinc, nickel, lithium, cadmium, beryllium, and flame retardants among others.[17]

In places like India, Ghana, Nigeria, and China, even young children climb massive mounds of discarded devices to locate valuable components they can sell to recyclers for a few dollars at a time. They smash computer batteries to recover cadmium, oblivious to the flecks that land on their skin and clothing as they work. Women bend over pots of molten lead as they "cook" circuit boards to extract slivers of silver or gold. They inadvertently inhale smoke as they burn plastic phone casings from the phones they dissemble, unaware that even low levels of mercury, cadmium and lead found in phones can cause drastic and irreversible neurological damage.

In China, where some villages have no alternative for viable jobs except to process e-waste flooding the country at record levels, women sort chips and components, making five or six dollars an hour, while inhaling toxic fumes 10 to 12 hours a day.[18] Noxious black smoke invades the air where men use industrial acids to melt down circuit skins in order to separate out the gold they contain, where eyes burn throughout the day. Too, many homes double as warehouses to store unsorted e-waste, exposing residents to hazardous components in their own habitations. The soil around the production areas turns as black as coal, rivers run black, and riverbanks become landfills as people scavenge the leftovers in hopes of finding something production workers missed.

Many of those exposed to debris from these sites report burns on their skin, infections, loss of hair, swollen skin, headaches, or constant sore throats. There are only a handful of men who don't bring their children to help search the remnants. Lead, as often is the case, is the largest source of affliction. A study of kindergarten children near the salvage sites in China, reveals that among 165 children, 82% have over 100 μg/dl, the standard for reporting lead in blood levels, when the standard for children is typically less than 10.[19] Many years of increasing e-waste in Taiwan has resulted in thousands of circuit boards which have aggregated to line the riverbanks, looking for all the world like rocks that are part of the eco-system, or perhaps the "bones" of the earth. Water near most landfill sites has become contaminated, and farms have become less fertile, villagers report. Most workers report they are "used to" the intense pollution and choose to earn wages over their health and the health of their families and communities.[20]

Clearly, the western industrialized consumer-based way of life allows us to accept the short life-cycle of our electronic devices without thinking much about the consequences of discarding them so fast. A colossal problem can be witnessed in the speed at which our technology is changing, and manufacturers release new and updated models of devices we already have and use. In 2013, the New York Times reported that Americans replace their cell phones every 22 months. Nearly 150 million phones were thrown away in 2010.[21] Worse, components needed to fix an ailing device are often nearly as expensive as repurchasing the entire device. In 2013, the cost of a new battery for an iPhone 5C cost $80, but you could buy a brand new phone for $100.[22] When I knocked a glass of water over on my laptop recently, it died immediately. The diagnosis? The motherboard was dead and a new one would cost me more than the computer was worth.

While many of us opt to re-sell working devices we no longer want using services like eBay or CraigsList, a far greater number of these items get stashed away until such time as they are useless. Devices that no longer work, even though the issues might be easily fixable, are similarly tossed away and replaced by new ones or newer models without any attempt at repair. Even finding technicians or those equipped to make required repairs is becoming more difficult in a culture where the technology is more and more complex, while new items are readily available and fairly affordable for the average general public. On the whole, we seem to have lost a tremendous amount of value and respect for the things we own, the possessions we sometimes work hard to buy. Unlike generations before this one, there is a plethora of products to choose from and a barrage of advertising incenting us to consume.

Thomas Berry points out that in the industrial culture in which we are embedded, the words we employ derive their significance and validation from an industrial framework. "Progress," for example, is a central and sustaining myth in our society. Berry notes what a fundamental role the concept possesses for us, saying,

> This word [progress] has great significance for increasing our scientific understanding of the universe, our personal and social development, our better health and longer life. Through modern technology, we can manufacture great quantities of products with greater facility. Human technology also enables us to travel faster and with greater ease. So on and on, endlessly, we see our increasing human advantage over the natural world.[23]

There is a downside to the importance we place on progress, however. Berry continues:

> But then we see that human progress has been carried out by desolating the natural world. This degradation of the earth is the very condition of the "progress" presently being made by humans. It is a kind of sacrificial

offering. Within the human community, however, there is little awareness of the misunderstanding of this word. The feeling that even the
most trivial modes of human progress are preferable to the survival of
the most sublime and even the most sacred aspects of the natural world
is so pervasive that the ecologist is at a loss as to how to proceed. The
language in which our values are expressed has been co-opted by the
industrial establishments and is used with the most extravagant modes
of commercial advertising to create the illusory world in which the
human community is now living.[24]

Jung also perceived the underlying risk that exists when systems get out of
control, however, saying, "Great organizations eat themselves up"[25] Psychologist
Ralph Metzner clearly articulates the connection between our increasing focus
on industry and technology and the environmental and ecological crisis we face:

> A growing chorus of voices is acknowledging that the fundamental roots
> of the environmental disaster lie in the attitudes, values, perceptions,
> and basic worldview that we humans of the industrial-technological
> global society have come to hold. Many now understand that the world
> view and associated attitudes and values of the industrial age have
> permitted and driven us to pursue exploitative, destructive, and wasteful
> applications of technology.[26]

The Empty Self

It is impossible not to wonder if the selfie phenomenon is related to our
profound need for making meaning. When we reach for the sky and turn the
lens on ourselves, we appear to be attempting to capture something in the image
that stares back at us after we click the shutter. What is there in the depths of
the pixels that speaks to the soul? While philosophers tell us meaning lies in the
phenomenology of being in the present moment, it is arguable that the individual
taking the selfie actually removes herself even further from the authenticity of
any given moment by looking through a lens. Still, what must be witnessed now
is the endeavor, the desire inherent in capturing the context around us so that
we might begin to piece together the puzzle of exactly what each of us is doing
here on planet Earth at this particular moment in time.

Philip Cushman perceives that the individual in modern culture suffers from
a condition he terms the "empty self" in which one is driven by a felt sense of
hollowness and a lack of meaning. The empty self originated from "the rise of the
industrial state, the attendant loss of community and the press of consumerism."[27]
Yearning for something it can't quite identify, the empty self desperately seeks

to fill itself up through increasing compulsive consumption of goods, services, technology, peak experiences, entertainment, celebrity and even psychotherapy. To alleviate the anxiety, depression, isolation, and suffering, psychosomatic disorders, or addiction, we automatically resist, turning to means of defense and denial. At the same time, we collectively attempt to fill the empty self by distracting ourselves, giving over to addiction, seeking and asserting power, individualism, and achievement.

All the time spent consuming to fill the empty self will never serve to mitigate the sense of separation that endures beneath the surface of our culture, nor the vast spiritual disconnect underlying the lives of virtually every individual. Juliet Schor, author of *Born to Buy*, laments, "We have become a nation that places a lower priority on teaching its children how to thrive socially, intellectually, even spiritually, than it does on training them to consume. The long-term consequences of this development are ominous."[28]

The personal hollowness articulated by Cushman[29] and referenced elsewhere in the documentaries, Century of the Self [30] and Consumed[31] among others, seeks liberation and the experience of success and fulfillment through consumption. Our increasing urge for immediate gratification is directly linked to the growing ecological crisis. "Man has the lost the capacity to foresee and to forestall," wrote Albert Schweitzer. "He will end up destroying the earth."[32]

Jung went further to suggest that what is needed is a healthy ability to say "no," to be able to rest, and to realize that most of what we seek is not necessary for our happiness but will lead, in fact, to neurosis, illness, or insanity. The desire for deep peace and ease is really at the root of our being:

> We are awakening a little to the feeling that something is wrong in the world, that our modern prejudice of overestimating the importance of the intellect and the conscious mind might bend false. We want simplicity. We are suffering in our cities, from a need of simple things. We would like to see our great railroad terminals deserted, the streets deserted, a great peace descend upon us.[33]

Similar to Jung, Freya Mathews, an environmental philosopher, mourns the loss of meaningful symbols in our culture. Symbols, which depth psychology has shown to be a connecting force between the ego and the unknown "other," help us make meaning. Without them, an enduring sense of exile takes a profound toll on our identity and connection to authenticity:

> A culture deprived of any symbolic representation of the universe and of its own relation to it will be a culture of non-plussed, unmotivated

individuals, set down inescapably in a world which makes no sense to them, and which accordingly baffles their agency. What are they to do in this world to which they do not belong? No natural directives appoint themselves. Self-interest is the only rational motive. Any other values smack of arbitrariness. Vocationless, such individuals must sink eventually into apathy and alienation, or into the mindless and joyless pursuit of material ends.[34]

Mathews goes on, potentially making the link to understanding the "selfie" phenomenon more explicit:

With no cosmological foundation for their identity, [such individuals] invent precarious individual self-pictures, self-stories, ego-images, but their sense of who they are is tenuous. Metaphysically adrift, these individuals experience insecurity; unless united by an external power, such a group does not offer the best prospect for stable community.[35]

We are each seeking meaning, desperate for context in an accelerated and often chaotic world where we no longer feel grounded in nature, as our ancestors did. Our longing for understanding and a sense of being embedded in a larger fabric of being is making itself manifest even in the midst of our quick adoption of the latest gadget or the most recent technological advance. It is as if the soul of the world, the *anima mundi*, is reaching out to us to fill the gap in the face of our loss of connection. In *The Red Book*, Jung put forth his own realization about an "empty self" and its corresponding loss of soul, writing,

He whose desire turns away from outer things, reaches the place of the soul. If he does not find the soul, the horror of emptiness will overcome him, and fear will drive him with a whip lashing time and again in a desperate endeavor and a blind desire for the hollow things of the world. He becomes a fool through his endless desire, and forgets the way of his soul, never to find her again. He will run after all things, and will seize hold of them, but he will not find his soul, since he would find her only in himself.[36]

Soul Loss

C. G. Jung wrote in detail about this pervasive psycho-spiritual deficit found in our culture, a condition Jung (and others) have referred to as "soul loss," which leaves us feeling profoundly ill-at-ease, experiencing depression, malaise, and a general loss of vitality.[37]

Mircea Eliade defines the loss of soul from an indigenous perspective in his seminal tome on shamanism, describing it as something which occurs when souls become lost or disoriented, resulting in a number of undesirable effects on a person including serious depression, malaise, or mental or physical illness.[38] In the psychological sense, the concept is related to "splitting," a term French psychologist Pierre Janet coined to describe the defensive mechanism through which the human mind is able to distance itself from the effects of trauma by severing the connection to thoughts, feelings, and memories that are in excess of what it can process at that time.[39]

When we feel unable to cope with information or experiences that overpower our customary methods and techniques, notes Donald Kalsched, a Jungian specialist on trauma, then disengaging, dismissing, and dropping those parts of ourselves that get overwhelmed is sometimes the only way we prevent ourselves from pain that might otherwise be unbearable.[40] This kind of fragmentation serves to undermine our energy and well-being, deflating and sometimes disorienting us, creating ever greater loss of connection and cohesiveness. Shamanic practitioner Sandra Ingerman describes it as "losing crucial parts of ourselves that provide life and vitality."[41]

Soul loss may be seen as a division between the individual ego and Jung's idea of the Self. June Singer, Jungian analyst and author, said when soul loss occurs, the soul has "ceased to be the connecting ribbon of a road between the conscious individual and the vast unknown and unknowable."[42] Jung felt soul loss transpires when the interaction between the ego and the unconscious fails.[43]

Jung died in 1961, but even in his day, he believed that, similar to individuals, our collective culture also suffers deeply from soul loss, manifesting in symptoms such as falling into conflict with one's self, fragmenting into splinters in the pursuit of goals, interests, and occupations, and forgetting one's own "origins and traditions . . . even losing all memory of his former self."[44] The rise of technology, which fragments our attention and decreases our ability to focus—combined with the pervasive lack of a sense of understanding among many of us in western, industrialized cultures—together serve to strip our lives of meaning and context. One desperate and unconcsious solution to fill that sense of an "empty self," and to repair our intimate relationships as part of nature ourselves, may well be to attempt to capture our own images by way of selfies.

It is worth noting that selfies are often taken in one of five key contexts that traditionally linked us back to meaning, weaving us into the world of fundamental being: in nature; with family, loved ones and friends; in historical sites (connecting us to both place and ancestors); eating, and thereby nourishing and nurturing ourselves; and in the presence of extraordinary feats or entertainment, linked to mystery, magic, and the unknown "other." This might seemingly provide a land-scape in which we might intensively inspect both our own faces and features in an attempt to understand the underlying emotion that may be hidden beneath the surface of our everyday egos, and also a way to assess our individual role in relationship to the setting in which we find ourselves suspended for eternity in the pixels of the modern age.

While we may unconsciously be turning to selfies to attempt to capture context, and thereby make meaning of our lives, not surprisingly, many individuals from earth-based, indigenous cultures were reluctant to have their photos taken, believing cameras could steal their souls.[45] Jung himself commented on this belief after spending time with the Elgonyis in Africa.[46] However, Carolyn J. Marr, an anthropologist and photo librarian at the Museum of History and Industry in Seattle, Washington, notes that some Native Americans "came to cherish photographs as links to ancestors and even integrated them into important ceremonies."[47]

Earth's Timeline

In the throes of unconscious trauma initiated by what is often latent despair about what we are collectively doing to the earth, and in the profound and ever-increasing need for re-rooting ourselves in nature so we feel connected to something larger, eternal, and imbued with sacred meaning, we need some hope. Jungian Fred Gustafson says we are lonesome for the earth, knowing we are, in truth, more separate than we can possibly stand.[48]

Our history of colonization and oppression of earth-based peoples, the proliferation of consumer cultures into the farthest reaches of the planet, and our own devastating practices that produce waste, and particularly electronic waste, in unimaginable amounts require that we correct past neglect and re-establish some kind of equilibrium in order to begin the process of restoring soul. If the longing we feel can be moved into and through by finding the interior—which we may consider indigenous aspects of ourselves—it may engender the feeling of being more grounded, more oriented, and finding more meaning in life than ever before.

Selfies have proliferated on social media, providing a vehicle that has propelled the phenomenon to a meteoric rise. Recently an image emerged on social media in the form of "elphie"—an elephant that reportedly took a selfie with her trunk.[49] It got me wondering: What would it look like if nature itself were trying to find context and meaning, to reconnect with humans in order to re-gain greatly-needed balance in much the same way (and for the same reasons) as humans do? What if the earth took a selfie and posted it?...How might that show up in a way that we could understand? At this critical time of acceleration and change in our planet's history, is the very earth itself also earnestly seeking to gain context for all the new and rapid changes taking place to her in the form of pollution, abuse, extinction, and loss?

One way, from a depth psychological perspective, would be for earth to post her selfies in our dreams, where the images we view at night in the dream-time may be observed, interpreted, read, and received as important updates on the social media "timeline" of the earth. Through dreams, symbols, reflection—and the context they provide if we only pay attention—we might yet be able to capture a snapshot of where we are now and what it means for our future, a future in which we literally *find* ourselves in the service of earth, embedded in community, and grounded in understanding. Only then might our current obsession with the selfie finally become clear.

Notes

1   Simon Hill, "From J-Phone to Lumina 1020: A Complete History of the Camera Phone," *Digital Trends*, 2013. http://www.digitaltrends.com/mobile/camera-phone-history

2   Robert Costanza, Lisa. J Graumlich, and Will Steffen. *Sustainability or Collapse? An Integrated History and Future of People on Earth*. Cambridge, MA: The MIT Press, 2007.

3   Ibid.

4   Thomas Berry, *The Great Work: Our Way into the Future* (1st ed.). New York, NY: Bell Tower, 1999, 67.

5   Carl Gustav Jung, *Memories, Dreams, Reflections*, 1989.

6   Ibid, 236.

7   Ibid, 236.

8   Adam Curtis, *Century of the Self*, Written/Produced by Adam Curtis. (United Kingdom: BBC, 2005), TV documentary.

9   Ibid.

10   Ibid.

11   Christopher Lasch, "The Culture of Consumerism," Artifact & Analysis. http://www.smithsonianeducation.org/idealabs/ap/essays/consume.htm

12   David T. Suzuki and Amanda McConnell, *The Sacred Balance: Rediscovering our Place in Nature. [Kindle version]*. Vancouver, BC: Greystone Books, 2009, 21.

13   Ibid, citing Victor Lebow.

14   Chris Carroll, "High Tech Trash," *National Geographic, 2008*. http://ngm.nationalgeographic.com/2008/01/high-tech-trash/carroll-text

15   Tanya Lewis. "World's E-Waste to Grow 33% by 2017, Says Global Report", on Live Science web site, December 15, 2013. http://www.livescience.com/41967-world-e-waste-to-grow-33-percent-2017.html

16   Ibid.

17   Chris Carroll, "High Tech Trash," *2008*.

18   Yunfeng Zhao, *eDump*. Directed and Produced by Yunfeng Zhao. 2008. http://www.movingimagefestival.com/2008/works_edump.html

19   Medline Plus, "Lead Levels—Blood", http://www.nlm.nih.gov/medlineplus/ency/article/003360.htm

20   Zhao, *eDump*, 2008

21   Leyla Acaroglu, "Where Do Old Cellphones Go to Die?" *New York Times*, May 4, 2013. http://www.nytimes.com/2013/05/05/opinion/sunday/where-do-old-cell-phones-go-to-die.html

22   Catherine Rampell, "Cracking the Apple Trap," *New York Times*, October 29, 2013. http://www.nytimes.com/2013/11/03/magazine/why-apple-wants-to-bust-your-iphone.html?_r=1&

23   Thomas Berry, "The Viable Human." *ReVision*, 16(2): 56, 1993.

24   Ibid.

25   Carl Gustav Jung, *Dream Analysis: Notes of the Seminar Given in 1928-1930*, edited by W. McGuire. Princeton, NJ: Princeton University Press, 1984, 543.

26   Ralph Metzner, *Green Psychology: Transforming our Relationship to the Earth*. Rochester, VT: Park Street Press, 1999.

27   Phillip Cushman *Constructing the Self, Constructing America: A Cultural History of Psychotherapy*. Boston, MA: Addison-Wesley, 1995, 245.

28   Juliet B. Schor, *Born to Buy: The Commercialized Child and the New Consumer Culture*. New York, NY: Scribner, 2004, 13.

29   Cushman, 1995.

30   Adam Curtis, *Century of the Self*

31   Richard Heap, *Consumed: Inside the Belly of the Beast*, directed by Richard Heap. (United Kingdom: Slackjaw Film, 2011), Documentary film. http://topdocumentaryfilms.com/consumed

32   Cited in Ann Cottrell Free, *Animals, Nature, and Albert Schweitzer*, The Flying Fox Press, Washington D.C., 1988, 60-61.

33   Carl Gustav Jung, *C. G. Jung Speaking: Interviews and* Encounters. Edited by William McGuire & R. F. C. Hull, *Bollingen Series XCVIM*. Princeton, NJ: Princeton University Press, 1993, 49.

34   Freya Mathews, *The Ecological Self [Kindle version]*. Oxon, England: Routledge, 2006, 13-14.

35   Ibid, 14.

36   Carl Gustav Jung, *The Red Book, Liber Novus*. Translated by Mark Kyburz, John Peck & Sonu Shamdasani. In Sonu Shamdasani (Ed.), New York, NY: Norton, 2009, 232.

37   Carl Gustav Jung, Archetypes of the Collective Unconscious. Edited by Herbert Read, Michael Fordham, Gerhard Adler & William McGuire, *The Collected Works of C. G. Jung. Translated by* R. F. C. Hull (2nd ed., Vol. 9i, 3-41). Princeton, NJ: Princeton University Press, 1990, (Original work published 1959), xvi.

38   Mircea Eliade, *Shamanism: Archaic Techniques of Ecstasy*. Princeton, NJ: Princeton University Press, 1974.

39   C. Michael Smith, *Jung and Shamanism in Dialogue: Retrieving the Soul / Retrieving the Sacred*. Victoria BC, Canada: Trafford, 2007.

40   Donald Kalsched, *The Inner World of Trauma: Archetypal Defenses of the Personal Spirit*. London: Routledge, 1996.

41   Sandra Ingerman, *Soul Retrieval: Mending the Fragmented Self*. San Francisco, CA: HarperCollins, 1991, 4

42   June Singer, *Boundaries of the Soul* (Rev. ed.). New York, NY: Anchor Books, 1994, 39

43 Carl Gustav Jung, "Concerning Rebirth". Edited by Herbert Read, Michael Fordham, Gerhard Adler & William McGuire, *The Collected Works of C. G. Jung. Translated by* R. F. C. Hull (2nd ed., Vol. 9i, pp. 113-147). Princeton, NJ: Princeton University Press, 1990. (Original work published 1939).

44 Carl Gustav Jung, "The Meaning of Psychology for Modern Man". In H. Read, M. Fordham, G. Adler & W. McGuire (Eds.), *The Collected Works of C. G. Jung*. Translated by R. F. C. Hall. (2nd ed., Vol. 10, pp. 134-156). Princeton, NJ: Princeton University Press, 1978. (Original work published 1933) 141

45 Carolyn J. Marr, "American Indians of the Pacific Northwest", Library Of Congress http://www.lcweb.loc.gov/teachers/classroommaterials/connections/pacific/thinking3.html, para. 1.

46 C. G. Jung, in Memories, Dreams, Reflections, p. 265

47 Carolyn J. Marr, "American Indians of the Pacific Northwest," para. 1.

48 Fred Gustafson, *Dancing Between Two Worlds: Jung and the Native American Soul.* New York, NY: Paulist Press, 1997.

49 "Elephant Snatches Man's Camera, Takes Amazing 'Elphie' ", Jethro Mullen, CNN, May 24, 2015: http://www.cnn.com/2015/05/24/travel/elephant-selfie-elphie-thailand/index.html

Bibliography

Acaroglu, Leyla. "Where Do Old Cellphones Go to Die?" *New York Times*, May 4, 2013. http://www.nytimes.com/2013/05/05/opinion/sunday/where-do-old-cellphones-go-to-die.html

Berry, Thomas. *The Great Work: Our Way into the Future* (1st ed.). New York, NY: Bell Tower, 1999.

Berry, Thomas. "The Viable Human." *ReVision, 16*(2), 1993.

Carroll, Chris. "High Tech Trash." *National Geographic, 2008.* http://ngm.nationalgeographic.com/2008/01/high-tech-trash/carroll-text

Costanza, Robert , Graumlich, Lisa. J, and Steffen, Will. *Sustainability or Collapse? An Integrated History and Future of People on Earth.* Cambridge, MA: The MIT Press, 2007.

Cottrell Free, Ann. *Animals, Nature, and Albert Schweitzer*, The Flying Fox Press, Washington D.C., 1988.

Curtis, Adam. *Century of the Self.* Written and produced by Adam Curtis. (United Kingdom: BBC, 2005), TV documentary.

Cushman, Phillip. *Constructing the Self, Constructing America: A Cultural History of Psychotherapy.* Boston, MA: Addison-Wesley, 1995.

Eliade, Mircea. *Shamanism: Archaic Techniques of Ecstasy.* Princeton, NJ: Princeton University Press, 1974.

Gustafson Fred. *Dancing Between Two Worlds: Jung and the Native American Soul.* New York, NY: Paulist Press, 1997.

Heap, Richard. *Consumed: Inside the Belly of the Beast.* Directed by Richard Heap. (United Kingdom: Slackjaw Film, 2011), Documentary film. http://topdocumentaryfilms.com/consumed

Simon Hill, "From J-Phone to Lumina 1020: A Complete History of the Camera Phone," *Digital Trends*, 2013. http://www.digitaltrends.com/mobile/camera-phone-history

Ingerman, Sandra. *Soul Retrieval: Mending the Fragmented Self.* San Francisco, CA: HarperCollins, 1991.

Jung, Carl Gustav. "Archetypes of the Collective Unconscious." In *The Collected Works of C. G. Jung ,*edited by Herbert Read, Michael Fordham, Gerhard Adler & William McGuire, and translated *by* R. F. C. Hull (2nd ed., Vol. 9i, 3-41). Princeton, NJ: Princeton University Press, 1990, (Original work published 1959).

Jung, Carl Gustav. "Concerning Rebirth." In *The Collected Works of C. G. Jung*, edited by Herbert Read, Michael Fordham, Gerhard Adler & William McGuire and translated by R. F. C. Hull (2nd ed., Vol. 9i, pp. 113-147). Princeton, NJ: Princeton University Press, 1990. (Original work published 1939).

Jung, Carl Gustav. *C. G. Jung Speaking: Interviews and Encounters*, edited by William McGuire & R. F. C. Hull, *Bollingen Series XCVIM*. Princeton, NJ: Princeton University Press, 1993.

Jung, Carl Gustav. *Dream Analysis: Notes of the Seminar Given in 1928-1930*, edited by William McGuire. Princeton, NJ: Princeton University Press, 1984.

Jung, Carl Jung. *Memories, Dreams, Reflections*, edited by Aniela Jaffé and translated by R. Winston & C. Winston. New York, NY: Random House, 1989.

Jung, Carl Gustav. "The Meaning of Psychology for Modern Man." In *The Collected Works of C. G. Jung*, edited by Herbert Read, Michael Fordham, Gerhard Adler & William McGuire, and translated by R. F. C. Hall. (2nd ed., Vol. 10, pp. 134-156). Princeton, NJ: Princeton University Press, 1978. (Original work published 1933).

Jung, Carl Gustav. *The Red Book, Liber Novus*, translated by Mark Kyburz, John Peck & Sonu Shamdasani and edited by Sonu Shamdasani. New York, NY: Norton, 2009.

Kalsched, Donald. *The Inner World of Trauma: Archetypal Defenses of the Personal Spirit*. London: Routledge, 1996.

Lasch, Christopher. "The Culture of Consumerism." *Artifact & Analysis*, n.d. http://www.smithsonianeducation.org/idealabs/ap/essays/consume.htm

Lewis, Tanya. "World's E-Waste to Grow 33% by 2017, Says Global Report." *Live Science*, December 15, 2013. http://www.livescience.com/41967-world-e-waste-to-grow-33-percent-2017.html

Mathews, Freya. *The Ecological Self [Kindle version]*. Oxon, England: Routledge, 2006.

Medline Plus, "Lead Levels—Blood," U.S. National Library of Medicine. http://www.nlm.nih.gov/medlineplus/ency/article/003360.htm

Marr, Carolyn J. "American Indians of the Pacific Northwest." Library Of Congress, n.d.. http://www.lcweb.loc.gov/teachers/classroommaterials/connections/pacific/thinking3.html

Metzner, Ralph. *Green Psychology: Transforming our Relationship to the Earth*. Rochester, VT: Park Street Press, 1999.

Mullen, Jethro. "Elephant Snatches Man's Camera, Takes Amazing 'Elphie.'" CNN, May 24, 2015. http://www.cnn.com/2015/05/24/travel/elephant-selfie-elphie-thailand/index.html

Rampell, Catherine. "Cracking the Apple Trap." *New York Times*, October 29, 2013. http://www.nytimes.com/2013/11/03/magazine/why-apple-wants-to-bust-your-iphone.html?_r=1&

Schor, Juliet B. *Born to Buy: The Commercialized Child and the New Consumer Culture*. New York, NY: Scribner, 2004.

Singer, June. *Boundaries of the Soul* (Rev. ed.). New York, NY: Anchor Books, 1994.

Smith, C. Michael. *Jung and Shamanism in Dialogue: Retrieving the Soul / Retrieving the Sacred*. Victoria BC, Canada: Trafford, 2007.

Suzuki, David T. and McConnell, Amanda. *The Sacred Balance: Rediscovering our Place in Nature [Kindle version]*. Vancouver, BC: Greystone Books, 2009.

Zhao, Yunfeng. *eDump*. Directed and produced by Yunfeng Zhao. Documentary film. 2008. http://www.movingimagefestival.com/2008/works_edump.html

Bonnie Bright, Ph.D., *spent fifteen years in the corporate world working in media and technology before earning Master's degrees in Psychology from Sonoma State University and in Depth Psychology from Pacifica Graduate Institute, where she also earned her Ph.D.*

She is s the founder of Depth Psychology Alliance, an online community for everyone interested in depth psychologies, and of DepthList.com, an free-to-search database of Jungian and depth psychology-oriented practitioners. She is the creator and executive editor of Depth Insights Journal, *and she regularly produces audio and video interviews on depth psychological topics. She has completed 2-year certifications in Archetypal Pattern Analysis via the Assisi Institute and in Indigenous African Spiritual Technologies with West African elder Malidoma Somé, and she has trained extensively in Holotropic Breathwork™ and the Enneagram.*

www.ingramcontent.com/pod-product-compliance
Lightning Source LLC
Chambersburg PA
CBHW061005280326
41935CB00009B/841